ALL SAINTS' DAY AND OTHER SERMONS

ALL SAINTS' DAY AND OTHER SERMONS

CHARLES KINGSLEY

Edited by the Rev. W. Harrison, M.A.

CHARLES KINGSLEY BOOKS

"Inheriting the zeal
And from the sanctity of elder times
Not deviating;—a priest, the like of whom
If multiplied, and in their stations set,
Would o'er the bosom of a joyful land
Spread true religion, and her genuine fruits."
The excursion—Book vi.

Published by Wildside Press LLC.
www.wildsidebooks.com

PREFACE

The following Sermons could not be arranged according to any proper sequence. Those, however, which refer to doctrine and the Church Seasons will mostly be found at the beginning of the volume, whilst those which deal with practical subjects are placed at the close.

A few of the Sermons have already appeared in "Good Words;" but by far the greater number were never prepared by their author for the press. They were written out very roughly—sometimes at an hour's notice, as occasion demanded—and were only intended for delivery from the pulpit.

The original MSS. have been adhered to as closely as possible.

It is thought that many to whom the late Rector of Eversley was dear will welcome the publication of these earnest words, and find them helpful in the Christian life.

"Blessed are the dead which die in the Lord from henceforth: Yea, saith the Spirit, that they may rest from their labours; and their works do follow them."

SERMON I

ALL SAINTS' DAY

Westminster Abbey. November 1, 1874.

Revelation vii. 9-12. "After this I beheld, and, lo, a great multitude, which no man could number, of all nations, and kindreds, and people, and tongues, stood before the throne, and before the Lamb, clothed with white robes, and palms in their hands; and cried with a loud voice, saying, Salvation to our God which sitteth upon the throne, and unto the Lamb. And all the angels stood round about the throne, and about the elders and the four beasts, and fell before the throne on their faces, and worshipped God, saying, Amen: Blessing, and glory, and wisdom, and thanksgiving, and honour, and power, and might, be unto our God for ever and ever. Amen."

To-day is All Saints' Day. On this day we commemorate—and, as far as our dull minds will let us, contemplate—the saints; the holy ones of God; the pure and the triumphant—be they who they may, or whence they may, or where they may. We are not bidden to define and limit their number. We are expressly told that they are a great multitude, which no man could number, of all nations, and kindreds, and peoples, and tongues; and most blessed news that is for all who love God and man. We are not told, again—and I beg you all to mark this well—that this great multitude consists merely of those who, according to the popular notion, have "gone to heaven," as it is called, simply because they have not gone to hell. Not so, not so! The great multitude whom we commemorate on All Saints' Day, are saints. They are the holy ones, the heroes and heroines of mankind, the elect, the aristocracy of grace. These are they who have kept themselves unspotted from the world. They are the pure who have washed their robes, and made them white in the blood of the Lamb, which is the spirit of self-sacrifice. They are those who carry the palm-branch of triumph, who have come out of great tribulation, who have dared, and fought, and suffered for God, and truth, and right. Nay, there are those among them, and many, thank God—weak women, too, among them—who have resisted unto blood, striving against sin.

And who are easy-going folk like you and me, that we should arrogate to ourselves a place in that grand company? Not so! What we should do on All Saints' Day is to place ourselves, with all humility, if but for an hour, where we can look afar off upon our betters, and see what they are like, and what they do.

And what are they like, those blessed beings of whom the text speaks? The Gospel for this day describes them to us; and we may look on that description as complete, for He who gives it is none other than our Lord

Himself. "Blessed are the poor in spirit; for their's is the kingdom of heaven. Blessed are they that mourn: for they shall be comforted. Blessed are the meek: for they shall inherit the earth. Blessed are they who hunger and thirst after righteousness: for they shall be filled. Blessed are the merciful: for they shall obtain mercy. Blessed are the pure in heart: for they shall see God. Blessed are the peace-makers: for they shall be called the children of God. Blessed are they which are persecuted for righteousness' sake: for their's is the kingdom of heaven. Blessed are ye, when men shall revile you, and persecute you, and shall say all manner of evil against you falsely, for my sake. Rejoice, and be exceeding glad: for great is your reward in heaven."

This is what they are like; and what we, I fear, too many of us, are not like. But in proportion as we grow like them, by the grace of God, just so far shall we enter into the communion of saints, and understand the bliss of that everlasting All Saints' Day which St John saw in heaven.

And what do they do, those blessed beings? Whatever else they do, or do not do, this we are told they do—they worship. They satisfy, it would seem, in perfection, that mysterious instinct of devotion—that inborn craving to look upward and adore, which, let false philosophy say what it will, proves the most benighted idolater to be a man, and not a brute—a spirit, and not a merely natural thing.

They have worshipped, and so are blest. They have hungered and thirsted after righteousness, and now they are filled. They have longed for, toiled for, it may be died for, the true, the beautiful, and the good; and now they can gaze upward at the perfect reality of that which they saw on earth, only as in a glass darkly, dimly, and afar; and can contemplate the utterly free, the utterly beautiful, and the utterly good in the character of God and the face of Jesus Christ. They entered while on earth into the mystery and the glory of self-sacrifice; and now they find their bliss in gazing on the one perfect and eternal sacrifice, and rejoicing in the thought that it is the cause and ground of the whole universe, even the Lamb slain before the foundation of the world.

I say not that all things are clear to them. How can they be to any finite and created being? They, and indeed angels and archangels, must walk for ever by faith, and not by sight. But if there be mysteries in the universe still hidden from them, they know who has opened the sealed book of God's secret counsels, even the Lamb who is the Lion, and the Lion who is the Lamb; and therefore, if all things are not clear to them, all things at least are bright, for they can trust that Lamb and His self-sacrifice. In Him, and through Him, light will conquer darkness, justice injustice, truth ignorance, order disorder, love hate, till God be all in all, and pain and sorrow and evil shall have been exterminated out of a world for which Christ stooped to die. Therefore they worship; and the very act of worship—understand it well—is that great reward in heaven which our Lord promised them. Adoration is their very bliss and life. It must be so. For what keener, what nobler enjoyment for rational and moral beings, than satisfaction with, and admiration of, a Being better than themselves? Therefore they worship; and their worship finds a natural vent in words most fit though few, but all expressing utter trust and utter satisfaction in the worthiness of God. Therefore they worship; and by worship enter into communion and harmony not only with each other, not only with angels and archangels, but with all the powers of nature, the four beings which are around the throne, and with every creature which is in heaven and in earth, and under the earth, and in the sea. For them, likewise, St John heard saying, "Blessing and glory, and honour, and power, be unto Him that sitteth on the throne, and to the Lamb for ever and ever."

And why? I think, with all humility, that the key to all these hymns—whether of angels or of men, or of mere natural things—is the first hymn of all; the hymn which shows that, however grateful to God for what He has done for them those are whom the Lamb has redeemed by His blood to God, out of every kindred, and nation, and tongue; yet, nevertheless, the hymn of hymns is that which speaks not of gratitude, but of absolute moral admiration—the hymn which glorifies God, not for that which He is to man, not for that which He is to the universe, but for that which He is absolutely and in Himself—that which He was before all worlds, and would be still, though the whole universe, all created things, and time, and space, and matter, and every created spirit likewise, should be annihilated for ever. And what is that?

"Holy, holy, holy, Lord God Almighty, which was, and is, and is to come."

Ah! what a Gospel lies within those words! A Gospel? Ay, if you will receive it, the root of all other possible Gospels, and good news for all created beings. What a Gospel! and what an everlasting fount of comfort! Surely of those words it is true, "blessed are they who, going through the vale of misery, find therein a well, and the pools are filled with water." Know you not what I mean? Happier, perhaps, are you—the young at least among you—if you do not know. But some of you must know too well. It is to them I speak. Were you never not merely puzzled—all thinking men are that—but crushed and sickened at moments by the mystery of evil? Sickened by the follies, the failures, the ferocities, the foulnesses of mankind, for ages upon ages past? Sickened by the sins of the unholy many—sickened, alas! by the imperfections even of the holiest few? And have you never cried in your hearts with longing, almost with impatience, Surely, surely, there is an ideal Holy One somewhere, or else how could have arisen in my mind the conception, however faint, of an ideal holiness? But where, oh where? Not in the world around, strewed with unholiness. Not in myself—unholy too, without and within—seeming to myself sometimes the very worst company of all the bad company I meet, because it is the only bad company from which I cannot escape. Oh, is there a Holy One, whom I may contemplate with utter delight? and if so, where is He? Oh, that I might behold, if but for a moment, His perfect beauty, even though, as in the fable of Semele of old, the lightning of His glance were death. Nay, more, has it not happened to some here—to clergyman, lawyer, physician, perhaps, alas! to some pure-minded, noble-hearted woman—to be brought in contact perforce with that which truly sickens them—with some case of human folly, baseness, foulness—which, however much their soul revolts from it, they must handle, they must toil over many weeks and months, in hope that that which is crooked may be made somewhat straight, till their whole soul was distempered, all but degraded, by the continual sight of sin, till their eyes seemed full of nothing but the dance of death, and their ears of the gibbering of madmen, and their nostrils with the odours of the charnel house, and they longed for one breath of pure air, one gleam of pure light, one strain of pure music, to wash their spirits clean from those foul elements into which their duty had thrust them down perforce?

And then, oh then, has there not come to such an one—I know that it has come—that for which his spirit was athirst, the very breath of pure air, the very gleam of pure light, the very strain of pure music, for it is the very music of the spheres, in those same words, "Holy, holy, holy, Lord God Almighty, which was, and is, and is to come;" and he has answered, with a flush of keenest joy, Yes. Whatever else is unholy, there is an Holy One, spotless and undefiled, serene and self-contained. Whatever else I cannot trust, there is One whom I can trust utterly. Whatever else I am dissatisfied with, there is One whom I can contemplate with utter satisfaction, and bathe my stained soul in that eternal fount of purity. And who is He? Who save the Cause and Maker, and Ruler of all things, past, present, and to come? Ah, Gospel of all gospels, that God Himself, the Almighty God, is the eternal and unchangeable realisation of all that I and all mankind, in our purest and our noblest moments, have ever dreamed concerning the true, the beautiful, and the good. Even though He slay me, the unholy, yet will I trust in Him. For He is Holy, Holy, Holy, and can do nothing to me, or any creature, save what He ought. For He has created all things, and for His pleasure they are and were created.

Whosoever has entered, though but for a moment, however faintly, partially, stupidly, into that thought of thoughts, has entered in so far into the communion of the elect; and has had his share in the everlasting All Saints' Day which is in heaven. He has been, though but for a moment, in harmony with the polity of the Living God, the heavenly Jerusalem; and with an innumerable company of angels, and the church of the first-born who are written in heaven; and with the spirits of just men made perfect, and with all past, present, and to come, in this and in all other worlds, of whom it is written, "Blessed are the poor in spirit: for theirs is the kingdom of heaven. Blessed are they who hunger and thirst after righteousness: for they shall be filled. Blessed are the pure in heart: for they shall see God. Blessed are they who are persecuted for righteousness' sake: for their's is the kingdom of heaven." Great indeed is their reward, for it is no less than the very beatific vision to contemplate and adore. That supreme moral beauty, of which all earthly beauty, all nature, all art, all poetry, all music, are but phantoms and parables, hints and hopes, dim reflected rays of the clear light of that everlasting day, of which it is written—that "the city had no need of the sun, neither of the moon, to shine in it: for the glory of God did lighten it, and the Lamb is the light thereof."

SERMON II

PREPARATION FOR ADVENT

Westminster Abbey. November 15, 1874.

Amos iv. 12. "Prepare to meet thy God, O Israel."

We read to-day, for the first lesson, parts of the prophecy of Amos. They are somewhat difficult, here and there, to understand; but nevertheless Amos is perhaps the grandest of the Hebrew prophets, next to Isaiah. Rough and homely as his words are, there is a strength, a majesty, and a terrible earnestness in them, which it is good to listen to; and specially good now that Advent draws near, and we have to think of the coming of our Lord Jesus Christ, and what His coming means. "Prepare to meet thy God," says Amos in the text. Perhaps he will tell us how to meet our God.

Amos is specially the poor man's prophet, for he was a poor man himself; not a courtier like Isaiah, or a priest like Jeremiah, or a sage like Daniel; but a herdsman and a gatherer of sycamore fruit in Tekoa, near Bethlehem, where Amos was born. Yet to this poor man, looking after sheep and cattle on the downs, and pondering on the wrongs and misery around, the word of the Lord came, and he knew that God had spoken to him, and that he must go and speak to men, at the risk of his life, what God had bidden, against all the nations round and their kings, and against the king and nobles and priests of Israel, and the king and nobles and priests of Judah, and tell them that the day of the Lord is at hand, and that they must prepare to meet their God. And he said what he felt he must say with a noble freedom, with a true independence such as the grace of God alone can give. Amaziah, the priest of Bethel, who was worshipping (absurd as it may seem to us) God and the golden calf at the same time in King Jeroboam's court, complained loudly, it would seem, of Amos's plain speaking. How uncourteous to prophesy that Jeroboam should die by the sword, and Israel be carried captive out of their own land! Let him go home into his own land of Judah, and prophesy there; but not prophesy at Bethel, for it was the king's chapel and the king's court. Amos went, I presume, in fear of his life. But he left noble words behind him. "I was no prophet," he said to Amaziah, "nor a prophet's son, but a herdsman, and a gatherer of wild figs. And the Lord took me as I followed the flock, and said, Go, prophesy unto my people Israel." And then he turned on that smooth court-priest Amaziah, and pronounced against him, in the name of the Lord, a curse too terrible to be repeated here.

Now what was the secret of this inspired herdsman's strength? What helped him to face priests, nobles, and kings? What did he believe? What did he preach? He believed and preached the kingdom of God and His righteousness; the simple but infinite difference between right and wrong; and the certain doom of wrong, if wrong was persisted in. He believed in the kingdom of God. He told the kings and the people of all the nations round, that they had committed cruel and outrageous sins, not against the Jews merely, but against each other. In the case of Moab, the culminating crime was an insult to the dead. He had burned the bones of the king of Edom into lime. In the case of Ammon, it was brutal cruelty to captive women; but in the cases of Gaza, of Tyre, and of Edom, it was slave-making and slave-trading invasions of Palestine. "Thus saith the Lord: For three transgressions of Gaza, and for four, I will not turn away the punishment thereof; because they carried away captive the whole captivity, to deliver them up to Edom. But I will send a fire upon the wall of Gaza, which shall devour the palaces thereof."

Yes. Slave-hunting and slave-trading wars—that was and is an iniquity which the just and merciful Ruler of the earth would not, and will not, pardon. And honour to those who, as in Africa of late, put down those foul deeds, wheresoever they are done; who, at the risk of their own lives, dare free the captives from their chains; and who, if interfered with in their pious work, dare execute on armed murderers and manstealers the vengeance of a righteous God. For the Lord God was their King, and their Judge, whether they knew it or not. And for three transgressions of theirs, and for four, the Lord would not turn away their punishment, but would send fire and sword among them, and they should be carried away captive, as they had carried others away. But to go back. Amos next turns to his own countrymen—to Judah and Israel, who were then two separate nations. For three transgressions of Judah, and for four, the Lord would not turn away their punishment, because they had despised the law of the Lord, and had not walked in His commandments. Therefore He would send a fire on Judah, and it should devour the palaces of Jerusalem. But Amos is most bitter against Israel, against the court of King Jeroboam at Samaria, and against the rich men of Israel, the bulls of Bashan, as he calls them. For three transgressions, and for four, the Lord would not turn away their punishment. And why?

Now see what I meant when I said that Amos believed not only in the kingdom of God, but in the righteousness of God. It was not merely that they were worshipping idols—golden calves at Dan, and Bethel, and Samaria, at the same time that they worshipped the true God. That was bad, but there was more behind. These men were bad, proud, luxurious, cruel; they were selling their countrymen for slaves—selling, he says so twice, as if it was some notorious and special case, an honest man for silver, and the poor for a pair of shoes. They were lying down on clothes taken on pledge by every altar. They were breaking the seventh commandment in an abominable way. They were falsifying weights and measures, and selling the refuse of the wheat. They stored up the fruits of violence and robbery in their palaces. They hated him who rebuked them, and abhorred him that spoke uprightly. They trod upon the poor and crushed the needy, and then said to their stewards, "Bring wine, and let us drink." Therefore though they had built houses of hewn stone, they should not live in them. They had planted pleasant vineyards, but should not drink of them. And all the while these superstitious and wicked rich men were talking of the day of the Lord, and hoping that the day of the Lord would appear.

You, if you have read your Bibles carefully and reverently, must surely be aware that the day of the Lord, either in the Old Testament or in the New, does not mean merely the final day of judgment, but any striking event, any great crisis in the world's history, which throws a divine light upon that history, and shows to men—at least to those who have eyes wherewith to see—that verily there is a God who judges the earth in righteousness, and ministers true judgment among the people;—a God whom men, and all their institutions, should always be prepared to meet, lest coming suddenly, He find them sleeping. If you are not aware of this, the real meaning of a day of the Lord, a day of the Son of Man, let me entreat you to go and search the Scriptures for yourselves; for in them ye think ye have eternal life, and they are they which testify of the Lord, of that Eternal Son of whom the second Psalm speaks, in words which mobs and tyrants, the atheist and the superstitious, are alike willing to forget.

In the time of Amos, the rich tyrants of Israel seem to have meant by the day of the Lord some vague hope that, in those dark and threatening times, God would interfere to save them, if they were attacked by foreign armies. But woe to you that desire the day of the Lord, says Amos the herdsman. What do you want with it? You will find it very different from what you expect. There is a day of the Lord coming, he says, therefore prepare to meet your God. But you are unprepared, and you will find the day of the Lord very different from what you expect. It will be a day in which you will learn the righteousness of God. Because He is righteous He will not suffer your unrighteousness. Because He is good, He will not permit you to be bad. The day of the Lord to you will be darkness and not light, not as you dream deliverance from the invaders, but ruin by the invaders, from which will be no escape. "As if a man did flee from a lion, and a bear met him; or went into the house and leaned his hand on the wall, and a serpent bit him." There will be no escape for those wicked men. Though they dug into hell, God's hand would take them; though they climbed up into heaven, God would fetch them down; though they hid in the bottom of the sea, God would command the serpent, and it should bite them. He would sift the house of Israel among all nations like corn in a sieve, and not a grain should fall to the earth. And all the sinners among God's people should die by the sword, who say, "The evil shall not overtake us."

This was Amos's notion of the kingdom of God and His righteousness. These Israelites would not obey the laws of God's kingdom, and be righteous and good. But Amos told them, they could not get rid of God's kingdom. The Lord was King, in spite of them, and they would find it out to their sorrow. If they would not seek His kingdom and His government, His government would seek them and find them, and find their evil-doings out. If they would not seek God's righteousness, His righteousness would seek them, and execute righteous judgment on them. No wonder that the Israelites thought Amos a most troublesome and insolent person. No wonder that the smooth priest Amaziah begged him to begone and talk in that way somewhere else. He saw plainly enough that either Amos must leave Samaria, or he must leave it. The two could no more work together than fire and water. Amos wanted to make men repent of their sins, while Amaziah wanted only to make them easy in their minds; and no man can do both at once.

So it was then, my friends, and so it will be till the end of this wicked world. The way to please men, and be popular, always was, and always will be, Amaziah's way; to tell men that they may worship God and the golden calf at the same time, that they may worship God and money, worship God and follow the ways of this wicked world which suit their fancy and their interest; to tell them the kingdom of God is not over you now, Christ is not ruling the world now; that the kingdom of God will only come, when Christ comes at the last day, and meanwhile, if people will only believe what they are told, and live tolerably respectable lives, they may behave in all things else as if there was no God, and no judgments of God. Seeking the righteousness of God, say these preachers of Amaziah's school, only means, that if Christ's righteousness is imputed to you need not be righteous yourselves, but will go to heaven without having been good men here on earth. That is the comfortable message which the world delights to hear, and for which the world will pay a high price to its flatterers.

But if any man dares to tell his fellow-men what Amos told them, and say, The kingdom of God is among you, and within you, and over you, whether you like or not, and you are in it; the Lord is King, be the people never so unquiet; and all power is given to Him in heaven and earth already; and at the last great day, when He comes in glory, He will show that He has been governing the world and the inhabitants thereof all along, whether they cared to obey Him or not:—if he tell men, that the righteousness of God means this—to pray for the Spirit of God and of Christ, that they may be perfect as their Father in heaven is perfect, and holy as Christ is holy, for without holiness no man shall see the Lord: if he tell men, that the wrath of God was revealed from heaven at the fall of man, and has been revealed continuously ever since, against all ungodliness and unrighteousness of men, that indignation and wrath, tribulation and anguish will fall upon every soul of man that doeth evil; and glory, honour, and peace to every man that worketh good:—when a man dares to preach that, he is no more likely to be popular with the wicked world (for it is a wicked world) than Amos was popular, or St Paul was popular, or our Lord Jesus Christ, who gave both to Amos and to St Paul their messages, was popular. False preachers will dislike that man, because he wishes to make sinners uneasy, while they wish to make them easy. Philosophers, falsely so-called, will dislike that man, because he talks of the kingdom of God, the providence of God, and they are busy—at least, just now—in telling men that there is no providence and no God—at least, no living God. The covetous and worldly will dislike that man, for they believe that the world is governed, not by God, but by money. Politicians will dislike that man, because they think that not God, but they, govern the world, by those very politics and knavish tricks, which we pray God to confound, whenever we sing "God save the Queen." And the common people—the masses—who ought to hear such a man gladly, for his words are to them, if they would understand them, a gospel, and good news of divine hope and deliverance from sin and ignorance, oppression and misery—the masses, I say, will dislike that man, because he tells them that God's will is law, and must be obeyed at all risks: and the poor fools have got into their heads just now that not God's will, but the will of the people, is law, and that not the eternal likeness of God, but whatever they happen to decide by the majority of the moment, is right.

And so such a preacher will not be popular with the many. They will dismiss him, at best, as they might a public singer or lecturer, with compliments and thanks, and so excuse themselves from doing what he tells them. And he must look for his sincere hearers in the hearts of those—and there are such, I verily believe, in this congregation—who have a true love and a true fear of Christ, their incarnate God—who believe, indeed, that Christ is their King, and the King of all the earth; who think that to please Him is the most blessed, as well as the most profitable, thing which man can do; to displease Him the most horrible, as well as the most dangerous, thing which man can do; and who, therefore, try to please Him by becoming like Him, by really renouncing the world and all its mean and false and selfish ways, and putting on His new pattern of man, which is created after God's likeness in righteousness and true holiness. Blessed are they, for of them it is written, "Blessed are they which do hunger and thirst after righteousness, for they shall be filled." Even Christ Himself shall fill them. Blessed are they, and all that they take in hand, for of them it is written, "Blessed are all they that fear the Lord, and walk in His ways. For thou shalt eat the labours of thine hands." "The Lord is righteous in all His ways, and holy in all His works. The Lord is nigh unto all them that call upon Him, yea, all such as call upon Him faithfully. He will fulfil the desire of them that fear Him. He also will hear their cry"—ay, "and will help them."

Happy, ay, blest will such souls be, let the day of the Lord appear when it will, or how it will. It may appear—the day of the Lord, as it has appeared again and again in history—in the thunder of some mighty war. It may appear after some irresistible, though often silent revolution, whether religious or intellectual, social or political. It will appear at last, as that great day of days, which will conclude, so we believe, the drama of human history, and all men shall give account for their own works. But, however and whenever it shall appear, they at least will watch its dawning, neither with the selfish assurance of modern Pharisaism, nor with the abject terror of mediæval superstition; but with that manful faith with which he who sang the 98th Psalm saw the day of the Lord dawn once in the far east, more than two thousand years ago, and cried with solemn joy, in the glorious words which you have just heard sung—words which the Church of England has embodied in her daily evening service, in order, I presume, to show her true children how they ought to look at days of judgment; and so prepare to meet their God:—

"Show yourselves joyful unto the Lord, all ye lands: sing, rejoice, and give thanks.

"Let the sea make a noise, and all that therein is: the round world, and they that dwell therein.

"Let the floods clap their hands, and let the hills be joyful together before the Lord: for He cometh to judge the earth.

"With righteousness shall He judge the world: and the people with equity.

"Glory be to the Father, and to the Son, and to the Holy Ghost;

"As it was in the beginning, is now and ever shall be, world without end. Amen."

SERMON III

THE PURIFYING HOPE

Eversley, 1869. Windsor Castle, 1869.

1 John iii. 2. "Beloved, now are we the sons of God, and it doth not yet appear what we shall be: but we know that, when he shall appear, we shall be like him; for we shall see him as he is. And every man that hath this hope in him purifieth himself, even as he is pure."

Let us consider this noble text, and see something, at least, of what it has to tell us. It is, like all God's messages, all God's laws, ay, like God's world in which we live and breathe, at once beautiful and awful; full of life-giving hope; but full, too, of chastening fear. Hope for the glorious future which it opens to poor human beings like us; fear, lest so great a promise being left us, we should fall short of it by our own fault. Behold what manner of love the Father hath bestowed on us, that we should be called the sons of God.

There is the root and beginning of all Christianity,—of all true religion. We are the sons of God, and the infinite, absolute, eternal Being who made this world, and all worlds, is our Father. We are the children of God. It is not for us to say who are not God's children. That is God's concern, not ours. All that we have to do with, is the awful and blessed fact that we are. We were baptised into God's kingdom, in the name of the Father, and of the Son, and of the Holy Ghost. Let us believe the Gospel and good news which baptism brings us, and say each of us;—Not for our own goodness and deserving; not for our own faith or assurance; not for anything which we have thought, felt, or done, but simply out of the free grace and love of God, seeking out us unconscious infants, we are children of God. "Beloved now are we the sons of God, and it doth not yet appear what we shall be." It doth not yet appear what the next life will be like, or what we shall be like in it. That there will be a next life,—that death does not end all for us, the New Testament tells us. Yea, our own hearts and reasons tell us. That sentiment of immortality, that instinct that the death of our body will not, cannot destroy our souls, or ourselves—all men have had that, except a few; and it is a question whether they had it not once, and have only lost it by giving way to their brute animal nature. But be that as it may, it concerns us, I think, very little. For we at least believe that we shall live again. That we shall live again in some state or other, is as certain to our minds as it was to the minds of our forefathers, even while they were heathens; as certain to us as it is that we are alive now. But in that future state, what we shall be like, we know not. St. John says that he did not know; and we certainly have no more means of knowing than St. John.

Therefore let us not feed our fancies with pictures of what the next world will be like,—pictures, I say, which are but waking dreams of men, intruding into those things which they have not seen, vainly puffed up in their fleshly minds—that is in their animal and mortal brain. Let us be content with what St. John tells us, which is a matter not for our brains, but for our hearts; not for our imaginations, but for our conscience, which is indeed our highest reason. Whatever we do not know about the next world, this, he says, we do know,—that when God in Christ shall appear, we shall be like Him. Like God. No more: No: but no less. To be like God, it appears, is the very end and aim of our being. That we might be like God, God our Father sent us forth from His eternal bosom, which is the ground of all life, in heaven and in earth. That we might be like God, He clothed us in mortal flesh, and sent us into this world of sense. That we might be like God, He called us, from our infancy, into His Church. That we might be like God, He gave us the divine sense of right and wrong; and more, by the inspiration of His holy spirit, that inward witness, that Light of God, which lightens every man that cometh into the world, He taught us to love the right and hate the wrong. That we might be like God, God is educating us from our cradle to our grave, by every event, even the smallest, which happens to us. That we might be like God, it is in God that we live, and move, and have our being; that as the raindrop which falls from heaven, rises again surely, soon or late, to heaven again; so each soul of man, coming forth from God at first, should return again to God, as many of them as have eternal life, having become like to God from whom it came at first. And how shall we become like God? or rather like Christ who is both God and man? To become like God the Father,—that is impossible for finite and created beings as we are. But to become somewhat, at least, like God the Son, like Jesus Christ our Lord, who is the brightness of His Father's glory, and the express image of His person, that is not impossible. For He has revealed Himself as a man, in the soul and body of a man, that our sinful souls might be made like His pure soul; our sinful bodies like His glorious body; and that so He might be the first born among many brethren. And how? "We know that when He appears, we shall be like Him, for we shall see Him as He is."

For we shall see Him as He is. Herein is a great mystery, and one which I do not pretend to fathom. Only this I can try to do—to shew how it may seem possible and reasonable, from what is called analogy, that is by judging of an unknown thing from a known thing, which is, at least, something like it. Now do we not all know how apt we are to become like those whom we see, with whom we spend our hours—and, above all, like those whom we admire and honour? For good and for evil, alas! For evil—for those who associate with evil or frivolous persons are too apt to catch not only their low tone, but their very manner, their very expression of face, speaking, and thinking, and acting. Not only do they become scornful, if they live with scorners; false, if they live with liars; mean, if they live with covetous men; but they will actually catch the very look of their faces. The companions of affected, frivolous people, men or women, grow to look affected frivolous. Indulging in the same passions, they mould their own countenances and their very walk, also the very tones of their voice, as well as their dress, into the likeness of those with whom they associate, nay, of those whose fashions (as they are called) they know merely by books and pictures. But thank God, who has put into the hearts of Christian people the tendency towards God—just in the same way does good company tend to make men good; high-minded company to make them high-minded; kindly company to make them kindly; modest company to make them modest; honourable company to make them honourable; and pure company to make them pure. If the young man or woman live with such, look up to such as their ideal, that is, the pattern which they ought to emulate—then, as a fact, the Spirit of God working in them does mould them into something of the likeness of those whom they admire and love. I have lived long enough to see more than one man of real genius stamp his own character, thought, even his very manner of speaking, for good or for evil, on a whole school or party of his disciples. It has been said, and truly, I believe, that children cannot be brought up among beautiful pictures,—I believe, even among any beautiful sights and sounds,—without the very expression of their faces becoming more beautiful, purer, gentler, nobler; so that in them are fulfilled the words of the great and holy Poet concerning the maiden brought up according to God, and the laws of God—

> "And she shall bend her ear
> In many a secret place,
> Where rivulets dance their wayward round,
> And beauty, born of murmuring sound,
> Shall pass into her face."

But if mere human beings can have this "personal influence," as it is called, over each others' characters, if even inanimate things, if they be beautiful, can have it—what must be the personal influence of our Lord Jesus Christ? Of Him, who is the Man of all men, the Son of Man, the perfect and ideal Man—and more, who is very God of very God; the Author of all life, power, wisdom, genius, in every human being, whether they use to good, or abuse to ill, His divine gifts; the Author, too, of all natural beauty, from the sun over our heads to the flower beneath our feet? Think of that steadily, accurately, rationally. Think of who Christ is, and what Christ is—and then think what His personal influence must be—quite infinite, boundless, miraculous. So that the very blessedness of heaven will not be merely the sight of our Lord; it will be the being made holy, and kept holy, by that sight. If only we be fit for it. For let us ask ourselves the question,—If St John's words come true of us, if we should see Him as He is, would the sight of His all-glorious countenance warm us into such life, love, longing for virtue and usefulness, as we never felt before? Or would it crush us into the very earth with utter shame and humiliation, full and awful knowledge of how weak and foolish, sinful and unworthy we were?—as it does to Gerontius in the poem, when he dreams that, after death, he demanded, rashly and ambitiously, to see our Lord, and had his wish.

That is the question which every one must try to answer for himself in fear and trembling, for, he that hath this hope in Him purifieth himself, even as He is pure. The common sense of men—which is often their conscience and highest reason—has taught them this, more or less clearly, in all countries and all ages. There are very few religions which have not made purifying of some kind a part of their duty. The very savage, when he enters (as he fancies) the presence of his god, will wash and adorn himself that he may be fit, poor creature, for meeting the paltry god which he has invented out of his own brain; and he is right as far as he goes. The Englishman, when he dresses himself in his best to go to church, obeys the same reasonable instinct. And, indeed, is not holy baptism a sign that this instinct is a true one?—that if God be pure, he who enters the presence of God must purify himself, even as God is pure? Else why, when each person, whether infant or adult, is received into Christ's Church, is washing with water, whether by sprinkling, as now, or, as of old, by immersion, the very sign and sacrament of his being received into God's kingdom? The instinct, I say, is reasonable, and has its root in the very heart of man. Whatsoever we respect and admire we shall also try to copy, if it be only for a time. If we are going into the presence of a wiser man than ourselves, we shall surely recollect and summon up what little wisdom or knowledge we may have; if into the presence of a holier person, we shall try to call up in ourselves those better and more serious thoughts which we so often forget, that we may be, even for a few minutes, fit for that good company. And if we go into the presence of a purer person than ourselves, we shall surely (unless we be base and brutal) call up our purest and noblest thoughts, and try to purify ourselves, even as they are pure. It is true what poets have said again and again, that there are women whose mere presence, whose mere look, drives all bad thoughts away—women before whom men dare no more speak, or act, nay, even think, basely, than they would dare before the angels of God.

But if it be so—and so it is—what must we be, to be fit to appear before Him who is Purity itself?—before that spotless Christ in whom is no sin and who knows what is in man; who is quick and piercing as a two-edged sword, even to the dividing asunder of the joints and marrow, so that all things are naked and open in the sight of Him with whom we have to do? What purity can we bring into His presence which will not seem impure to Him? What wisdom which will not seem folly? What humility which will not seem self-conceit? What justice which will not seem unjust? What love which will not seem hardness of heart, in the sight of Him who charges His angels with folly, and the very heavens are not clean in His sight? Who loved Him better, and whom did He love better, than St John? Yet, what befel St John when, in the spirit, he saw Him even somewhat as He is?—"And I fell at His feet as dead." If St John himself was struck down with awe, what shall we feel, even the best and purest among us? All we can do is to cast ourselves, now and for ever, in life, in death, and in the day of judgment, on His boundless mercy and love—who stooped from heaven to die for us and cry, God be merciful to me a sinner.

Therefore, I have many fears for some who are ready enough to talk of their fulness of hope and their assurance of salvation, and to join in hymns which express weariness of this life and longings for the joys of heaven, and prayers that they may depart and be with Christ. If they are not in earnest in such words they mock God; but if they are in earnest, some of them, I fear much, tempt God. What if He took them at their word? What if He gave them their wish? What if they departed and entered the presence of Christ, only to meet with a worse fate than that of Gerontius? Only to be overwhelmed with shame and terror, because, though they have been talking of being with Christ, they have not been trying to be like Christ; because they have not sought after holiness, without which no man shall see the Lord; because they have not tried to purify themselves, even as He is pure; and have, poor, heedless souls, gone out of the world, with all their sins upon their head, to enter a place for which they will find themselves utterly unfit, because it is a place into which nothing can enter which defileth, or committeth abomination, or maketh a lie, and from which the covetous are specially excluded; and in which will be fulfilled the parable of the man who came to the feast, not having on a wedding garment,—Take him, bind him hand and foot, and cast him into the outer darkness. There shall be wailing and gnashing of teeth.

Assurance, my friends, may be reasonable enough when it is founded on repentance and hatred of evil, and love and practice of what is good. But, again, assurance may be as unreasonable as it is offensive. We blame a man who has too much assurance about earthly things. Let us beware that we have not too much assurance about heavenly things. For our assurance will surely be too great, unreasonable, built upon the sand, if it be built on mere self-conceit of our own orthodoxy, and our own privileges, or our own special connection with God.

Meanwhile it has been my comfort to meet with some—would God they were more numerous—who, instead of talking of their assurance of salvation, lived in a state of noble self-discontent and holy humility; who could see nothing but their own faults and failings; who, though they were holier than others, considered themselves as unholy; though they were do-ing more good than others, thought themselves useless; whose standard of duty was so lofty, that they could think of nothing, but how far they had failed in reaching it; who measured themselves, not by other men, but by Christ Himself; and, doing that, had nought to say, save, "God be merciful to me a sinner." And for such people I have had full assurance, just because they had no assurance themselves. And I have said in my heart, These are worthy, just because they think themselves unworthy. These are fit to appear in the presence of God, just because they believe themselves unfit. These are they who will cry at the day of judgment, in wondering humility,—Lord, when saw we Thee hungry, or thirsty, or naked, or in prison, and visited Thee? And will receive for answer,—"Inasmuch as ye have done it unto one of the least of these my brethren, ye have done it unto Me." "Thou hast been faithful over a few things, I will make thee ruler over many things. Enter into the joy of thy Lord."

To which end may God of His mercy bring us, and all we love. Amen.

SERMON IV

THE LORD COMING TO HIS TEMPLE

Westminster Abbey. November, 1874.

Malachi iii. 1, 2. "The Lord, whom ye seek, shall suddenly come to His temple. . . . But who may abide the day of His coming? and who shall stand when He appeareth? for He is like a refiner's fire, and like fuller's sope."

We believe that this prophecy was fulfilled at the first coming of our Lord Jesus Christ. We believe that it will be fulfilled again, in that great day when He shall judge the quick and the dead. But it is of neither of these events I wish to speak to you just now. I wish to speak of an event which has not (as far as we know) happened; which will probably never happen; but which is still perfectly possible; and one, too, which it is good for us to face now and then, and ask ourselves, If this thing came to pass, what should I think, and what should I do?

I shall touch the question with all reverence and caution. I shall try to tread lightly, as one who is indeed on hallowed ground. For the question which I have dared to ask you and myself is none other than this—If the Lord suddenly came to this temple, or any other in this land; if He appeared among us, as He did in Judea eighteen hundred years ago, what should we think of Him? Should we recognise, or should we reject, our Saviour and our Lord? It is an awful thought, the more we look at it. But for that very reason it may be the more fit to be asked, once and for all.

Now, to put this question safely and honestly, we must keep within those words which I just said—as He appeared in Judea eighteen hundred years ago. We must limit our fancy to the historic Christ, to the sayings, doings, character which are handed down to us in the four Gospels; and ask ourselves nothing but—What should I think if such a personage were to meet me now? To imagine Him—as has been too often done—as doing deeds, speaking words, and even worse, entertaining motives, which are not written in the four Gospels, is as unfair morally, as it is illogical critically. It creates a phantom, a fictitious character, and calls that Christ. It makes each writer, each thinker—or rather dreamer—however shallow his heart and stupid his brain—and all our hearts are but too shallow, and all our brains too stupid—the measure of a personage so vast and so unique, that all Christendom for eighteen hundred years has seen in Him, and we of course hold seen truly, the Incarnate God. No; we must think of nothing save what is set down in Holy Writ.

And yet, alas! we cannot use in our days, that which eighteen hundred years ago was the most simple and obvious test of our Lord's truthfulness, namely His miraculous powers. The folly and sin of man have robbed us of what is, as it were, one of the natural rights of reasoning, man. Lying prodigies and juggleries, forged and pretended miracles, even—oh, shame!—imitations of His most sacred wounds, have, up to our own time, made all rational men more and more afraid of aught which seems to savour of the miraculous; till most of us, I think, would have to ask forgiveness—as I myself should have to ask,—if, tantalized and insulted again and again by counterfeit miracles, we failed to recognise real miracles, and Him who performed them. Therefore, for good or evil, we should be driven back upon that test alone, which, after all, perhaps, is the most sure as well as the most convincing—the moral test—the test of character. What manner of personage would He be did He condescend to appear among us? Of that, thank God, the Gospels ought to leave us in no doubt. What acts He might condescend to perform, what words He might condescend to speak, it is not for such beings as we to guess. But how He would demean Himself we know; for Holy Writ has told us how He demeaned Himself in Judea eighteen hundred years ago; and He is the same yesterday, to-day, and for ever, and can be only like Himself. But should we know Him merely by His bearing and character? Should we see in Him an utterly ideal personage— The Son of Man, and therefore, ere we lost sight of Him once more, the Son of God? Let us think. First, therefore, we must believe that—as in Judea of old—Christ would meet men with all consideration and courtesy. He would not break the bruised reed, nor quench the smoking flax. He would not strive, nor cry, nor let His voice be heard in the streets. He would not cause any of God's little ones to offend, to stumble. In plain words, He would not shock and repel them by any conduct of His. Therefore, as in Judea of old, He would be careful of, even indulgent to, the usages of society, as long as they were innocent. He would never outrage the code of manners, however imperfect, however conventional, which this or any other civilised nation may have agreed on, to express and keep up respect, self-restraint, delicacy, of man toward man, of man toward woman, of the young ward the old, of the living toward the dead. No.

As I said just now, He would never cause, by any act or word of His, one of God's little ones to stumble and fall away.

I used just now that word manners. Let me beg your very serious attention to it. I use it, remember, in its true, its ancient—that is, in its moral and spiritual sense. I use it as the old Greeks, the old Romans, used their corresponding words; as our wise forefathers used it, when they said well, that "Manners maketh man;" that manners are at once the efficient cause of a man's success, and the proof of his deserving to succeed: the outward and visible sign of whatsoever inward and spiritual grace, or disgrace, there may be in him. I mean by the word what our Lord meant when He reproved the pushing and vulgar arrogance of the Scribes and Pharisees, and laid down the golden rule of all good manners, "Whosoever will be great among you, let him be your minister; and whosoever will be chief among you, let him be your servant."

Next, I beg you to remember that all, or almost all, good manners which we have among us—courtesies, refinements, self-restraint, and mutual respect—all which raises us, socially and morally, above our forefathers of fifteen hundred years ago—deep-hearted men, valiant and noble, but coarse, and arrogant, and quarrelsome—all that, or almost all, we owe to Christ, to the influence of His example, and to that Bible which testifies of Him. Yes, the Bible has been for Christendom, in the cottage as much as in the palace, the school of manners; and the saying that he who becomes a true Christian becomes a true gentleman, is no rhetorical boast, but a solid historic fact.

Now imagine Christ to reappear on earth, with that perfect outward beauty of character—with what Greeks and Romans, and our own ancestors, would have called those perfect manners—which, if we are to believe the Gospels, He shewed in Judea of old, which won then so many hearts, especially of the common people, sounder judges often of true nobility than many who fancy themselves their betters. Conceive—but which of us can conceive?—His perfect tenderness, patience, sympathy, graciousness, and grace, combined with perfect strength, stateliness, even awfulness, when awe was needed. Remember that, if, again, the Gospels are to be believed. He alone, of all personages of whom history tells us, solved in His own words and deeds the most difficult paradox of human character—to be at once utterly conscious, and yet utterly unconscious, of self; to combine with perfect self-sacrifice a perfect self-assertion. Whether or not His being able to do that proved Him to have been that which He was, the Son of God, it proves Him at least to have been the Son of Man—the unique and unapproachable ideal of humanity, utterly inspired by the Holy Spirit of God.

But again: He condescended, in His teaching of old, to the level of Jewish, knowledge at that time. We may, therefore, believe that He would condescend to the level of our modern knowledge; and what would that involve? It would leave Him, however less than Himself, at least master of all that the human race has thought or discovered in the last eighteen hundred years. Think of that. And think again, that if He condescended, as in Judea of old, to employ that knowledge in teaching men—He who knew what was in man, and needed not that any should bear witness to Him of man—He would manifest a knowledge of human nature to which that of a Shakspeare would be purblind and dull; a knowledge of which the Scripture nobly says that "The Word of God is quick and powerful, and sharper than any two-edged sword, even to the dividing asunder of soul and spirit, and of the joints and marrow, and is a discerner of the thoughts and intents of the heart;" so that all "things are naked and opened unto the eyes of Him with whom we have to do." And consider that, in the light of that knowledge, He might adapt himself as perfectly to us of this great city, as He did to the villagers of Galilee, or to the townsmen of Jerusalem.

Consider, again, that He who spoke as never man yet spake in Jerusalem, might speak as man never yet spoke on English soil; that He who was listened to gladly once, because He spake with authority, and not as the scribes, at second hand, and by rule and precedent, might be listened to gladly here once more. For He might speak here, not as we poor scribes can speak at best, but with an authority, originality, earnestness, as well as an eloquence, which might exercise a fascination, which would be, to all with whom He came in contact, what Malachi calls it, "a refiner's fire"—most purifying, though often most painful to the very best; a fascination which might be to every one who came under its spell a veritable Judgment and Day of the Lord, shewing each man with fearful clearness to which side he really inclined at heart in the struggle between truth and falsehood, good and evil; a fascination, therefore, equally attractive to those who wished to do right, and intolerable to those who wished to do wrong.

Consider that last thought. And consider, too, that those to whom the fascination of such a personage might be so intolerable, that it might turn to utter hate, would probably be those whose moral sense was so perverted, that they thought they were doing right when they were doing wrong, and speaking truth when they were telling lies. It is an awful thought. But we know that there were such men, and too many, among the scribes and Pharisees of Jerusalem. And human nature is the same in every age. Be that as it may—however retired His life, He could not long be hid. He would shortly exercise, almost without attempting it, an enormous public influence.

But yet, as in Judea of old, would He not be only too successful? Would He not be at once too liberal for some, and too exacting for others? Would He not, as in Judea of old, encounter not merely the active envy of the vain and the ambitious, which would follow one who spoke as never man spoke; not merely the active malignity of those who wish their fellow-creatures to be bad and not good; not merely the bigotry of every sect and party; but that mere restless love of new excitements, and that dull fear and suspicion of new truths, and even of old truths in new words, which beset the uneducated of every rank and class, and in no age more than in our own? And therefore I must ask, in sober sadness, how long would His influence last? It lasted, we know, in Judea of old, for some three years. And then—. But I am not going to say that any such tragedy is possible now. It would be an insult to Him; an insult to the gracious influences of His Spirit, the gracious teaching of His Church, to say that of our generation, however unworthy we may be of our high calling in Christ. And yet, if He had appeared in any country of Christendom only four hundred years ago, might He not have endured an even more dreadful death than that of the cross?

But doubtless, no personal harm would happen to Him here. Only there might come a day, in which, as in Judea of old, "after He had said these things, many were offended, and walked no more with Him:" when his hearers and admirers would grow fewer and more few, some through bigotry, some through envy, some through fickleness, some through cowardice, till He was left alone with a little knot of earnest disciples; who might diminish, alas, but too rapidly, when they found at He, as in Judea of old, did not intend to become the head of a new sect, and to gratify their ambition and vanity by making them His delegates. And so the world, the religious world as well as the rest, might let Him go His way, and vanish from the eyes and minds of men, leaving behind little more than a regret that one so gifted and so fascinating should have proved—I hardly like to say the words, and yet they must be said—so unsafe and so unsound a teacher.

I shall not give now the reasons which have led me, and not in haste, to this melancholy conclusion. I shall only say that I have come to it, with pain, and shame, and fear. With shame and fear. For when I ask you the solemn question, Would you know Christ if He came among you? do I not ask myself a question which I dare not answer? How can I tell whether I should recognise, after all, my Saviour and my Lord? How do I know that if He said (as He but too certainly might), something which clashed seriously with my preconceived notions of what He ought to say, I should not be offended, and walk no more with Him? How do I know that if He said, as in Judea of old, "Will ye too go away?" I should answer with St Peter, "Lord, to whom shall we go? Thou hast the words of eternal life, and we believe and are sure that thou art the Christ, the Son of the living God?" I dare not ask that question of myself. How then dare I ask it of you? I know not. I can only say, "Lord, I believe: help thou mine unbelief." I know not. But this I know—that in this or any other world, if you or I did recognise Him, it would be with utter shame and terror, unless we had studied and had striven to copy either Himself, or whatsoever seems to us most like Him. Yes; to study the good, the beautiful, and the true in Him, and wheresoever else we find it—for all that is good, beautiful, and true throughout the universe are nought but rays from Him, the central sun—to obey St. Paul of old, and "whatsoever things are true, venerable, just, pure, lovely, and of good report—if there be any virtue and if there be any praise, to think on these things,"—on these scattered fragmentary sacraments of Him whose number is not two, nor seven, "but seventy-times seven;" that is the way—I think, the only way—to be ready to recognise our Saviour, and to prepare to meet our God; that He may be to us, too, as a refiner's fire, and refine us—our thoughts, our deeds, our characters throughout.

And I think, too, that this is the way, perhaps the only way, to rid ourselves of the fancy that we can be accounted righteous before God for any works or deservings of our own. Those in whom that fancy lingers must have but a paltry standard of what righteousness is, a mean conception of moral—that is, spiritual—perfection. But those who look not inwards, but upwards; not at themselves, but at Christ and all spiritual perfection—they become more and more painfully aware of their own imperfections. The beauty of Christ's character shows them the ugliness of their own. His purity shows them their own foulness. His love their own hardness. His wisdom their own folly. His strength their own weakness. The higher their standard rises, the lower falls their estimate of themselves; till, in utter humiliation and self-distrust, they seek comfort ere alone it can be found—in faith—in utter faith and trust in that very moral perfection of Christ which shames and dazzles them, and yet is their only hope. To trust in Him for themselves and all they love. To trust that, just because Christ is so magnificent, He will pity, and not despise, our meanness. Just because He is so pure, and righteous, and true, and lovely, He will appreciate, and not abhor, our struggles after purity, righteousness, truth, love, however imperfect, however soiled with failure—and with worse. Just because He is so unlike us, He will smile graciously upon out feeblest attempts to be like Him. Just because He has borne the sins and carried the sorrows of mankind, therefore those who come to Him He will in no wise cast out. Amen.

SERMON V

ADVENT LESSONS

Westminster Abbey, First Sunday in Advent, 1873.

Romans vii. 22-25. "I delight in the law of God after the inward man: but I see another law in my members, warring against the law of my mind, and bringing me into captivity to the law of sin which is in my members. O wretched man that I am! who shall deliver me from the body of this death? I thank God through Jesus Christ our Lord."

This is the first Sunday in Advent. To-day we have prayed that God would give us grace to put away the works of darkness, and put on us the armour of light. Next Sunday we shall pray that, by true understanding of the Scriptures, we may embrace and hold fast the blessed hope of everlasting life. The Sunday after that the ministers and stewards of God's mysteries may prepare His way by turning the hearts of the disobedient to the wisdom of the just—the next, that His grace and mercy may speedily help and deliver us from the sins which hinder us in running the race set before us. But I do not think that we shall understand those collects, or indeed the meaning of Advent itself, or the reason why we keep the season of Advent year by year, unless we first understand the prayer which we offered up last Sunday, "Stir up, O Lord, the wills of Thy faithful people,"—and we shall understand that prayer just in proportion as we have in us the Spirit of God, or the spirit of the world, which is the spirit of unbelief.

Worldly people say—and say openly, just now—that this prayer is all a dream. They say God will not stir up men's wills to do good any more than to do harm. He leaves men to themselves to get through life as they can. This Heavenly Father of whom you speak will not give His holy spirit to those who ask Him. He does not, as one of your Collects says, put into men's minds good desires—they come to a man entirely from outside a man, from his early teaching, his youthful impressions, as they are called now-a-days. He does not either give men grace and power to put these desires into practice. That depends entirely on the natural strength of a man's character; and that, again, depends principally on the state of his brain. So, says the world, if you wish your own character to improve, you must improve it yourself, for God will not improve it for you. But, after all, why should you try to improve? why not be content to be just what you are? you did not make yourself, and you are not responsible for being merely what God has chosen to make you.

This is what worldly men say, or at least what they believe and act on; and this is the reason why there is so little improvement in the world, because men do not ask God to improve their hearts and stir up their wills. I say, very little improvement. Men talk loudly of the enlightenment of the age, and the progress of the species, and the spread of civilisation, and so forth: but when I read old books, and compare old times with these, I confess I do not see so much of it as all this hopeful talk would lead me to expect. Men in general have grown more prudent, more cunning, from long experience. They have found out that certain sins do not pay—that is, they interfere with people's comfort and their power of making money, and therefore they prudently avoid them themselves, and put them down by law in other men's cases. Men have certainly grown more good-natured, in some countries, in that they dislike more than their ancestors did, to inflict bodily torture on human beings; but they are just as ready, or even more ready, to inflict on those whom they dislike that moral and mental torture which to noble souls is worse than any bodily pain. As for any real improvement in human nature—where is it? There is just as much falsehood, cheating, and covetousness, I believe, in the world as ever there was; just as much cant and hypocrisy, and perhaps more; just as much envy, hatred, malice and all uncharitableness. Is not the condition of the masses in many great cities as degraded and as sad as ever was that of the serfs in the middle ages? Do not the poor still die by tens of thousands of fevers, choleras, and other diseases, which we know perfectly how to prevent, and yet have not the will to prevent? Is not the adulteration of food just now as scandalous as it is unchecked? The sins and follies of human nature have been repressed in one direction only to break out another. And as for open and coarse sin, people complain even now, and I fear with justice, that there is more drunkenness in England at this moment than there ever was. So much for our boasted improvement.

Look again at the wars of the world. Five-and-twenty years ago, one used to be told that the human race was grown too wise to go to war any more, and that we were to have an advent of universal peace and plenty, and since then we have seen some seven great wars, the last the most terrible of all,—and ever since, all the nations of Europe have been watching each other in distrust and dread, increasing their armaments, working often night and day at forging improved engines of destruction, wherewith to kill their fellow-men. Not that I blame that. It is necessary. Yes! but the hideous thing is, that it should be necessary. Does that state of things look much like progress of the human race? Can we say that mankind is much improved, either in wisdom or in love, while all the nations of Europe are spending millions merely to be ready to fight they know not whom, they know not why?

No, my good friends, obey the wise man, and clear your minds of cant— man's pretensions, man's boastfulness, man's power of blinding his own eyes to plain facts—above all, to the plain fact that he does not succeed, even in this world of which he fancies himself the master, because he lives without God in the world. All this saddens, I had almost said, sickens, a thoughtful man, till he turns away from this noisy sham improvement of mankind—the wages of sin, which are death, to St John's account of the true improvement of mankind, the true progress of the species,—the gift of God which is eternal life. "And I saw a new heaven and a new earth: for the first heaven and the first earth were passed away. And I saw the Holy City—New Jerusalem, coming down from God out of heaven, prepared as a bride adorned for her husband. And I heard a great voice out of heaven, saying, Behold the tabernacle of God is with men, and He will dwell with them, and they shall be His people, and God Himself shall be with them, and be their God. And God shall wipe away all tears from their eyes; and there shall be no more death, neither sorrow nor crying, neither shall there be any more pain: for the former things are passed away."

Does that sound much like a general increase of armaments? or like bills for the prevention of pestilence, or of drunkenness,—which, even if they pass, will both probably fail to do the good which they propose? No. And if this wicked world is to be mended, then God must stir up the wills of His faithful people, and we must pray without ceasing for ourselves, and for all for whom we are bound to pray, that He would stir them up. For what we want is not knowledge; we have enough of that, and too much. Too much; for knowing so much and doing so little, what an account will be required of us at the last day!

No. It is the will which we want, in a hundred cases. Take that of pestilential dwelling-houses in our great towns. Every one knows that they ought to be made healthy; every one knows that they can be made healthy. But the will to make them healthy is not here, and they are left to breed disease and death. And so, as in a hundred instances, shallow philosophers are proved, by facts, to be mistaken, when they tell us that man will act up to the best of his knowledge without God's help. For that is exactly what man does not. What is wrong with the world in general, is wrong likewise more or less with you and me, and with all human beings; for after all, the world is made up of human beings; and the sin of the world is nothing save the sins of each and all human beings put together; and the world will be renewed and come right again, just as far and no farther, as each human being is renewed and comes right. The only sure method, therefore, of setting the world right, is to begin by setting our own little part of the world right—in a word, setting ourselves right.

But if we begin to try, that, we find, is just what we cannot do. When a man begins to hunger and thirst after righteousness, and, discontented with himself, attempts to improve himself, he soon begins to find a painful truth in many a word of the Bible and the Prayer Book to which he gave little heed, as long as he was contented with himself, and with doing just what pleased him, right or wrong. He soon finds out that he has no power of himself to help himself, that he is tied and bound with the burden of his sins, and that he cannot, by reason of his frailty, stand upright—that he actually is sore let and hindered by his own sins, from running the race set before him, and doing his duty where God has put him. All these sayings come home to him as actual facts, most painful facts, but facts which he cannot deny. He soon finds out the meaning and the truth of that terrible struggle between the good in him and the evil in him, of which St Paul speaks so bitterly in the text. How, when he tries to do good, evil is present with him. How he delights in the law of God with his inward mind, and yet finds another law in his body, warring against the law of God, and bringing him into captivity to the law of sin. How he is crippled by old bad habits, weakened by cowardice, by laziness, by vanity, by general inability of will, till he is ready,—disgusted at himself and his own weakness,—to cry, Who shall deliver me from the body of this death?

Let him but utter that cry honestly. Let him once find out that he wants something outside himself to help him, to deliver him, to strengthen him, to stir up his weak will, to give him grace and power to do what he knows instead of merely admiring it, and leaving it undone. Let a man only find out that. Let him see that he needs a helper, a deliverer, a strengthener—in one word, a Saviour—and he will find one. I verily believe that, sooner or later, the Lord Jesus Christ will reveal to that man what He revealed to St Paul; that He Himself will deliver him; and that, like St Paul, after crying "O wretched man that I am, who shall deliver me from the body of this death?" he will be able to answer himself, I thank God—God will, through Jesus Christ our Lord. Christ will deliver me from the bonds of my sins, Christ will stir up this weak will of mine, Christ will give me strength and power, faithfully to fulfil all my good desires, because He Himself has put them into my heart not to mock me, not to disappoint me—not to make me wretched with the sight of noble graces and virtues to which I cannot attain, but to fulfil His work in me. What He has begun in me He will carry on in me. He has sown the seed in me, and He will make it bear fruit, if only I pray to Him, day by day, for strength to do what I know I ought to do, and cry morning and night to Him, the fount of life, Stir up my will, O Lord, that I may bring forth the fruit of good works, for then by Thee I shall be plentifully rewarded.

So the man gains hope and heart for himself, and so, if he will but think rationally and humbly, he may gain hope and heart for this poor sinful world. For what has come true for him may come true for any man. Who is he that God should care more for him than for others? Who is he that God should help him when he prays, more than He will help His whole church if it will but pray? He says to himself, all this knowledge of what is right; all these good desires, all these longings after a juster, purer, nobler, happier state of things; there they are up and down the world already, though, alas! they have borne little enough fruit as yet. Be it so. But God put them into my heart. And who save God has put them into the world's heart? It was God who sowed the seed in me; surely it is God who has sowed it in other men? And if God has made it bear even the poorest fruit in me, why should He not make it bear fruit in other men and in all the world? All they need is that God should stir up their wills, that they may do the good they know, and attain the blessedness after which they long.

And then, if the man have a truly human, truly reasonable heart in him— he feels that he can pray for others as well as for himself. He feels that he must pray for them, and cry,—Thou alone canst make men strong to do the right thing, and Thou wilt make them. Stir up their wills, O Lord! Thou canst not mean that all the good seed which is sown about the world should die and wither, and bring no fruit to perfection. Surely Thy word will not return to Thee void, but be like the rain which comes down from heaven, and gives seed to the sower and bread to the eater. Oh, strengthen such as stand, and comfort and help the weak-hearted, and raise up them that fall, and, finally, beat down Satan and all the powers of evil under our feet, and pour out thy spirit on all flesh, that so their Father's name may be hallowed, His kingdom come, His will be done on earth as it is in heaven. And so will come the one and only true progress of the human race—which is, that all men should become faithful and obedient citizens of the holy city, the kingdom of God, which is the Church of Christ. To which may God in His mercy bring us all, and our children after us. Amen.

This, then, is the lesson why we are met together this Advent day. We are met to pray that God would so help us by His grace and mercy that we may bring forth the fruit of good works, and that when our Lord Jesus Christ shall come in His glorious majesty to judge the quick and the dead, we, and our descendants after us, may be found an acceptable people in His sight.

We are met to pray, in a National Church, for the whole nation of England, that all orders and degrees therein may, each in his place and station, help forward the hallowing of God's name, the coming of His kingdom, the doing of His will on earth. We are met to pray for the Queen and all that are in authority, that these Advent collects may be fulfilled in them, and by them, for the good of the whole people; for the ministers and stewards of Christ's mysteries, that the same collects may be fulfilled by them and in them, till they turn the hearts of the disobedient to the wisdom of the just; for the Commons of this nation, that each man may he delivered, by God's grace and mercy, from the special sin which besets him in this faithless and worldly generation and hinders him from running the race of duty which is set before him, and get strength from God so to live that in that dread day he may meet his Judge and King, not in tenor and in shame, but in loyalty and in humble hope.

But more—we are here to worship God in Christ, both God and man. To confess that without Him we can do nothing, that unless He enlighten our understandings we are dark, unless He stir up our wills we are powerless for good. To confess that though we have forgotten Him, yet He has not forgotten us. That He is the same gracious and generous Giver and Saviour. That though we deny Him He cannot deny Himself. That He is the same yesterday, to-day, and for ever as when He came to visit this earth in great humility. That the Lord is King, though the earth be moved. He sitteth upon His throne, be the nations never so unquiet. We are here to declare to ourselves and all men, and the whole universe, that we at least believe that the heavens and earth are full of His glory. We are here to declare that, whether or not the kings of the earth are wise enough, or the judges of it learned enough, to acknowledge Christ for their king, we at least will worship the Son lest He be angry, and so we perish from the right way; for if His wrath be kindled, yea but a little, then blessed are they, and they only, who put their trust in Him. We are here to join our songs with angels round the throne, and with those pure and mighty beings who, in some central sanctuary of the universe, cry for ever, "Thou art worthy, O Lord, to receive glory and honour and power: for Thou hast created all things, and for Thy pleasure they are and were created."

We do so in ancient words, ancient music, ancient ceremonies, for a token that Christ's rule and glory is an ancient rule and an eternal glory; that it is no new discovery of our own, and depends not on our own passing notions and feelings about it, but is like Christ, the same now as in the days of our forefathers, the same as it was fifteen hundred years ago, the same as it has been since the day that He stooped to be born of the Virgin Mary, the same that it will be till He shall come in His glory to judge the quick and the dead. Therefore we delight in the ancient ceremonial, as like as we can make it, to that of the earlier and purer ages of the Church, when Christianity was still, as it were, fresh from the hand of its Creator, ere yet it had been debased and defiled by the idolatrous innovations of the Church of Rome. For so we confess ourselves bound by links of gratitude to the Apostles, and the successors of the Apostles, and to all which has been best, purest, and truest in the ages since. So we confess that we worship the same God-man of whom Apostles preached, of whom fathers philosophised, and for whom martyrs died. That we believe, like them, that He alone is King of kings and Lord of lords; that there is no progress, civilization, or salvation in this life or the life to come, but through His undeserved mercy and His strengthening grace; that He has reigned from the creation of the world, reigns now, and will reign unto that last dread day, when He shall have put all enemies under His feet, and delivered up the kingdom to God, even the Father, that God may be all in all. Unto which day may He in His mercy bring us all through faith and good works: Amen.

SERMON VI

CAPITAL PUNISHMENT

*Eversley. **Quinquagesima Sunday, 1872.***

Genesis ix. 1, 3, 4, 5, 6. "And God blessed Noah and his sons, and said unto them, Be fruitful, and multiply, and replenish the earth. . . . Every moving thing that liveth shall be meat for you . . . But flesh with the life thereof, which is the blood thereof, shall ye not eat. And surely your blood of your lives will I require: at the hand of every beast will I require it, and at the hand of man; at the hand of every man's brother will I require the life of man. Whoso sheddeth man's blood, by man shall his blood be shed. for in the image of God made he man."

This is God's blessing on mankind. This is our charter from God, who made and rules this earth. This is the end and duty of our mortal life:—to be fruitful and multiply and replenish the earth, and subdue it. But is that all? Is there no hint in this blessing of God of something more than our mortal life—something beyond our mortal life? Surely there is. Those words—"in the image of God made He man," must mean, if they mean anything, that man can, if he will but be a true man, share the eternal life of God. But I will not speak of that to-day, but rather of a question about his mortal life in this world, which is this:—What is the reason why man has a right over the lives of animals? why he may use them for his food? and at the same time, what is the reason why he has not the same right over the lives of his fellow-men? why he may not use them for food?

It is this—that "in the image of God made He man." Man is made in the image and likeness of God, therefore he is a sacred creature; a creature, not merely an animal, and the highest of all animals, only cunninger than all animals, more highly organised, more delicately formed than all animals; but something beyond an animal. He is in the likeness of God, therefore he is consecrated to God. He is the one creature on earth whom God, so far as we know, is trying to make like Himself. Therefore, whosoever kills a man, sins not only against that man, nor against society: he sins against God. And God will require that man's blood at the hand of him who slays him. But how? At the hand of every beast will He require it, and at the hand of every man.

What that first part of the law means I cannot tell. How God will require from the lion, or the crocodile, or the shark, who eats a human being, the blood of their victims, is more than I can say. But this I can say—that the feeling, not only of horror and pity, but of real rage and indignation, with which men see (what God grant you never may see) a wild beast kill a man, is a witness in man's conscience that the text is true somehow, though how we know not. I received a letter a few weeks since from an officer, a very remarkable person, in which he described his horror and indignation at seeing a friend of his struck down and eaten by a tiger, and how, when next day he stood over what had been but the day before a human being, he looked up to heaven, and kept repeating the words of the text, "in the image of God made He man," in rage and shame, and almost accusing God for allowing His image to be eaten by a brute beast. It shook, for the moment, his faith in God's justice and goodness. That man was young then, and has grown calmer and wiser now, and has regained a deeper and sounder faith in God. But the shock, he said, was dreadful to him. He felt that the matter was not merely painful and pitiable, but that it was a wrong and a crime; and on the faith of this very text, a wrong and a crime I believe it to be, and one which God knows how to avenge and to correct when man cannot. Somehow—for He has ways of which we poor mortals do not dream—at the hand of every beast will He require the blood of man.

But more; at the hand of every man will He require it. And how? The text tells us, "Whoso sheddeth man's blood, by man shall his blood be shed: for in the image of God made He man." Now, I do not doubt but that the all-seeing God, looking back on what had most probably happened on this earth already, and looking forward to what would happen, and happens, alas! too often now, meant to warn men against the awful crime of cannibalism, of eating their fellow-men as they would eat an animal. By so doing, they not only treated their fellow-men as beasts, but they behaved like beasts themselves. They denied that their victim was made in the likeness of God; they denied that they were made in the likeness of God; they willingly and deliberately put on the likeness of beasts, and as beasts they were to perish. Now, this is certain, that savages who eat men—and alas! there are thousands even now who do so—usually know in their hearts that they are doing wrong. As soon as their consciences are the least awakened, they are ashamed of their cannibalism; they lie about it, try to conceal it; and as soon as God's grace begins to work on them, it is the very first sin that they give up. And next, this is certain, that there is a curse upon it. No cannibal people, so far as I can find, have ever risen or prospered in the world; and the cannibal peoples now-a-days, and for the last three hundred years, have been dying out. By their own vices, diseases, and wars, they perish off the face of the earth, in the midst of comfort and plenty; and, in spite of all the efforts of missionaries, even their children and grand-children, after giving up the horrid crime, and becoming Christians, seem to have no power of living and increasing, but dwindle away, and perish off the earth. Yes, God's laws work in strange and subtle ways; so darkly, so slowly, that the ungodly and sinners often believe that there are no laws of God, and say—"Tush, how should God perceive it? Is there knowledge in the Most High?" But the laws work, nevertheless, whether men are aware of them or not. "The mills of God grind slowly," but sooner or later they grind the sinner to powder.

And now I will leave this hateful subject and go on to another, on which I am moved to speak once and for all, because it is much in men's minds just now—I mean what is vulgarly called "capital punishment," the punishing of murder by death. Now the text, which is the ancient covenant of God with man, speaks very clearly on this point. "Whosoever sheddeth man's blood, by man shall his blood be shed." Man is made in the likeness of God. That is the ground of our law about murder, as it is the ground of all just and merciful law; that gives man his right to slay the murderer; that makes it his duty to slay the murderer. He has to be jealous of God's likeness, and to slay, in the name of God, the man who, by murder, outrages the likeness of God in himself and in his victim.

You all know that there is now-a-days a strong feeling among some persons about capital punishment; that there are those who will move heaven and earth to interfere with the course of justice, and beg off the worst of murderers, on any grounds, however unreasonable, fanciful, even unfair; simply because they have a dislike to human beings being hanged. I believe, from long consideration, that these persons' strange dislike proceeds from their not believing sufficiently that man is made in the image of God. And, alas! it proceeds, I fear, in some of them, from not believing in a God at all—believing, perhaps, in some mere maker of the world, but not in the living God which Scripture sets forth. For how else can they say, as I have known some say, that capital punishment is wrong, because "we have no right to usher a man into the presence of his Maker."

Into the presence of his Maker! Why, where else is every man, you and I, heathen and Christian, bad and good, save in the presence of his Maker already? Do we not live and move and have our being in God? Whither can we go from His spirit, or whither can we flee from His presence? If we ascend into heaven, He is there. If we go down to hell He is there also. And if the law puts a man to death, it does not usher him into the presence of his Maker, for he is there already. It simply says to him, "God has judged you on earth, not we. God will judge you in the next world, not we. All we know is, that you are not fit to live in this world. All our duty is to send you out of it. Where you will go in the other world is God's matter, not ours, and the Lord have mercy on your soul."

And this want of faith in a living God lies at the bottom of another objection. We are to keep murderers alive in order to convert and instruct and amend them. The answer is, We shall be most happy to amend anybody of any fault, however great: but the experience of ages is that murderers are past mending; that the fact of a man's murdering another is a plain proof that he has no moral sense, and has become simply a brute animal Our duty is to punish not to amend, and to say to the murderer, "If you can be amended; God will amend you, and so have mercy on your soul. God must amend you, if you are to be amended. If God cannot amend you, we cannot. If God will not amend you, certainly we cannot force Him to do so, if we kept you alive for a thousand years." That would seem reasonable, as well as reverent and faithful to God. But men now-a-days fancy that they love their fellow creatures far better than God loves them, and can deal far more wisely and lovingly with them than God is willing to deal. Of these objections I take little heed. I look on them as merely loose cant, which does not quite understand the meaning of its own words, and I trust to sound, hard, English common sense to put them aside.

But there is another objection to capital punishment, which we must deal with much more respectfully and tenderly; for it is made by certain good people, people whom we must honour, though we differ from them, for no set of people have done more (according to their numbers) for education, for active charity, and for benevolence, and for peace and good will among the nations of the earth. And they say, you must not take the life of a murderer, just because he is made in God's image. Well, I should have thought that God Himself was the best judge of that. That, if God truly said that man was made in His image, and said, moreover, as it were at the same moment, that, therefore, whoso sheds man's blood, by man shall his blood be shed—our duty was to trust God, to obey God, and to do our duty against the murderer, however painful to our feelings it might be. But I believe these good people make their mistake from forgetting this; that if the murderer be made in God's image and likeness, so is the man whom he murders; and so also is the jury who convict him, the judge who condemns him, and the nation (the society of men) for whom they act.

And this, my dear friends, brings us to the very root of the meaning of law. Man has sense to make laws (which animals cannot do), just because he is made in the likeness of God, and has the sense of right and wrong. Man has the right to enforce laws, to see right done and wrong punished, just because he is made in the likeness of God. The laws of a country, as far as they are just and righteous, are the copy of what the men of that country have found out about right and wrong, and about how much right they can get done, and how much wrong punished. So, just as the men of a country are (in spite of all their sins) made in the likeness of God, so the laws of a country (in spite of all their defects) are a copy of God's will, as to what men should or should not do. And that, and no other, is the true reason why the judge or magistrate has authority over either property, liberty, or life. He is God's servant, the servant of Christ, who is King of this land and of all lands, and of all governments, and all kings and rulers of the earth. He sits there in God's name, to see God's will done, as far as poor fallible human beings can get it done. And, because he is, not merely as a man, but, by his special authority, in the likeness of God, who has power over life and death, therefore he also, as far as his authority goes, has power over life and death. That is my opinion, and that was the opinion of St. Paul. For what does he say—and say not (remember always) of Christian magistrates in a Christian country, but actually of heathen Roman magistrates? "Let every soul be subject unto the higher powers. For there is no power but of God: the powers that be are ordained of God. Whosoever therefore resisteth the power, resisteth the ordinance of God: and they that resist shall receive to themselves damnation." Thus spoke out the tenderest-hearted, most Christ-like human being, perhaps, who ever trod this earth, who, in his intense longing to save sinners, endured a life of misery and danger, and finished it by martyrdom. But there was no sentimentality, no soft indulgence in him.

He knew right from wrong; common sense from cant; duty from public opinion; and divine charity from the mere cowardly dislike of witnessing pain, not so much because it pains the person punished, as because it pains the spectator. He knew that Christ was King of kings, and what Christ's kingdom was like. He had discovered the divine and wonderful order of men and angels. He saw that one part of that order was—"the soul that sinneth, it shall die."

But some say that capital punishment is inconsistent with the mild religion of Christ—the religion of mercy and love. "The mild religion of Christ!" Do these men know of Whom they talk? Do they know that, if the Bible be true, the God who said, "Whoso sheddeth man's blood, by man shall his blood be shed," is the very same Being, the very same God, who was born of the Virgin Mary, crucified under Pontius Pilate—the very same Christ who took little children up in His arms and blessed them, the very same Word of God, too, of whom it is written, that out of His mouth goeth a two-edged sword, that He may smite the nations, and He shall rule them with a rod of iron, and He treadeth the wine press of the fierceness and wrath of Almighty God? These are awful words, but, my dear friends, I can only ask you if you think them too awful to be true? Do you believe the Christian religion? Do you believe the Creeds? Do you believe the Bible? For if you do, then you believe that the Lord Christ, who was born of the Virgin Mary, and crucified under Pontius Pilate, is the Maker, the Master, the Ruler of this world, and of all worlds. By what laws He rules other worlds we know not, save that they are, because they must be—just and merciful laws. But of the laws by which He rules this world we do know, by experience, that His laws are of most terrible and unbending severity, as I have warned you again and again, and shall warn you, as long as there is a liar or an idler, a drunkard or an adulteress in this parish.

And if this be so—if Christ be a God of severity as well as a God of love, a God who punishes sinners as well as a God who forgives penitents—what then? We are, He tells us, made in His likeness. Then, according to His likeness we must behave. We must copy His love, by helping the poor and afflicted, the weak and the oppressed. But we must copy His severity, by punishing whenever we have the power, without cowardice or indulgence, all wilful offenders; and, above all, the man who destroys God's image in himself, by murdering and destroying the mortal life of a man made in the image of God. And more; if we be made in the likeness of God and of Christ, we must remember, morning and night, and all day long, that most awful and most blessed fact. We must say to ourselves, again and again, "I am not a mere animal, and like a mere animal I must not behave; I dare not behave like a mere animal, for I was made in the likeness of God; and when I was baptised the Spirit of God took possession of me to restore me to God's likeness, and to call out and perfect God's likeness in me all my life long. Therefore, I am no mere animal; and never was intended to be. I am the temple of God; my body and soul belong to God, and not to my own fancies and passions and lusts, and whosoever defiles the temple of God, him will God destroy."

Therefore, this is our duty, this is our only hope or safety—to do our best to keep alive and strong the likeness of God in ourselves; to try to grow, not more and more mean, and brutal, and carnal, but more and more noble, and human, and spiritual; to crush down our base passions, our selfish inclinations, by the help of the Spirit of God, and to think of and to pray for, whatsoever is like Christ and like God; to pray for a noble love of what is good and noble, for a noble hate of what is bad; and whatsoever things are pure and lovely and of good report to think of these things. And to pray, too, for forgiveness from Christ, and for the sake of Christ, whenever we have yielded to our low passions, and defiled the likeness of God in us, and grieved His Spirit, lest at the last day it be said to us, if not in words yet in acts, which there will be no mistaking, no escaping,—"I made thee in My likeness in the beginning of the creation, I redeemed thee into My likeness on the cross, I baptised thee into My likeness by my Holy Spirit; and what hast thou hast done with My likeness? Thou hast cast it away, thou hast let it die out in thee, thou hast lived after the flesh and not after the spirit, and hast put on the likeness of the carnal man, the likeness of the brute. Thou hast copied the vanity of the peacock, the silliness of the ape, the cunning of the fox, the rapacity of the tiger, the sensuality of the swine; but thou hast not copied God, thy God, who died that thou mightest live, and be a man. Then, thou hast destroyed God's likeness, for thou hast destroyed it in thyself. Thou hast slain a man, for thou hast slain thy own manhood, and art thine own murderer, and thine own blood shall be required at thy hand. That which thou hast done to God's likeness in thee, shall be done to that which remains of thee in a second death."

And from that may Christ in His mercy deliver us all. Amen.

SERMON VII

TEMPTATION

Eversley, 1872. Chester Cathedral, 1872.

St Matt. iv. 3. "And when the tempter came to Him, he said, If Thou be the Son of God, command that these stones be made bread."

Let me say a few words to-day about a solemn subject, namely, Temptation. I do not mean the temptations of the flesh—the temptations which all men have to yield to the low animal nature in them, and behave like brutes. I mean those deeper and more terrible temptations, which our Lord conquered in that great struggle with evil which is commonly called His temptation in the wilderness. These were temptations of an evil spirit—the temptations which entice some men, at least, to behave like devils.

Now these temptations specially beset religious men—men who are, or fancy themselves, superior to their fellow-men, more favoured by God, and with nobler powers, and grander work to do, than the common average of mankind. But specially, I say, they beset those who are, or fancy themselves, the children of God. And, therefore, I humbly suppose our Lord had to endure and to conquer these very temptations because He was not merely a child of God, but the Son of God—the perfect Man, made in the perfect likeness of His Father. He had to endure these temptations, and to conquer them, that He might be able to succour us when we are tempted, seeing that He was tempted in like manner as we are, yet without sin.

Now it has been said, and, I think, well said, that what proves our Lord's three temptations to have been very subtle and dangerous and terrible, is this—that we cannot see at first sight that they were temptations at all. The first two do not look to us to be wrong. If our Lord could make stones into bread to satisfy His hunger, why should He not do so? If He could prove to the Jews that He was the Son of God, their divine King and Saviour, by casting Himself down from the pinnacle of the temple, and being miraculously supported in the air by angels—if He could do that, why should He not do it? And lastly, the third temptation looks at first sight so preposterous that it seems silly of the evil spirit to have hinted at it. To ask any man of piety, much less the Son of God Himself, to fall down and worship the devil, seems perfectly absurd—a request not to be listened to for a moment, but put aside with contempt.

Well, my friends, and the very danger of these spiritual temptations is—that they do not look like temptations. They do not look ugly, absurd, wrong, they look pleasant, reasonable, right.

The devil, says the apostle, transforms himself at times into an angel of light. If so, then he is certainly far more dangerous than if he came as an angel of darkness and horror. If you met some venomous snake, with loathsome spots upon his scales, his eyes full of rage and cunning, his head raised to strike at you, hissing and showing his fangs, there would be no temptation to have to do with him. You would know that you had to deal with an evil beast, and must either kill him or escape from him at once. But if, again, you met, as you may meet in the tropics, a lovely little coral snake, braided with red and white, its mouth so small that it seems impossible that it can bite, and so gentle that children may take it up and play with it, then you might be tempted, as many a poor child has been ere now, to admire it, fondle it, wreathe it round the neck for a necklace, or round the arm for a bracelet, till the play goes one step too far, the snake loses its temper, gives one tiny scratch upon the lip or finger, and that scratch is certain death. That would be a temptation indeed; one all the more dangerous because there is, I am told, another sort of coral snake perfectly harmless, which is so exactly like the deadly one, that no child, and few grown people, can know them apart.

Even so it is with our worst temptations. They look sometimes so exactly like what is good and noble and useful and religious, that we mistake the evil for the good, and play with it till it stings us, and we find out too late that the wages of sin are death. Thus religious people, just because they are religious, are apt to be specially tempted to mistake evil for good, to do something specially wrong, when they think they are doing something specially right, and so give occasion to the enemies of the Lord to blaspheme; till, as a hard and experienced man of the world once said: "Whenever I hear a man talking of his conscience, I know that he is going to do something particularly foolish; whenever I hear of a man talking of his duty, I know that he is going to do something particularly cruel."

Do I say this to frighten you away from being religious? God forbid. Better to be religious and to fear and love God, though you were tempted by all the devils out of the pit, than to be irreligious and a mere animal, and be tempted only by your own carnal nature, as the animals are. Better to be tempted, like the hermits of old, and even to fall and rise again, singing, "Rejoice not against me, O mine enemy, when I fall I shall arise;" than to live the life of the flesh, "like a beast with lower pleasures, like a beast with lower pains." It is the price a man must pay for hungering and thirsting after righteousness, for longing to be a child of God in spirit and in truth. "The devil," says a wise man of old, "does not tempt bad men, because he has got them already; he tempts good men, because he has not got them, and wants to get them."

But how shall we know these temptations? God knows, my friends, better than I; and I trust that He will teach you to know, according to what each of you needs to know. But as far as my small experience goes, the root of them all is pride and self-conceit. Whatsoever thoughts or feelings tempt us to pride and self-conceit are of the devil, not of God. The devil is specially the spirit of pride; and, therefore, whatever tempts you to fancy yourself something different from your fellow-men, superior to your fellow men, safer than them, more favoured by God than them, that is a temptation of the spirit of pride. Whatever tempts you to think that you can do without God's help and God's providence; whatever tempts you to do anything extraordinary, and show yourself off, that you may make a figure in the world; and above all, whatever tempts you to antinomianism, that is, to fancy that God will overlook sins in you which He will not overlook in other men—all these are temptations from the spirit of pride. They are temptations like our Lord's temptations. These temptations came on our Lord more terribly than they ever can on you and me, just because He was the Son of Man, the perfect Man, and, therefore, had more real reason for being proud (if such a thing could be) than any man, or than all men put together. But He conquered the temptations because He was perfect Man, led by the Spirit of God; and, therefore, He knew that the only way to be a perfect man was not to be proud, however powerful, wise, and glorious He might be; but to submit Himself humbly and utterly, as every man should do, to the will of His Father in Heaven, from whom alone His greatness came.

Now the spirit of pride cannot understand the beauty of humility, and the spirit of self-will cannot understand the beauty of obedience; and, therefore, it is reasonable to suppose the devil could not understand our Lord. If He be the Son of God, so might Satan argue, He has all the more reason to be proud; and, therefore, it is all the more easy to tempt Him into shewing His pride, into proving Himself a conceited, self-willed, rebellious being—in one word, an evil spirit.

And therefore (as you will see at first sight) the first two temptations were clearly meant to tempt our Lord to pride; for would they not tempt you and me to pride? If we could feed ourselves by making bread of stones, would not that make us proud enough? So proud, I fear, that we should soon fancy that we could do without God and His providence, and were masters of nature and all her secrets. If you and I could make the whole city worship and obey us, by casting ourselves off this cathedral unhurt, would not that make us proud enough? So proud, I fear, that we should end in committing some great folly, or great crime in our conceit and vainglory.

Now, whether our Lord could or could not have done these wonderful deeds, one thing is plain—that He would not do them; and, therefore, we may presume that He ought not to have done them. It seems as if He did not wish to be a wonderful man: but only a perfectly good man, and He would do nothing to help Himself but what any other man could do. He answered the evil spirit simply out of Scripture, as any other pious man might have done. When He was bidden to make the stones into bread, He answers not as the Eternal Son of God, but simply as a man. "It is written:"—it is the belief of Moses and the old prophets of my people that man doth not live by bread alone, but by every word that proceedeth out of the mouth of God.— as much as to say, If I am to be delivered out of this need, God will deliver me by some means or other, just as He delivers other men out of their needs. When He was bidden cast Himself from the temple, and so save Himself, probably from sorrow, poverty, persecution, and the death on the cross, He answers out of Scripture as any other Jew would have done. "It is written again, Thou shalt not tempt the Lord thy God." He says nothing—this is most important—of His being the eternal Son of God. He keeps that in the background. There the fact was; but He veiled the glory of His godhead, that He might assert the rights of His manhood, and shew that mere man, by the help of the Spirit of God, could obey God, and keep His commandments.

I say these last words with all diffidence and humility, and trusting that the Lord will pardon any mistake which I may make about His Divine Words. I only say them because wiser men than I have often taken the same view already. Of course there is more, far more, in this wonderful saying than we can understand, or ever will understand. But this I think is plain—that our Lord determined to behave as any and every other man ought to have done in His place; in order to shew all God's children the example of perfect humility and perfect obedience to God.

But again, the devil asked our Lord to fall down and worship him. Now how could that be a temptation to pride? Surely that was asking our Lord to do anything but a proud action, rather the most humiliating and most base of all actions. My friends, it seems to me that if our Lord had fallen down and worshipped the evil spirit, He would have given way to the spirit of pride utterly and boundlessly; and I will tell you why.

The devil wanted our Lord to do evil that good might come. It would have been a blessing, that all the kingdoms of the world and the glory of man should be our Lord's,—the very blessing for this poor earth which He came to buy, and which He bought with His own precious blood. And here the devil offered Him the very prize for which He came down on earth, without struggle or difficulty, if He would but do, for one moment, one wrong thing. What temptation that would be to our Lord as God, I dare not say. But that to our Lord as Man, it must have been the most terrible of all temptations, I can well believe: because history shews us, and, alas! our own experience in modern times shews us, persons yielding to that temptation perpetually; pious people, benevolent people, people who long to spread the Bible, to convert sinners, to found charities, to amend laws, to set the world right in some way or other, and who fancy that therefore, in carrying out their fine projects, they have a right to do evil that good may come.

This is a very painful subject; all the more painful just now, because I sometimes think it is the special sin of this country and this generation, and that God will bring on us some heavy punishment for it. But all who know the world in its various phases, and especially what are called the religious world, and the philanthropic world, and the political world, know too well that men, not otherwise bad men, will do things and say things, to carry out some favourite project or movement, or to support some party, religious or other, which they would (I hope) be ashamed to say and do for their own private gain. Now what is this, but worshipping the evil spirit, in order to get power over this world, that they may (as they fancy) amend it? And what is this but self-conceit—ruinous, I had almost said, blasphemous? These people think themselves so certainly in the right, and their plans so absolutely necessary to the good of the world, that God has given them a special licence to do what they like in carrying them out; that He will excuse in them falsehoods and meannesses, even tyranny and violences which He will excuse in no one else.

Now, is not this self-conceit? What would you think of a servant who disobeyed you, cheated you, and yet said to himself—No matter, my master dare not turn me off: I am so useful that he cannot do without me. Even so in all ages, and now as much as, or more than ever, have men said, We are so necessary to God and God's cause, that He cannot do without us; and therefore though He hates sin in everyone else, He will excuse sin in us, as long as we are about His business.

Therefore, my dear friends, whenever we are tempted to do or say anything rash, or vain, or mean, because we are the children of God; whenever we are inclined to be puffed up with spiritual pride, and to fancy that we may take liberties which other men must not take, because we are the children of God; let us remember the words of the text, and answer the tempter, when he says, If thou be the Son of God, do this and that, as our Lord answered him—"If I be the Child of God, what then? This—that I must behave as if God were my Father. I must trust my God utterly, and I must obey Him utterly. I must do no rash or vain thing to tempt God, even though it looks as if I should have a great success, and do much good thereby. I must do no mean or base thing, nor give way for a moment to the wicked ways of this wicked world, even though again it looks as if I should have a great success, and do much good thereby. In one word, I must worship my Father in heaven, and Him only must I serve. If He wants me, He will use me. If He does not want me, He will use some one else. Who am I, that God cannot govern the world without my help? My business is to refrain my soul, and keep it low, even as a weaned child, and not to meddle with matters too high for me. My business is to do the little, simple, everyday duties which lie nearest me, and be faithful in a few things; and then, if Christ will, He may make me some day ruler over many things, and I shall enter into the joy of my Lord, which is the joy of doing good to my fellow men. But I shall never enter into that by thrusting myself into Christ's way, with grand schemes and hasty projects, as if I knew better than He how to make His kingdom come. If I do, my pride will have a fall. Because I would not be faithful over a few things, I shall be tempted to be unfaithful over many things; and instead of entering into the joy of my Lord, I shall be in danger of the awful judgment pronounced on those who do evil that good may come, who shall say in that day, Lord, Lord, have we not prophesied in thy name? and in thy name cast out devils? and in thy name done many wonderful works? And then will He protest unto them—I never knew you. Depart from me, ye that work iniquity."

Oh, my friends, in all your projects for good, as in all other matters which come before you in your mortal life, keep innocence and take heed to the thing that is right. For that, and that alone, shall bring a man peace at the last.

To which, may God in His mercy bring us all. Amen.

SERMON VIII

MOTHER'S LOVE

Eversley, Second Sunday in Lent, 1872.

St Matthew xv. 22-28. "And, behold, a woman of Canaan came out of the same coasts, and cried unto him, saying, Have mercy on me, O Lord, thou son of David; my daughter is grievously vexed with a devil. But he answered her not a word. And his disciples came and besought him, saying, Send her away; for she crieth after us. But he answered and said, I am not sent but unto the lost sheep of the house of Israel. Then came she and worshipped him, saying, Lord, help me. But he answered and said, It is not meet to take the children's bread, and to cast it to dogs. And she said, Truth, Lord: yet the dogs eat of the crumbs which fall from their master's table. Then Jesus answered and said unto her, O woman, great is thy faith: be it unto thee even as thou wilt. And her daughter was made whole from that very hour."

If you want a proof from Scripture that there are two sides to our blessed Lord's character—that He is a Judge and an Avenger as well as a Saviour and a Pardoner—that He is infinitely severe as well as infinitely merciful—that, while we may come boldly to His throne of grace to find help and mercy in time of need, we must, at the same time, tremble before His throne of justice—if you want a proof of all this, I say, then look at the Epistle and the Gospel for this day. Put them side by side, and compare them, and you will see how perfectly they shew, one after the other, the two sides.

The Epistle for the day tells men and women that they must lead moral, pure, and modest lives. It does not advise them to do so. It does not say, It will be better to do so, more proper and conducive to the good of society, more likely to bring you to heaven at last. It says, You must, for it is the commandment of the Lord Jesus, and the will of God. Let no man encroach on or defraud his brother in the matter, says St Paul; by which he means, Thou shalt not covet thy neighbour's wife. And why? "Because that the Lord is the avenger of all such, as we also have forewarned you and testified."

My friends, people talk loosely of the Thunder of Sinai and the rigour of Moses' law, and set them against what they call the gentle voice of the Gospel, and the mild religion of Christ. Why, here are the Thunders of Sinai uttered as loud as ever, from the very foot of the Cross of Christ; and the terrible, "Thou shalt not," of Moses' law, with the curse of God for a penalty on the sinner, uttered by the Apostle of Faith, and Freedom, in the name of Christ and of God. St Paul is not afraid to call Christ an Avenger. How could he be? He believed that it was Christ who spoke to Moses on Sinai—the very same Christ who prayed for His murderers, "Father, forgive them, for they know not what they do." And he knew that Christ was the eternal Son of God, the same yesterday, to-day, and for ever; that He had not changed since Moses' time, and could never change; that what He forbade in Moses' time, hated in Moses' time, and avenged in Moses' time, He would forbid, and hate, and avenge for ever. And that, therefore, he who despises the warnings of the Law despises not man merely, but God, who has also given to us His Holy Spirit to know what is unchangeable, the everlastingly right, from what is everlastingly wrong. So much for that side of our Lord's character; so much for sinners who, after their hardness and impenitent hearts, treasure up for themselves wrath against the day of wrath and revelation of the righteous judgment of God, in the day when God shall judge the secrets of men by Jesus Christ, according to St Paul's Gospel.

But, when we turn to the Gospel for the day, we see the other side of our Lord's character, boundless condescension and boundless charity. We see Him there still a Judge, as He always is and always will be, judging the secrets of a poor woman's heart, and that woman a heathen. He judges her openly, in public, before His disciples. But He is a Judge who judges righteous judgment, and not according to appearances; who is no respecter of persons; who is perfectly fair, even though the woman be a heathen: and, instead of condemning her and driving her away, He acquits her, He grants her prayer, He heals her daughter, even though that daughter was also a heathen, and one who knew Him not. I say our Lord judged the woman after He had tried her, as gold is tried in the fire. Why He did so, we cannot tell. Perhaps He wanted, by the trial, to make her a better woman, to bring out something noble which lay in her heart unknown to her, though not to Him who knew what was in man. Perhaps He wished to shew his disciples, who looked down on her as a heathen dog, that a heathen, too, could have faith, humility, nobleness, and grace of heart. Be that as it may, when the poor woman came crying to Him, He answered her not a word. His disciples besought Him to send her away—and I am inclined to think that they wished Him to grant her what she asked, simply to be rid of her. "Send her away," they said, "for she crieth after us." Our Lord, we learn from St Mark, did not wish to be known in that place just then. The poor woman, with her crying, was drawing attention to them, and, perhaps, gathering a crowd. Somewhat noisy and troublesome, perhaps she was, in her motherly eagerness. But our Lord was still seemingly stern. He would not listen, it seemed, to His disciples any more than to the heathen woman. "I am not sent but unto the lost sheep of the house of Israel." So our Lord said, and (what is worth remembering) if He said so, what He said was true. He was the King of the people of Israel, the Royal Prince of David's line; and, as a man, His duty was only to His own people. And this woman was a Greek, a Syro-phenician by nation—of a mixed race of people, notoriously low and profligate, and old enemies of the Jews.

Then, it seems, He went into a house, and would have no man know it. But, says St Mark, "He could not be hid." The mother's wit found our Lord out, and the mother's heart urged her on, and, in spite of all His rebuffs, she seems to have got into the house and worshipped Him. She "fell at His feet," says St Mark—doubtless bowing her forehead to the ground, in the fashion of those lands—an honour which was paid, I believe, only to persons who were royal or divine. So she confessed that He was a king—perhaps a God come down on earth—and again she cried to Him, "Lord, help me." And what was our Lord's answer—seemingly more stern than ever? "Let the children first be filled: for it is not meet to take the children's bread and cast it unto the dogs." Hard words. Yes: but all depends on how they were spoken. All depends on our Lord's look as He spoke them, and, even more, on the tone of His voice. We all know that two men may use the very same words to us;—and the one shall speak sneeringly, brutally, and raise in us indignation or despair; another shall use the same words, but solemnly, tenderly, and raise in us confidence and hope. And so it may have been—so, I fancy, it must have been—with the tone of our Lord's voice, with the expression of His face. Did He speak with a frown, or with something like a smile? There must have been some tenderness, meaningness, pity In His voice which the quick woman's wit caught instantly, and the quick mother's heart interpreted as a sign of hope.

Let Him call her a dog if He would. What matter to a mother to be called a dog, if she could thereby save her child from a devil? Perhaps she was little better than a dog. They were a bad people these Syrians, quick-witted, highly civilised, but vicious, and teaching vice to other nations, till some of the wisest Romans cursed the day when the Syrians first spread into Rome, and debauched the sturdy Romans with their new-fangled, foreign sins. They were a bad people, and, perhaps, she had been as bad as the rest. But if she were a dog, at least she felt that the dog had found its Master, and must fawn on Him, if it were but for the hope of getting something from Him.

And so, in the poor heathen mother's heart, there rose up a whole heaven of perfect humility, faith, adoration. If she were base and mean, yet our Lord was great, and wise, and good; and that was all the more reason why He should be magnanimous, generous, condescending, like a true King, to the basest and meanest of His subjects. She asked not for money, or honour, or this world's fine things: but simply for her child's health, her child's deliverance from some mysterious and degrading illness. Surely there was no harm in asking for that. It was simply a mother's prayer, a simply human prayer, which our Lord must grant, if He were indeed a man of woman born, if He had a mother, and could feel for a mother, if He had human tenderness, human pity in Him. And so, with her quick Syrian wit, she answers our Lord with those wonderful words—perhaps the most pathetic words in the whole Bible—so full of humility, of reverence, and yet with a certain archness, almost playfulness, in them, as it were, turning our Lord's words against Him; and, by that very thing, shewing how utterly she trusted Him,—"Truth, Lord: yet the dogs eat of the crumbs which fall from their masters' table."

Those were the beautiful words—more beautiful to me than whole volumes of poetry—which our Lord had as it were crushed out of the woman's heart. Doubtless, He knew all the while that they were in her heart, though not as yet shaped into words. Doubtless, He was trying her, to shew His disciples—and all Christians who should ever read the Bible—what was in her heart, what she was capable of saying when it came to the point. So He tried her, and judged her, and acquitted her. Out of the abundance of her heart her mouth had spoken. By her words she was justified. By those few words she proved her utter faith in our Lord's power and goodness—perhaps her faith in His godhead. By those words she proved the gentleness and humility, the graciousness and gracefulness of her own character. By those words she proved, too,—and oh, you that are mothers, is that nothing?—the perfect disinterestedness of her mother's love. And so she conquered—as the blessed Lord loves to be conquered—as all noble souls who are like their blessed Lord, love to be conquered—by the prayer of faith, of humility, of confidence, of earnestness, and she had her reward. "O woman," said He, the Maker of all heaven and earth, "great is thy faith. For this saying go thy way. Be it unto thee even as thou wilt. The devil is gone out of thy daughter." She went, full of faith; and when she was come to her house, she found the devil gone out, and her daughter laid upon the bed.

One word more, and I have done. I do not think that any one who really took in the full meaning of this beautiful story, would ever care to pray to Saints, or to the Blessed Virgin, for help; fancying that they, and specially the Blessed Virgin, being a woman, are more humane than our Lord, and can feel more quickly, if not more keenly, for poor creatures in distress. We are not here to judge these people, or any people. To their own master they stand or fall. But for the honour of our Lord, we may say, Does not this story shew that the Lord is humane enough, tender enough, to satisfy all mankind? Does not this story shew that even if He seem silent at first, and does not grant our prayers, yet still He may be keeping us waiting, as He kept this heathen woman, only that He may be gracious to us at last? Does not this story shew us especially that our Lord can feel for mothers and with mothers; that He actually allowed Himself to be won over—if I may use such a word in all reverence—by the wit and grace of a mother pleading for her child? Was it not so? "O woman, great is thy faith. For this saying go thy way. Be it unto thee even as thou wilt." Ah! are not those gracious words a comfort to every mother, bidding her, in the Lord's own name, to come boldly where mothers—of all human beings—have oftenest need to come, to the throne of Christ's grace, to find mercy, and grace to help in time of need?

Yes, my friends, such is our Lord, and such is our God. Infinite in severity to the scornful, the proud, the disobedient: infinite in tenderness to the earnest, the humble, the obedient. Let us come to Him, earnest, humble, obedient, and we shall find Him, indeed, a refuge of the soul and body in spirit and in truth.

Thou, O Lord, art all I want.

All and more in thee I find. Amen.

SERMON IX

GOOD FRIDAY

Eversley, 1856.

St. Luke xxiv. 5, 6. "Why seek ye the living among the dead? He is not here, but is risen."

This is a very solemn day; for on this day the Lord Jesus Christ was crucified. The question for us is, how ought we to keep it? that is, what sort of thoughts ought to be in our minds upon this day? Now, many most excellent and pious persons, and most pious books, seem to think that we ought to-day to think as much as possible of the sufferings of our Blessed Lord; and because we cannot, of course, understand or imagine the sufferings of His Spirit, to think of what we can, that is, His bodily sufferings. They, therefore, seem to wish to fill our minds with the most painful pictures of agony, and shame, and death, and sorrow; and not only with our Lord's sorrows, but with those of His Blessed Mother, and of the disciples, and the holy women who stood by His cross; they wish to stir us up to pity and horror, and to bring before us the saddest parts of Holy Scripture, such as the Lamentations of Jeremiah; as well as dwell at great length upon very painful details, which may be all quite true, but of which Scripture says nothing; as so to make this day a day of darkness, and sorrow, and horror, just such as it would have been to us if we had stood by Christ's cross, like these holy women, without expecting Him to rise again, and believing that all was over—that all hope of Israel's being redeemed was gone, and that the wicked Jews had really conquered that perfectly good, and admirable Saviour, and put Him out of the world for ever.

Now, I judge no man; to his own master he standeth or falleth; yea, and he shall stand, for God is able to make him stand. But it does seem to me that these good people are seeking the living among the dead, and forgetting that Christ is neither on the cross nor in the tomb, but that He is risen; and it seems to me better to bid you follow to-day the Bible and the Church Service, and to think of what they tell you to think of.

Now the Bible, it is most remarkable, never enlarges anywhere upon even the bodily sufferings of our dear and blessed Lord. The evangelists keep a silence on that point which is most lofty, dignified, and delicate. What sad and dreadful things might not St. John, the beloved apostle as he was, have said, if he had chosen, about what he saw and what he felt, as he stood by that cross on Calvary—words which would have stirred to pity the most cruel, and drawn tears from a heart of stone? And yet all he says is, "They crucified Him, and two other with him, on either side one, and Jesus in the midst." He passes it over, as it were, as a thing which he ought not to dwell on; and why should we put words into St. John's mouth which he did not think fit to put into his own? He wrote by the Spirit of God; and therefore he knew best what to say, and what not to say. Why should we try and say anything more for him? Scripture is perfect. Let us be content with it. The apostles, too, in their Epistles, never dwell on Christ's sufferings. I entreat you to remark this. They never mention His death except in words of cheerfulness and triumph. They seem so full of the glorious fruits of His death, that they have, as it were, no time to speak of the death itself. "Who, for the joy which was set before Him, endured the cross, despising the shame, and is set down at the right hand of the throne of God." That is the apostles' key-note. For God's sake let it be ours too, unless we fancy that we can improve on Scripture, or that we can feel more for our Lord than St. Paul did. In the Lessons, the Psalms, the Epistle, and Gospel for this day, you find just the same spirit. All except one Psalm are songs of hope, joy, deliverance, triumph. The Collects for this day, which are particularly remarkable, being three in number, and evidently meant to teach us the key-note of Good Friday, make no mention of our Lord's sufferings, save to say that He was contented, "contented to be betrayed, and given up into the hands of wicked men, and to suffer death upon the cross," but are full of prayers that the glorious fruits of His death may be fulfilled, not only in us and all Christians, but in the very heathen who have not known Him; drawing us away, as it were, from looking too closely upon the cross itself, lest we should forget what the cross meant, what the cross conquered, what the cross gained, for us and mankind.

Surely, this was not done without a reason. And I cannot but think the reason was to keep us from seeking the living among the dead; to keep us from knowing Christ any longer after the flesh, and spending tears and emotions over His bodily sufferings; to keep us from thinking and sorrowing too much over the dead Christ, lest we should forget, as some do, that He is alive for evermore; and while they weep over the dead Christ or the crucifix, go to the blessed Virgin and the saints to do for them all that the living Christ is longing to do for them, if they would but go straight to Him to whom all power is given in heaven and earth; whom St John saw, no longer hanging on the accursed tree, but with His hair as white as snow, and His eyes like a flame of fire, and His voice like the sound of many waters, and His countenance as the sun when he shineth in his strength, saying unto him, "Fear not, I am the first and the last; I am He that liveth and was dead, and behold I am alive for evermore." This is what Christ is now. In this shape He is looking at us now. In this shape He is hearing me speak. In this shape He is watching every feeling of your hearts, discerning your most secret intents, seeing through and through the thoughts which you would confess to no human being, hardly even to yourselves. This is He, a living Christ, an almighty Christ, an all-seeing Christ, and yet a most patient and loving Christ. He needs not our pity; but our gratitude, our obedience, our worship. Why seek Him among the dead? He is not there, He is risen! He is not there, He is here! Bow yourselves before Him now; for He is in the midst of you; and those eyes of His, more piercing than the mid-day sunbeams, are upon you, and your hearts, and your thoughts, and upon mine also. God have mercy upon me a sinner.

Yes, my friends, why seek the living among the dead? He is not there, but here. We may try to put ourselves in the place of the disciples and the Virgin Mary, as they stood by Jesus' cross; but we cannot do it, for they saw Him on the cross, and thought that He was lost to them for ever; they saw Him die, and gave up all hope of His rising again. And we know that Christ is not lost to us for ever. We know Christ is not on the cross, but at the right hand of God in bliss and glory unspeakable. We may be told to watch with the three Maries at the tomb of Christ: but we cannot do as they did, for they thought that all was over, and brought sweet spices to embalm His body, which they thought was in the tomb; and we know that all was not over, that His body is not in the tomb, that the grave could not hold Him, that His body is ascended into heaven; that instead of His body needing spices to embalm it, it is His body which embalms all heaven and earth, and is the very life of the world, and food which preserves our souls and bodies to everlasting life. We are not in the place of those blessed women; God has not put us in their place, and we cannot put ourselves into their place; and if we could and did, by any imaginations of our own, we should only tell ourselves a lie. Good Friday was to them indeed a day of darkness, horror, disappointment, all but despair; because Easter Day had not yet come, and Christ had not yet risen. But Good Friday cannot be a day of darkness to us, because Christ has risen, and we know it, and cannot forget it; we cannot forget that Easter dawn, when the Sun of Righteousness arose, never to set again. Has not the light of that Resurrection morning filled with glory the cross and the grave, yea the very agony in the Garden, and hell itself, which Christ harrowed for us? Has it not risen a light to lighten the Gentiles, a joy to angels and archangels, and saints, and all the elect of God; ay, to the whole universe of God, so that the very stars in their courses, the trees as they bud each spring, yea, the very birds upon the bough, are singing for ever, in the ears of those who have ears to hear, "Christ is risen?" And shall we, under pretence of honouring Christ and of bestowing on Him a pity which He needs least of all, try to spend Good Friday and Passion Week in forgetting Easter Day; try to think of Christ's death as we should if He had not risen, and try to make out ourselves and the world infinitely worse off than we really know that we are? Christ has died, but He has risen again; and we must not think of one without the other. Heavenly things are too important, too true, too real—Christ is too near us, and too loving to us, too earnest about our salvation, for us to spend our thoughts on any such attempts (however reverently meant) at imaginative play-acting in our own minds about His hanging on His cross, while we know that He is not on His cross; and about watching by His tomb, when we know that He is not in His tomb. Let us thank Him, bless Him, serve Him, die for Him, if need be, in return for all He endured for us: but let us keep our sorrow and our pity, and our tears, for our own daily sins—we have enough of them to employ all our sorrow, and more;—and not in voluntary humility and will-worship, against which St Paul warns us, lose sight of our real Christ, of Him who was dead and is alive for evermore, and dwells in us by faith; now and for ever, amen; and hath the keys of death and hell, and has opened them for us, and for our fathers before us, and for our children after us, and for nations yet unborn.

True, this is a solemn day, for on it the Son of God fought such a fight, that He could only win it at the price of His own life's blood; and a humiliating day, for our sins helped to nail Him on the cross—and therefore a day of humiliation and of humility. Proud, self-willed thoughts are surely out of place to-day (and what day are they in place?) On this day God agonised for man: but it is a day of triumph and deliverance; and we must go home as men who have stood by and seen a fearful fight—a fight which makes the blood of him who watches it run cold; but we have seen, too, a glorious victory—such a victory as never was won on earth before or since; and we therefore must think cheerfully of the battle, for the sake of the victory that was won; and remember that on this day death was indeed swallowed up in victory—because death was the victory itself.

The question on which the fate of the whole world depended was, whether Christ dare die; and He dared die. Whether Christ would endure to the end; and He did endure. Whether He would utterly drink the cup which His Father had given Him; and He drank it to the dregs; and so by His very agony He showed Himself noble, beautiful, glorious, adorable, beyond all that words can express. And so the cross was His throne of glory; the prints of the nails in His hands and feet were the very tokens of His triumph; His very sorrows were His bliss; and those last words, "It is finished," were no cry of despair, but a trumpet-call of triumph, which rang from the highest heaven to the lowest hell, proclaiming to all created things, that the very fountain of life, by dying, had conquered death, that good had conquered evil, love had conquered selfishness, God had conquered man, and all the enemies of man; and that He who died was the first begotten from the dead, and the King of all the princes of the earth, who was going to fulfil, more and more, as the years and the ages rolled on, the glorious prayer which we have prayed this day, graciously to behold that family for whom He had been contented to die; and wisely and orderly to call each man to a vocation and a ministry, in which he might duly serve God and be a blessing to all around him, by the inspiration of Christ's Holy Spirit; and to have mercy, in His own good time, upon all Jews, Turks, heathens, and infidels, and bring them home to His flock, that they may be saved, and made one fold under one Shepherd—Him who was dead and is alive for evermore.

Therefore, my dear friends, if we wish to keep Good Friday in spirit and in truth, we cannot do so better than by trying to carry out the very end for which Christ died on this day; and doing our part, small though it be, toward bringing those poor heathens home into Christ's fold, and teaching them the gospel and good news that for them, too, Christ died, and over them, too, Christ reigns alive for evermore; and bringing them home into His flock, that they, too, may find a place in His great family, and have their calling and ministry appointed to them among the nations of those who are saved and walk in the light of God and of the Lamb.

I have refrained till now from speaking to you much about missionaries, and the duty which lies on us all of helping missions. It seemed to me that I must first teach you to understand these first and second collects before I went on. to the third; that I must first teach you that you belonged to Christ's family, and that He had called each of you, and appointed each of you to some order and degree in His Holy Church. But now, if indeed you have learnt that—if my preaching here for fourteen years has had any effect to teach you who and what you are, and what your duty is, let me entreat you to go on, and take the lesson of that third collect, and think of those poor Jews, Turks, infidels, and heretics, who still—many a million of them—sit, or rather wander, and fall, and lie, miserably wallowing in darkness and the shadow of death, and think whether you cannot do something toward helping them. What you can do, and how it is to be done, I will tell you hereafter; and, by God's grace, I hope to see men of God in this pulpit, who having been missionaries themselves, can tell you better than I, what remains to be done, and how you can help to do it. But take home this one thought with you, this Good Friday,—Christ, who liveth and was dead, and behold He is alive for evermore, if He be indeed precious to you, if you indeed feel for His sufferings, if you indeed believe that what He bought by those sufferings was a right to all the souls on earth, then do what you can toward repaying Him for His sufferings, by seeing of the travail of His soul, and being satisfied. All the reward He asks, or ever asked, is the hearts of sinners, that He may convert them; the souls of sinners, that He may save them; and they belong to Him already, for He bought them this day with His own most precious blood. Do something, then, toward helping Christ to His own.

SERMON X

THE IMAGE OF THE EARTHLY AND THE HEAVENLY

Eversley, Easter Day, 1871.

1 Cor. xv. 49. "As we have borne the image of the earthy, we shall also bear the image of the heavenly."

This season of Easter is the most joyful of all the year. It is the most comfortable time, in the true old sense of that word; for it is the season which ought to comfort us most—that is, it gives us strength; strength to live like men, and strength to die like men, when our time comes. Strength to live like men. Strength to fight against the temptation which Solomon felt when he said: "I have seen all the works which are done under the sun, and behold all is vanity and vexation of spirit. For what has a man of all his labour, and of the vexation of his heart, wherein he has laboured under the sun? For all his days are sorrow, and his travail grief. Yea, his heart taketh not rest in the night. This also is vanity. For that which befalleth the sons of men befalleth beasts: as the one dieth, so dieth the other: yea, they have all one breath: so that a man has no pre-eminence over a beast; for all is vanity. All go to one place: all are of the dust, and all turn to dust again. Who knoweth the spirit of man that it goeth upward, and the spirit of the beast that it goeth downward to the earth?" So thought Solomon in his temptation, and made up his mind that there was nothing better for a man than that he should eat and drink, and make his soul enjoy good in his labour.

So thought Solomon, in spite of all his wisdom, because he had not heard the good news of Easter day. And so think many now, who are called wise men and philosophers; because they, alas! for them, will not believe the good news of Easter day.

But what says Easter day? Easter day says, Man has pre-eminence over a beast. The man is redeemed from the death of the beasts by Christ, who rose on Easter day. Easter day says, Wherever the spirit of the beast goes, wherever the spirit of the brutal and the wicked man goes, the spirit of the true Christian goes upward, to Christ, who bought it with His precious blood. Easter day says, The body may turn to the dust from which it was taken, but the spirit lives for ever before God, who shall give it another body, as it shall please Him, as He gives to every seed its own body. And, therefore, Easter day says, There is something better for a man than to eat and drink and enjoy himself, for to-morrow he may die, and all be over; and that something is, to labour not merely for the meat which perishes with the perishing body, but to labour after the fruits of the spirit—love, joy, peace, long-suffering, gentleness, goodness, faith, meekness, temperance. These the life of the body does not give us; and these the death of the body not take away from us; for they are spiritual and heavenly, eternal and divine; and he who has them cannot die for ever. And therefore, we may comfort ourselves in all our labour, if only we labour at the one useful work on earth, to be good, and to do good, and to make others good likewise.

True it is, as St. Paul says, that if in this life only we have hope in Christ we are of all men most miserable. For we do not care to be of the earth, earthy: we long to be of the heaven, heavenly. We do not care to spend our time in eating and drinking, mean covetousness, ambition, and the base pleasures of the flesh: we long after high and noble things, which we cannot get on earth, or at best only in fragments, and at rare moments; after the holiness and the blessedness of ourselves and our fellow-creatures. But we have hope in Christ for the next life as well as for this. Hope that in the next life He will give us power to succeed, where we failed here; that He will enable us to be good and to do good, and, if not to make others good (for there, we trust, all will be good together), to enjoy the fulness of that pleasure for which we have been longing on earth—the pleasure of seeing others good, as Christ is good and perfect, as their Father in heaven is perfect.

To be good ourselves, and to live for ever in good company—ah my friends, that is true bliss. If we cannot reach that after death, it were better for us that death should make an end of us, and that when our body decays in the grave we should be annihilated, and become nothing for ever.

But Easter day says to us, If you labour to create good company in this life, by trying to make other people round you good, you shall enjoy for ever in the next world the good company which you have helped to make. If you labour to make yourself good in this life, you shall enjoy the fruit of your labour in the next life by being good, and, therefore, blessed for ever. Easter day says, Your labour is not vanity and vexation of spirit. It is solid work, which shall receive solid pay from God hereafter. Easter day is a pledge—I may say a sacrament—from God to us, that He will righteously reward all righteous work; and that, therefore, it is worth any man's while to labour, to suffer, if need be even to die, in trying to be good, noble, useful, self-sacrificing, as Christ toiled and suffered and died and sacrificed Himself to do good. For then he will share Christ's reward, as he has shared Christ's labour, and be rewarded, as Christ was, by resurrection to eternal life.

And so Easter day should give us strength to live like men—the only truly manly, truly human life; the life of being good and doing good.

And strength to die. Men are afraid of dying, principally, I believe, because they fear the unknown. It is not that they are afraid of the pain of dying. It is not that they are afraid of going to hell; for in all my experience, at least, I have met with but one person who thought that he was going to hell. Neither is it that they are afraid of not going to heaven. Their expectation almost always is, that they are going thither. But they do not care much to go to heaven. They are willing enough to go there, because they know that they must go somewhere. But their notions of what heaven will be like are by no means clear. They have sung rapturous hymns in church or chapel about the heavenly Jerusalem, and passing Jordan safe to Canaan's shore, with no very clear notion of what the words meant—and small blame to them.

But when they think of actually dying, they feel as if to go into the next world was to be turned out into the dark night, into an unknown land, away from house and home, and all they have known, and all they have loved; and they are ready to say with the good old heathen emperor, when he lay a-dying—

> *"Little soul of mine, wandering, kindly,*
> *Companion and guest of my body;*
> *Into what place art thou now departing,*
> *Shivering, naked, and pale?"*

And so they shrink from death. They must shrink from death, unless they will believe with their whole hearts the good news of Easter day. The more thoughtful and clever they are, the more they will shrink from death, and dread the thought of losing their bodies. They have always had bodies here on earth. They only know themselves as souls embodied, living in bodies; and they cannot think of themselves in the next world with any comfort, if they may not think of themselves as having bodies.

And the more loving and affectionate they are, the more they will shrink from death, unless they believe with their whole hearts the good news of Easter day. For those whom they have loved on earth have bodies. Through their bodies—through their voices, their looks, their actions, they have known them, and thus they have loved them; and if their beloved ones are to have no bodies in the world to come, how shall they see them? how shall they know them? how shall they converse with them? It seems to them in that case neither they, nor those they love, would be the same persons in the world to come they are here; and that thought is lonely and dreadful, till they accept the good news of Easter day, the thrice blessed words of St. Paul, in his Epistle to the Corinthians, which they hear at the burial of those whom they love and lose. Oh, blessed news for us, and for those we love; those without whose company the world to come would be lonely and cheerless to us. For now we can say, Tell me not that as the beast dies, so dies the man. Tell me not that as Adam died because of sin, so must I die, and all I love. Tell me not that it is the universal law of nature that all things born in time must die in time; and that every human being, animal, and plant carries in itself from its beginning to its end a law of death, the seed of its own destruction. I know all that; but I care little for it, because I know more than that. I know that the man's body dies as the beast's body dies; but I know that the body is not the man, but only the husk, the shell of the man; that the true man, the true woman, lives on after the loss of his mortal body; and that there is an eternal law of life, which conquers the law of death; and by that law a fresh body will grow up round the true man, the immortal spirit, and will be as fit—ay, far fitter—to do his work, than this poor mortal body which has turned to death on earth. Tell me not that because I am descended from a mortal and sinful old Adam, of whom it is written that he was of the earth, earthly, therefore my soul is a part of my body, and dies when my body dies. I belong not to the old Adam, but to the new Adam—the new Head of men, who is the Lord from heaven, the author of eternal life to all who obey Him. Do not tell me that I have nothing in me but the likeness of the old Adam, for that seems to me and to St. Paul nothing but the likeness of the fallen savage and the brute in human form. I know I have more in me—infinitely more—than that. What may be in store for the savage, the brutal, the wicked, is God's concern, not mine. But what is in store for me I know—that as I have borne the image of the earthly, so shall I bear the image of the heavenly, if only the Spirit of Christ, the new Adam, be in me. For if Christ be in us, "the body is dead because of sin; but the Spirit is life because of righteousness." And if the Spirit of Him which raised up Jesus from the dead dwell in us, He that raised up Christ from the dead shall also quicken our mortal bodies by His Spirit that dwelleth in us. How He will do it I know not; neither do I care to know. When He will do it I know not; but it will be when it ought to be; and that is enough for me. That He can do it I know, for He is the Maker of the universe, and to Him all power is given in heaven and earth; and as for its being strange, wonderful, past understanding, that matters little to me. That will be but one wonder more in a world where all is wonderful—one more mystery in an utterly mysterious universe.

And so, as Easter day has given us strength to live, let Easter day, too, give us strength to die.

SERMON XI

EASTER DAY

Chester Cathedral. 1870.

St John xii. 24, 25. "Verily, verily, I say unto you, except a corn of wheat fall into the ground and die, it abideth alone: but if it die, it bringeth forth much fruit. He that loveth his life shall lose it; and he that hateth his life in this world shall keep it unto life eternal."

This is our Lord's own parable. In it He tells us that His death, His resurrection, His ascension, is a mystery which we may believe, not only because the Bible tells us of it, but because it is reasonable, and according to the laws of His universe; a fulfilment, rather say the highest fulfilment, of one of those laws which runs through the world of nature, and through the spiritual and heavenly world likewise. "Except a corn of wheat fall into the ground and die, it abideth alone;"—barren, useless, and truly dead to the rest of the world around it, because it is shut up in itself, and its hidden life, with all its wondrous powers of growth and fertility, remains undeveloped, and will remain so, till it decays away, a worthless thing, into worthless dust. But if it be buried in the earth a while, then the rich life which lay hid in it is called out by that seeming death, and it sprouts, tillers, and flowers, and ripens its grain—forty-fold, sixty-fold, an hundred-fold; and so it shows God's mind and will concerning it. It shows what is really in it, and develops the full capabilities of its being. Even so, says our Lord, would His death, His resurrection, His ascension be.

He speaks of His own resurrection and ascension; yes, but He speaks first of His own death. Before the corn can bring forth fruit, and show what is in it, fulfilling the law of its being, it must fall into the ground and die. Before our Lord could fulfil the prophecy, "Thou wilt not leave my soul in hell, neither wilt Thou suffer Thy Holy One to see corruption," He must fulfil the darker prophecy of that awful 88th Psalm, the only one of all the psalms which ends in sorrow, in all but despair, "My soul is full of trouble, and my life draweth nigh unto hell. I am counted as one of them that go down into the pit: and I have been even as a man that hath no strength. Free among the dead, like unto them that are wounded and lie in the grave, who are out of remembrance, and are cut away from thy hand." So it was to be. So, we may believe, it needed to be. Christ must suffer before He entered into His glory. He must die, before He could rise. He must descend into hell, before He ascended into heaven. For this is the law of God's kingdom. Without a Good Friday, there can be no Easter Day. Without self-sacrifice, there can be no blessedness, neither in earth nor in heaven. He that loveth his life will lose it. He that hateth his life in this paltry, selfish, luxurious, hypocritical world, shall keep it to life eternal. Our Lord Jesus Christ fulfilled that law;

because it is the law, the law not of Moses, but of the kingdom of heaven, and must be fulfilled by him who would fulfil all righteousness, and be perfect, even as his Father in heaven is perfect.

Bear this in mind, I pray you, and whenever you think of our Lord's resurrection and ascension, remember always that the background to His triumph is—a tomb. Remember that it is the triumph over suffering; a triumph of One who still bears the prints of the nails in His hands and in His feet, and the wound of the spear in His side; like many a poor soul who has followed Him triumphant at last, and yet scarred, and only not maimed in the hard battle of life. Remember for ever the adorable wounds of Christ. Remember for ever that St John saw in the midst of the throne of God the likeness of a lamb, as it had been slain. For so alone you will learn what our Lord's resurrection and ascension are to all who have to suffer and to toil on earth. For if our Lord's triumph had had no suffering before it,—if He had conquered as the Hindoos represent their gods as conquering their enemies, without effort, without pain, destroying them, with careless case, by lightnings, hurled by a hundred hands and aided by innumerable armies of spirits,—what would such a triumph have been to us? What comfort, what example to us here struggling, often sinning, in this piecemeal world? We want—and blessed be God, we have—a Captain of our salvation, who has been made perfect by sufferings. We want—and blessed be God, we have—an High Priest who can be touched with the feeling of our infirmities, because He has been tempted in all things like as we are, yet without sin. We want—and blessed be God, we have—a King who was glorified by suffering, that, if we are ever called on to sacrifice ourselves, we may hope, by suffering, to share His glory. And when we have remembered this, and fixed it in our minds, we may go on safely to think of His glory, and see that (as I said at first) His resurrection and ascension satisfy our consciences,—satisfy that highest reason and moral sense within us, which is none other than the voice of the Holy Spirit of God.

For see. Our Lord proved Himself to be the perfectly righteous Being, by His very passion. He proved it by being righteous utterly against His own interest; by enduring shame, torment, death, for righteousness' sake. But we feel that our Lord's history could not, must not, end there. Our conscience, which is our highest reason, shrinks from that thought. If our Lord had died and never risen, then would His history be full of nothing but despair to all who long to copy Him and do right at all costs. Our consciences demand that God should be just. We say with Abraham, "Shall not the Judge of all the earth do right?" Shall not He, who suffered without hope of reward, have His reward nevertheless? Shall not He who cried, "My God! my God! why hast Thou forsaken Me?" be justified by having it proved to all the world that God had not forsaken Him? But we surely cannot be more just than God. If we expect God to do right, we shall surely "find that He has done right, and more right than we could expect or dream. Therefore we may believe—I say that we must believe, if we be truly reasonable beings—what the Bible tells us; that Christ, who suffered more than all, was rewarded more than all; that Christ, who humbled Himself more than all, was exalted more than all; and that His resurrection and ascension, as St Paul tells us again and again, was meant to show men this,—to show them that God the Father has been infinitely just to the infinite merits of God the Son, Jesus Christ our Lord,—to justify our Lord to all mankind by His triumph over death and hell, and in justifying Him to justify His Father and our Father, his God and our God.

And what is true of Christ must be true of us, the members of Christ. He is entered into His rest, and you desire to enter into it likewise. You have a right to desire it, for it is written, "There remaineth a rest for the people of God." Remember, then, that true rest can only be attained as He attained it, through labour. You desire to be glorified with Christ. Remember that true glory can only be attained in earth or heaven through self-sacrifice. Whosoever will save his life shall lose it; whosoever will lose his life shall save it. If that eternal moral law held good enough for the sinless Christ, who, though He were a son, yet learned obedience by the things which He suffered, how much more must it hold good of you and me and all moral and rational beings,—yea, for the very angels in heaven. They have not sinned. That we know; and we do not know; and I presume cannot know, that they have ever suffered. But this at least we know, that they have submitted. They have obeyed and have given up their own wills to be the ministers of God's will. In them is neither self-will nor selfishness; and therefore by faith, that is, by trust and loyalty, they stand. And so, by consenting to lose their individual life of selfishness, they have saved their eternal life in God, the life of blessedness and holiness; just as all evil spirits have lost their eternal life by trying to save their selfish life, and be something in themselves and of themselves without respect to God.

This is a great mystery; indeed, it is the mystery of the eternal, divine, and blessed life, to which God of His mercy bring us all. And therefore Good Friday, Easter Day, Ascension Day, are set as great lights in the firmament of the spiritual year,—to remind us that we are not animals, born to do what we like, and fulfil the sinful lusts of the flesh, the ways whereof are death; but that we are moral and rational beings, members of Christ, children of God, inheritors of the kingdom of heaven; and that, therefore, I say it again, like Christ our Lord, we must die in order to live, stoop in order to conquer. They remind us that honour must grow out of humility; that freedom must grow out of discipline; that sure conquest must be born of heavy struggles; righteous joy out of righteous sorrow; pure laughter out of pure tears; true strength out of the true knowledge of our own weakness; sound peace of mind out of sound contrition; and that the heart which has a right to cry, "The Lord is on my side, I will not fear what man doeth unto me," must be born out of the heart which has cried, "God be merciful to me a sinner!" They remind us that in all things, as says our Lord, there cannot be joy, because a man is born into the world, unless there first be sorrow, because the hour of birth is come; and that he who would be planted into the likeness of Christ's resurrection, must, like the corn of wheat, be first planted into the likeness of His death, and die to sin and self, that he may live to righteousness and to God; and, like the corn of wheat, become truly living, truly strong, truly rich, truly useful, and develop the hidden capabilities of his being, fulfilling the mind and will of God concerning him. Again, I say, this is a great mystery. But again, I say, this is the law, not Moses' law, but the Gospel law;—the law of liberty, by which a man becomes truly free, because he has trampled under foot the passions of his own selfish flesh, till his immortal spirit can ascend free into the light of God, and into the love of God, and into the beneficence of God. My dear friends, remember these words, for they are true. Remember that St Paul always couples with the resurrection and ascension of our bodies in the next life the resurrection and ascension of our souls in this life; for without that, the resurrection of our bodies would be but a resurrection to fresh sin, and therefore to fresh misery and ruin. Remember his great words about that moral resurrection and ascension of our wills, our hearts, our characters, our actions. "God," he says, "who is rich in mercy, for His great love, wherewith He loved us, even when we were dead in sins, hath quickened us together with Christ, (by grace are ye saved;) and hath raised us up together, and made us sit together in heavenly places in Christ Jesus."

And what are those heavenly places? And what is our duty in them? Let St Paul himself answer. "If ye then be risen with Christ, seek those things which are above, where Christ sitteth at the right hand of God."

And what are they? Let St Paul answer once more; who should know better than he, save Christ alone? "Whatsoever things are true, honest, just, pure, lovely, of good report. If there be any virtue, and if there be any praise, think on these things."

Yes, think of these things,—and, thinking of them, ask the Holy Spirit of God to inspire you, and make a Whitsuntide in your hearts, even as He has made, I trust, a Good Friday and an Eastertide and an Ascension Day; that so, knowing these things, you may be blessed in doing them; that so—and so only—may be fulfilled in you and me or any rational being, those blessed promises which were fulfilled in Christ our Lord. "They that sow in tears shall reap in joy." "He that now goeth on his way weeping, and beareth forth good seed, shall doubtless come again with joy, and bring his sheaves with him." "Blessed is the man whose strength is in Thee, in whose heart are Thy ways; who going through the vale of misery, use it for a well, and the pools are filled with water. They will go from strength to strength: and unto the God of gods appeareth every one of them in Sion." To which may God in His great mercy bring us all. Amen.

SERMON XII

PRESENCE IN ABSENCE

Eversley, third Sunday after Easter. 1862.

St John xvi. 16. "A little while, and ye shall not see me: and again, a little while, and ye shall see me, because I go to the Father."

Divines differ, and, perhaps, have always differed, about the meaning of these words. Some think that our Lord speaks in them of His death and resurrection. Others that He speaks of His ascension and coming again in glory. I cannot decide which is right. I dare not decide. It is a very solemn thing—too solemn for me—to say of any words of our Lord's they mean exactly this or that, and no more. For if wise men's words have (as they often have) more meanings than one, and yet all true, then surely the words of Jesus, the Son of God, who spake as never man spake—His words, I say, may have many meanings; yea, meanings without end, meanings which we shall never fully understand, perhaps even in heaven, and yet all alike true.

But I think it is certain that most of the early Christians understood these words of our Lord's ascension and coming again in glory. They believed that He was coming again in a very little while during their own life-time, in a few months or years, to make an end of the world and to judge the quick and the dead. And as they waited for His coming, one generation after another, and yet He did not come, a sadness fell upon them. Christ seemed to have left the world. The little while that He had promised to be away seemed to have become a very long while. Hundreds of years passed, and yet Christ did not come in glory. And, as I said, a sadness fell on all the Church. Surely, they said, this is the time of which Christ said we were to weep and lament till we saw Him again—this is the time of which He said that the bridegroom should be taken from us, and we should fast in those days. And they did fast, and weep, and lament; and their religion became a very sad and melancholy one—most sad in those who were most holy, and loved their Lord best, and longed most for His coming in glory.

What happened after that again I could tell you, but we have nothing to do with it to-day. We will rather go back, and see what the Lord's disciples thought He meant when He said,—"A little while, and ye shall not see me; and again, a little while, and ye shall see me, because I go to the Father." One would think, surely, that they must have taken those words to mean His death and resurrection. They heard Him speak them on the very night that He was betrayed. They saw Him taken from them that very night. In horror and agony they saw Him mocked and scourged, crucified, dead, and buried, as they thought for ever, and the world around rejoicing over His death. Surely they wept and lamented then. Surely they thought that He had gone away and left them then.

And the third day, beyond all hope or expectation, they beheld Him alive again, unchanged, perfect, and glorious—as near them and as faithful to them as ever. Surely that was seeing Him again after a little while. Surely then their sorrow was turned to joy. Surely then a man, the man of all men, was born into the world a second time, and in them was fulfilled our Lord's most exquisite parable—most human and yet most divine—of the mother remembering no more her anguish for joy that a man is born into the world.

I think, too, that we may see, by the disciples' conduct, that they took these words of the text to speak of Christ's death and resurrection. For when He ascended to heaven out of their sight, did they consider that was seeing Him no more? Did they think that He had gone away and left them? Did they, therefore, as would have been natural, weep and lament? On the contrary, we are told expressly by St Luke that they "returned to Jerusalem with great joy; and were continually in the temple," not weeping and lamenting, but praising and blessing God. Plainly they did not consider that Christ was parted from them when He ascended into heaven. He had been training them during the forty days between Easter Day and Ascension Day to think of Him as continually near them, whether they saw Him or not. Suddenly He came and went again. Mysteriously He appeared and disappeared. He showed them that though they saw not Him, He saw them, heard their words, knew the thoughts and intents of their hearts. He was always near them they felt; with them to the end of the world, whether in sight or out of sight. And when they saw Him ascend into heaven, it seemed to them no separation, no calamity, no change in His relation to them. He was gone to heaven. Surely He had been in heaven during those forty days, whenever they had not seen Him. He had gone to the Father. Might He not have been with the Father during those forty days, whenever they had not seen Him? Nay; was He not always in heaven? Was not heaven very near them? Did not Christ bring heaven with Him whithersoever He went? Was He not always with the Father, the Father who fills all things, in whom all created things live, and move, and have their being? How could they have thought otherwise about our Lord, when almost His last words to them were not, Lo, I leave you alone, but, "Lo, I am with you alway, even to the end of the world."

My friends, these may seem deep words to some—doubtless they are, for they are the words of the Bible—so deep that plain, unlearned people can make no use of them, and draw no lesson from them. I do not think so. I think it is of endless use and endless importance to you how you think about Christ; and, therefore, how you think about these forty days between our Lord's resurrection and ascension. You may think of our Lord in two ways. You may think of Him as having gone very far away, millions of millions of miles into the sky, and not to return till the last day,—and then, I do not say that you will weep and lament. There are not many who have that notion about our Lord, and yet love Him enough to weep and lament at the thought of His having gone away. But your religion, when it wakes up in you, will be a melancholy and terrifying one. I say, when it wakes up in you—for you will be tempted continually to let it go to sleep. There will come over you the feeling—God forgive us, does it not come over us all but too often?—Christ is far away. Does He see me? Does He hear me? Will He find me out? Does it matter very much what I say and do now, provided I make my peace with Him before I die? And so will come over you not merely a carelessness about religious duties, about prayer, reading, church-going, but worse still, a carelessness about right and wrong. You will be in danger of caring little about controlling your passions, about speaking the truth, about being just and merciful to your fellow-men. And then, when your conscience wakes you up at times, and cries, Prepare to meet thy God! you will be terrified and anxious at the thought of judgment, and shrink from the thought of Christ's seeing you. My friends, that is a fearful state, though a very common one. What is it but a foretaste of that dreadful terror in which those who would not see in Christ their Lord and Saviour will call on the mountains to fall on them, and the hills to cover them, from Him that sitteth on the throne, and from the anger of the Lamb?

But, again: you may think of Christ as His truest servants, though they might have been long in darkness, in all ages and countries have thought of Him, sooner or later. And they thought of Him, as the disciples did; as of One who was about their path and about their bed, and spying out all their ways; as One who was in heaven, but who, for that very reason, was bringing heaven down to earth continually in the gracious inspirations of His Holy Spirit; as One who brought heaven down to them as often as He visited their hearts and comforted them with sweet assurance of His love, His faithfulness, His power—as God grant that He may comfort those of you who need comfort. And that thought, that Christ was always with them, even to the end of the world, sobered and steadied them, and yet refreshed and comforted them. It sobered them. What else could it do? Does it not sober us to see even a picture of Christ crucified? How must it have sobered them to carry, as good St Ignatius used to say of himself, Christ crucified in his heart. A man to whom Christ, as it were, showed perpetually His most blessed wounds, and said, Behold what I have endured—how dare he give way to his passion? How dare he be covetous, ambitious, revengeful, false? And yet it cheered and comforted them. How could it do otherwise, to know all day long that He who was wounded for their iniquities, and by whose stripes they were healed, was near them day and night, watching over them as a father over his child, saying to them,—"Fear not, I am He that was dead, and am alive for evermore, and I hold the keys of death and hell. Though thou walkest through the fires, I will be with thee. I will never leave thee nor forsake thee." Yes, my friends, if you wish your life—and therefore your religion, which ought to be the very life of your life—to be at once sober and cheerful, full of earnestness and full of hope, believe our Lord's words which He spoke during these very forty days,—"Lo, I am with you alway, even to the end of the world." Believe that heaven has not taken Him away from you, but brought Him nearer to you; and that He has ascended up on high, not that He, in whom alone is life, might empty this earth of His presence, but that He might fill all things, not this earth only, but all worlds, past, present, and to come. Believe that wherever two or three are gathered together in Christ's name, there He is in the midst of them; that the holy communion is the sign of His perpetual presence; and that when you kneel to receive the bread and wine, Christ is as near you—spiritually, indeed, and invisibly, but really and truly—as near you as those who are kneeling by your side.

And if it be so with Christ, then it is so with those who are Christ's, with those whom we love. It is the Christ in them which we love; and that Christ in them is their hope of glory; and that glory is the glory of Christ. They are partakers of His death, therefore they are partakers of His resurrection. Let us believe that blessed news in all its fulness, and be at peace. A little while and we see them; and again a little while and we do not see them. But why? Because they are gone to the Father, to the source and fount of all life and power, all light and love, that they may gain life from His life, power from His power, light from His light, love from His love—and surely not for nought?

Surely not for nought, my friends. For if they were like Christ on earth, and did not use their powers for themselves alone, if they are to be like Christ when they shall see Him as He is, then, more surely, will they not use their powers for themselves, but, as Christ uses His, for those they love.

Surely, like Christ, they may come and go, even now, unseen. Like Christ, they may breathe upon our restless hearts and say, Peace be unto you—and not in vain. For what they did for us when they were on earth they can more fully do now that they are in heaven. They may seem to have left us, and we, like the disciples, may weep and lament. But the day will come when the veil shall be taken from our eyes, and we shall see them as they are, with Christ, and in Christ for ever; and remember no more our anguish for joy that a man is born into the world, that another human being has entered that one true, real, and eternal world, wherein is neither disease, disorder, change, decay, nor death, for it is none other than the Bosom of the Father.

SERMON XIII

ASCENSION DAY

Eversley. Chester Cathedral. 1872.

St John viii. 58. "Before Abraham was, I am."

Let us consider these words awhile. They are most fit for our thoughts on this glorious day, on which the Lord Jesus ascended to His Father, and to our Father, to His God, and to our God, that He might be glorified with the glory which He had with the Father before the making of the world. For it is clear that we shall better understand Ascension Day, just as we shall better understand Christmas or Eastertide, the better we understand Who it was who was born at Christmas, suffered and rose at Eastertide, and, as on this day, ascended into heaven. Who, then, was He whose ascent we celebrate? What was that glory which, as far as we can judge of divine things, He resumed as on this day?

Let us think a few minutes, with all humility, not rashly intruding ourselves into the things we have not seen, or meddling with divine matters which are too hard for us, but taking our Lord's words simply as they stand, and where we do not understand them, believing them nevertheless.

Now it is clear that the book of Exodus and our Lord's words speak of the same person. The Old Testament tells of a personage who appeared to Moses in the wilderness, and who called Himself "the Lord God of Abraham, Isaac and Jacob." But this personage also calls Himself "I AM." "I AM THAT I AM:" "and He said, Thus shalt thou say unto the children of Israel, I AM hath sent me unto you."

In the New Testament we read of a personage who calls Himself the Son of God, is continually called the Lord, and who tells His disciples to call Him by that name without reproving them, though they and He knew well what it meant—that it meant no less than this, that He, Jesus of Nazareth, poor mortal man as He seemed, was still the Lord, the God of Abraham, Isaac, and Jacob. I do not say that the disciples saw that at first, clearly or fully, till after our Lord's resurrection. But there was one moment shortly before His death, when they could have had no doubt who He assumed Himself to be. For the unbelieving Jews had no doubt, and considered Him a blasphemer; and these were His awful and wonderful words,—I do not pretend to understand them—I take them simply as I find them, and believe and adore. "Your father Abraham rejoiced to see my day, and he saw it, and was glad. Then said the Jews unto Him, Thou art not yet fifty years old, and hast Thou seen Abraham?" One cannot blame them for asking that question, for Abraham had been dead then nearly two thousand years. But what is our Lord's solemn answer? "Verily, verily, I say unto you, before Abraham was, I am."

"I Am." The same name by which our Lord God had revealed Himself to Moses in the wilderness, some sixteen hundred years before. If these words were true,—and the Lord prefaces them with Verily, verily, Amen, Amen, which was as solemn an asseveration as any oath could be—then the Lord Jesus Christ is none other than the God of Abraham, the God of Moses, the God of the Jews, the God of the whole universe, past, present, and to come.

Let us think awhile over this wonder of all wonders. The more we think over it, we shall find it not only the wonder of all wonders, but the good news of all good news.

The deepest and soundest philosophers will tell us that there must be an "I Am." That is, as they would say, a self-existent Being; neither made nor created, but who has made and created all things; who is without parts and passions, and is incomprehensible, that is cannot be comprehended, limited, made smaller or weaker, or acted on in any way by any of the things that He has made. So that this self-existing Being whom we call God, would be exactly what He is now, if the whole universe, sun, moon, and stars, were destroyed this moment; and would be exactly what He is now, if there had never been any universe at all, or any thing or being except His own perfect and self-existent Self. For He lives and moves and has His being in nothing. But all things live and move and have their being in Him. He was before all things, and by Him all things consist. And this is the Catholic Faith; and not only that, this is according to sound and right reason. But more: the soundest philosophers will tell you that God must be not merely a self-existent Being, but the "I Am:" that if God is a Spirit, and not merely a name for some powers and laws of brute nature and matter, He must be able to say to Himself, "I Am:" that He must know Himself, that He must be conscious of Himself, of who and what He is, as you and I are conscious of ourselves, and more or less of who and what we are. And this, also, I believe to be true, and rational, and necessary to the Catholic Faith.

But they will tell you again—and this, too, is surely true—that I Am must be the very name of God, because God alone can say perfectly, "I Am," and no more. You and I dare not, if we think accurately, say of ourselves, "I am." We may say, I am this or that; I am a man; I am an Englishman; but we must not say, "I am;" that is, "I exist of myself." We must say—not I am; but I become, or have become; I was made; I was created; I am growing, changing; I depend for my very existence on God and God's will, and if He willed, I should be nothing and nowhere in a moment. God alone can say, I Am, and there is none beside Me, and never has, nor can be. I exist, absolutely, and simply; because I choose to exist, and get life from nothing; for I Am the Life, and give life to all things. But you may say, What is all this to us? It is very difficult to understand, and dreary, and even awful. Why should we care for it, even if it be true? Yes, my friends; philosophy may be true, and yet be dreary, and awful, and have no gospel and good news in it at all. I believe it never can have; that only in Revelation, and in the Revelation of our Lord Jesus Christ, can poor human beings find any gospel and good news at all. And sure I am, that that is an awful thought, a dreary thought, a crushing thought, which makes a man feel as small, and worthless, and help-less, and hopeless, as a grain of dust, or a mote in the sunbeam—that thought of God for ever contained in Himself, and saying for ever to Himself, "I Am, and there is none beside Me."

But the Gospel, the good news of the Old Testament, the Gospel, the good news of the New Testament, is the Revelation of God and God's ways, which began on Christmas Day, and finished on Ascension Day: and what is that? What but this? That God does not merely say to Himself in Majesty, "I Am;" but that He goes out of Himself in Love, and says to men, "I Am." That He is a God who has spoken to poor human beings, and told them who He was; and that He, the I Am, the self-existent One, the Cause of life, of all things, even the Maker and Ruler of the Universe, can stoop to man—and not merely to perfect men, righteous men, holy men, wise men, but to the enslaved, the sinful, the brutish—that He may deliver them, and teach them, and raise them from the death of sin, to His own life of righteousness.

Do you not see the difference, the infinite difference, and the good news in that? Do you not see a whole heaven of new hope and new duty is opened to mankind in that one fact—God has spoken to man. He, the I Am, the Self-Existent, who needs no one, and no thing, has turned aside, as it were, and stooped from the throne of heaven, again and again, during thousands of years, to say to you, and me, and millions of mankind, I Am your God. How do you prosper?—what do you need?—what are you doing?—for if you are doing justice to yourself and your fellow-men, then fear not that I shall be just to you.

And more. When that I Am, the self-existent God, could not set sinful men right by saying this, then did He stoop once more from the throne of the heavens to do that infinite deed of love, of which it is written, that He who called Himself "I Am," the God of Abraham, was conceived of the Holy Ghost, born of the Virgin Mary, crucified under Pontius Pilate, rose again the third day, and ascended into heaven,—that He might send down the Spirit of the "I Am," the Holy Spirit who proceedeth from the Father and the Son, upon all who ask Him; that they may be holy as God is holy, and perfect as God is perfect. Yes, my dear friends, remember that, and live in the light of that; the gospel of good news of the Incarnation of Jesus Christ, very God of very God begotten. Know that God has spoken to you as He spoke to Abraham, and said,—I am the Almighty God, walk before Me, and be thou perfect. Know that He has spoken to you as He spoke to Moses, saying,—I am the Lord thy God, who have brought you, and your fathers before you, out of the spiritual Egypt of heathendom, and ignorance, sin, and wicked-ness, into the knowledge of the one, true, and righteous God. But know more, that He has spoken to you by the mouth of Jesus Christ, saying,—I am He that died in the form of mortal man upon the cross for you. And, behold, I am alive for evermore; and to me all power is given in heaven and earth.

Yes, my friends, let us lay to heart, even upon this joyful day, the awful warnings of the Epistle to the Hebrews,—God, the I Am, has spoken to us; God, the I Am, is speaking to us now. See that you refuse not Him that speaketh; for if they escaped not who refused Moses that spake on earth, much more shall not we escape if we turn away from Him that speaketh from heaven; wherefore follow peace with all men, and holiness, without which no man shall see the Lord, and have grace, whereby we may serve God acceptably, with reverence and godly fear. For our God is a consuming fire. To those who disobey Him, eternal wrath; to those who love Him, eternal love.

Yes, my friends. Let us believe that, and live in the light of that, with reverence and godly fear, all the year round. But let us specially to-day, as far as our dull feelings and poor imaginations will allow us; let us, I say, adore the ascended Saviour, who rules for ever, a Man in the midst of the throne of the universe, and that Man—oh, wonder of wonders!—slain for us; and let us say with St Paul of old, with all our hearts and minds and souls:—Now to the King of the Ages, immortal, invisible, with the Father and the Holy Spirit, be honour and glory, for ever and ever. Amen!

SERMON XIV

THE COMFORTER

Eversley. Sunday after Ascension Day. 1868.

St John xv. 26. "When the Comforter is come, whom I will send unto you from the Father, even the Spirit of truth, which proceedeth from the Father, he shall testify of me."

Some writers, especially when they are writing hymns, have fallen now-a-days into a habit of writing of the Holy Spirit of God, in a tone of which I dare not say that it is wrong or untrue; but of which I must say, that it is one-sided. And if there are two sides to a matter, it must do us harm to look at only one of them. And I think that it does people harm to hear the Holy Spirit of God, the Holy Ghost, the Comforter, spoken of in terms, not of reverence, but of endearment. For consider: He is the

> "Creator-Spirit, by whose aid
> The world's foundations first were laid,"

the life-giving Spirit of whom it is written, Thou sendest forth Thy Spirit, and things live, and Thou renewest the face of the earth.

But He is the destroying Spirit too; who can, when He will, produce not merely life, but death; who can, and does send earthquakes, storm, and pestilence; of whom Isaiah writes—"All flesh is as grass, and all the goodliness thereof is as the flower of the field. The grass withereth, the flower fadeth; because the Spirit of the Lord bloweth upon it." I think it does people harm to hear this awful and almighty being, I say, spoken of merely as the "sweet Spirit," and "gentle dove"—words which are true, but only true, if we remember other truths, equally true of Him, concerning whom they are spoken. The Spirit of God, it seems to me, is too majestic a being to be talked of hastily as "sweet." Words may be true, and yet it may not be always quite reverent to use them. An earthly sovereign may be full of all human sweetness and tenderness, yet we should not dare to address him as "sweet."

But, indeed, some of this talk about the Holy Spirit is not warranted by Scripture at all. In one of the hymns, for instance, in our hymn-book—an excellent hymn in other respects, there is a line which speaks of the Holy Spirit as possessing "The brooding of the gentle dove."

Now, this line is really little but pretty sentiment, made up of false uses of Scripture. The Scripture speaks once of the Holy Spirit of God brooding like a bird over its nest. But where? In one of the most mysterious, awful, and important of all texts. "And the earth was without form and void. And the Spirit of God moved (brooded) over the face of the deep." What has this—the magnificent picture of the Life-giving Spirit brooding over the dead world, to bring it into life again, and create from it sea and land, heat and fire, and cattle and creeping things after their kind, and at last man himself, the flower and crown of things;—what has that to do with the brooding of a gentle dove?

But the Holy Spirit is spoken of in Scripture under the likeness of a dove? True, and here is another confusion. The Dove is not the emblem of gentleness in the Bible: but the Lamb. The dove is the emblem of something else, pure and holy, but not of gentleness; and therefore the Holy Spirit is not spoken of in Scripture as brooding as a gentle dove; but very differently, as it seems to me. St Matthew and St John say, that at our Lord's baptism the Holy Spirit was seen, not brooding, but descending from heaven as a dove. To any one who knows anything of doves, who will merely go out into the field or the farm-yard and look at them, and who will use his own eyes, that figure is striking enough, and grand enough. It is the swiftness of the dove, and not its fancied gentleness that is spoken of. The dove appearing, as you may see it again and again, like a speck in the far off sky, rushing down with a swiftness which outstrips the very eagle; returning surely to the very spot from which it set forth, though it may have flown over hundreds of miles of land, and through the very clouds of heaven. It is the sky-cleaving force and swiftness, the unerring instinct of the dove, and not a sentimental gentleness to which Scripture likens that Holy Spirit, which like the rushing mighty wind bloweth whither it listeth, and thou hearest the sound thereof, but canst not tell whence it cometh, or whither it goeth;—that Holy Spirit who, when He fell on the apostles, fell in tongues of fire, and shook all the house where they were sitting; that Holy Spirit of whom one of the wisest Christians who ever lived, who knew well enough the work of the Spirit, arguing just as I am now against the fancy of associating the Holy Spirit merely with pretty thoughts of our own, and pleasant feelings of our own, and sentimental raptures of our own, said, "Wouldst thou know the manner of spiritual converse? Of the way in which the Spirit of God works in man? Then it is this: He hath taken me up and dashed me down. Like a lion, I look, that He will break all my bones. From morning till evening, Thou wilt make an end of me."

But people are apt to forget this. And therefore they fall into two mistakes. They think of the Holy Spirit as only a gentle, and what they call a dove-like being; and they forget what a powerful, awful, literally formidable being He is. They lose respect for the Holy Spirit. They trifle with Him; and while they sing hymns about His gentleness and sweetness, they do things which grieve and shock Him; forgetting the awful warning which He, at the very outset of the Christian Church, gave against such taking of liberties with God the Holy Ghost:—how Ananias and Sapphira thought that the Holy Spirit was One whom they might honour with their lips, and more, with their outward actions, but who did not require truth in the inward parts, and did not care for their telling a slight falsehood that they might appear more generous than they really were in the eyes of men; and how the answer of the Holy Spirit of God was that He struck them both dead there and then for a warning to all such triflers, till the end of time.

Another mistake which really pious and good people commit, is, that they think the Holy Spirit of God to be merely, or little beside, certain pleasant frames, and feelings, and comfortable assurances, in their own minds. They do not know that these pleasant frames and feelings really depend principally on their own health: and, then, when they get out of health, or when their brain is overworked, and the pleasant feelings go, they are terrified and disheartened, and complain of spiritual dryness, and cry out that God's Spirit has deserted them, and are afraid that God is angry with them, or even that they have committed the unpardonable sin: not knowing that God is not a man that He should lie, nor a son of man that He should repent; that God is as near them in the darkness as in the light; that whatever their own health, or their own feelings may be, yet still in God they live, and move, and have their being; that to God's Spirit they owe all which raises them above the dumb animals; that nothing can separate them from the love of Him who promised that He would not leave us comfortless, but send to us His Holy Ghost to comfort us, and exalt us to the same place whither He has gone before.

Now, why do I say all this? To take away comfort from you? To make you fear and dread the Spirit of God? God forbid! Who am I, to take away comfort from any human being! I say it to give yon true comfort, to make you trust and love the Holy Spirit utterly, to know Him—His strength and His wisdom as well as His tenderness and gentleness.

You know that afflictions do come—terrible bereavements, sorrows sad and strange. My sermon does not make them come. There they are, God help us all, and too many of them, in this world. But from whom do they come? Who is Lord of life and death? Who is Lord of joy and sorrow? Is not that the question of all questions? And is not the answer the most essential of all answers? It is the Holy Spirit of God; the Spirit who proceedeth from the Father and the Son; the Spirit of the Father who so loved the world that He spared not His only begotten Son; the Spirit of the Son who so loved the world, that He stooped to die for it upon the Cross; the Spirit who is promised to lead you into all truth, that you may know God, and in the knowledge of Him find everlasting life; the Spirit who is the Comforter, and says, I have seen thy ways and will heal thee, I will lead thee also, and restore comforts to thee and to thy mourners. I speak peace to him that is near, and to him that is far off, saith the Lord; and I will heal him. Is it not the most blessed news, that He who takes away, is the very same as He who gives? That He who afflicts is the very same as He who comforts? That He of whom it is written that, "as a lion, so will He break all my bones; from day even to night wilt Thou make an end of me;" is the same as He of whom it is written, "He shall gather the lambs in His arms, and carry them, and shall gently lead those that are with young;" and, again, "as a beast goeth down into the valley, so the Spirit of the Lord caused him to rest?" That He of whom it is written, "Our God is a consuming fire," is the same as He who has said, "When thou walkest through the fire, thou shalt not be burned?" That He who brings us into "the valley of the shadow of death," is the same as He of whom it is said, "Thy rod and Thy staff they comfort me?" Is not that blessed news? Is it not the news of the Gospel; and the only good news which people will really care for, when they are tormented, not with superstitious fears and doctrines of devils which man's diseased conscience has originated, but tormented with the real sorrows, the rational fears of this stormy human life.

We all like comfort. But what kind of comfort do we not merely like but need? Merely to be comfortable?—To be free from pain, anxiety, sorrow?—To have only pleasant faces round us, and pleasant things said to us? If we want that comfort, we shall very seldom have it. It will be very seldom good for us to have it. The comfort which poor human beings want in such a world as this, is not the comfort of ease, but the comfort of strength. The comforter whom we need is not one who will merely say kind things, but give help—help to the weary and heavy laden heart which has no time to rest. We need not the sunny and smiling face, but the strong and helping arm. For we may be in that state that smiles are shocking to us, and mere kindness,—though we may be grateful for it—of no more comfort to us than sweet music to a drowning man. We may be miserable, and unable to help being miserable, and unwilling to help it too. We do not wish to flee from our sorrow, we do not wish to forget our sorrow. We dare not; it is so awful, so heartrending, so plain spoken, that God, the master and tutor of our hearts must wish us to face it and endure it. Our Father has given us the cup—shall we not drink it? But who will help us to drink the bitter cup? Who will be the comforter, and give us not mere kind words, but strength? Who will give us the faith to say with Job, "Though He slay me, yet will I trust in Him?" Who will give us the firm reason to look steadily at our grief, and learn the lesson it was meant to teach? Who will give us the temperate will, to keep sober and calm amid the shocks and changes of mortal life? Above all, I may say—Who will lead us into all truth? How much is our sorrow increased—how much of it is caused by simple ignorance! Why has our anxiety come? How are we to look at it? What are we to do? Oh, that we had a comforter who would lead us into all truth:—not make us infallible, or all knowing, but lead us into truth; at least put us in the way of truth, put things in their true light to us, and give us sound and rational views of life and duty. Oh, for a comforter who would give us the spirit of wisdom and understanding, the spirit of counsel and ghostly strength, the spirit of knowledge and true godliness, and fill us with that spirit of God's holy fear, which would make us not superstitious, not slavish, not anxious, but simply obedient, loyal and resigned.

If we had such a Comforter as that, could we not take evil from his hands, as well as good? We have had fathers of our flesh who corrected us, and we gave them reverence. They chastised us, but we loved and trusted them, because we knew that they loved and trusted us—chastised us to make us better—chastised us because they trusted us to become better. But if we can find a Father of our spirits, of our souls, shall we not rather be in subjection to Him and live? If He sent us a Comforter, to comfort and guide, and inspire, and strengthen us, shall we not say of that Comforter—"Though He slay me, yet will I trust in Him."

If we had such a Comforter as that, we should not care, if He seemed at times stern, as well as kind; we could endure rebuke and chastisement from Him, if we could only get from Him wisdom to understand the rebuke, and courage to bear the chastisement. Where is that Comforter? God answers:—That Comforter am I, the God of heaven and earth. There are comforters on earth who can help thee with wise words and noble counsel, can be strong as man, and tender as woman. Then God can be more strong than man, and more tender than woman likewise. And when the strong arm of man supports thee no longer, yet under thee are the everlasting arms of God.

Oh, blessed news, that God Himself is the Comforter. Blessed news, that He who strikes will also heal: that He who gives the cup of sorrow, will also give the strength to drink it. Blessed news, that chastisement is not punishment, but the education of a Father. Blessed news, that our whole duty is the duty of a child—of the Son who said in His own agony, "Father, not my will, but thine be done." Blessed news, that our Comforter is the Spirit who comforted Christ the Son Himself; who proceeds both from the Father and from the Son; and who will therefore testify to us both of the Father and the Son, and tell us that in Christ we are indeed, really and literally, the children of God who may cry to Him, "Father," with full understanding of all that that royal word contains. Blessed, too, to find that in the power of the Divine Majesty, we can acknowledge the unity, and know and feel that the Father, Son and Holy Ghost are all one in love to the creatures whom they have made—their glory equal, for the glory of each and all is perfect charity, and their majesty co-eternal, because it is a perfect majesty; whose justice is mercy, whose power is goodness, its very sternness love, love which gives hope and counsel, and help and strength, and the true life which this world's death cannot destroy.

SERMON XV

THOU ART WORTHY

Eversley, 1869. Chester Cathedral, 1870. Trinity Sunday.

Revelation iv. 11. "Thou art worthy, O Lord, to receive glory and honour and power: for Thou hast created all things, and for Thy pleasure they are and were created."

I am going to speak to you on a deep matter, the deepest and most important of all matters, and yet I hope to speak simply. I shall say nothing which you cannot understand, if you will attend. I shall say nothing, indeed, which you could not find out for yourselves, if you will think, and use your own common sense. I wish to speak to you of Theology—of God Himself. For this Trinity Sunday of all the Sundays of the year, is set apart for thinking of God Himself—not merely of our own souls, though we must never forget them, nor of what God has done for our souls, though we must never forget that—but of what God is Himself, what He would be if we had no souls—if there were, and had been from the beginning, no human beings at all upon the earth.

Now, if we look at any living thing—an animal, say, or a flower, and consider how curiously it is contrived, our common sense will tell us at once that some one has made it; and if any one answers—Oh! the flower was not made, it grew—our common sense would tell us that that was only a still more wonderful contrivance, and that there must be some one who gave it the power of growing, and who makes it grow. And so our common sense would tell us, as it told the heathens of old, that there must be gods—beings whom we cannot see, who made the world. But if we watch things more closely, we should find out that all things are made more or less upon the same plan; that (and I tell you that this is true, strange as it may seem) all animals, however different they may seem to our eyes, are made upon the same plan; all plants and flowers, however different they may seem, are made upon the same plan; all stones, and minerals, and earths, however different they may seem, are made upon the same plan. Then common sense would surely tell us, one God made all the animals, one God made all the plants, one God made all the earths and stones. But if we watch more closely still, we should find that the plants could not live without the animals, nor the animals without the plants, nor either of them without the soil beneath our feet, and the air and rain above our heads. That everything in the world worked together on one plan, and each thing depended on everything else. Then common sense would tell us, one God must have made the whole world. But if we watched more closely again, or rather, if we asked the astronomers, who study the stars and heavens, they would tell us that all the worlds over our heads, all the stars that spangle the sky at night, were made upon the same plan as our earth—that sun and moon, and all the host of heaven, move according to the same laws by which our earth moves, and as far as we can find out, have been made in the same way as our earth has been made, and that these same laws must have been going on, making worlds after worlds, for hundreds of thousands of years, and ages beyond counting, and will, in all probability, go on for countless ages more. Then common sense will tell us, the same God has made all worlds, past, present, and to come. There is but one God, the same yesterday, to-day, and for ever.

So we should learn something of how all things were made; and then would come a second question, why all things were made? Why did God make the worlds?

Let us begin with a very simple example. Simple things will often teach us most. You see a flower growing, not in a garden, but wild in a field or wood. You admire its beautiful colours, or if it is fragrant, its sweet scent. Now, why was that flower put there? You may answer, "to please me." My dear friends, I should be the last person to deny that. I can never see a child picking a nosegay, much less a little London child, born and bred and shut up among bricks and mortar, when it gets for the first time into a green field, and throws itself instinctively upon the buttercups and daisies, as if they were precious jewels and gold;—I never can see that sight, I say, without feeling that there are such things as final causes—I mean that the great Father in heaven put those flowers into that field on purpose to give pleasure to His human children. But then comes the question, Of all the flowers in a single field, is one in ten thousand ever looked at by child or by men? And yet they are just as beautiful as the rest; and God has, so to speak, taken just as much pains with the many beautiful things which men will never see, as with the few, very few, which men may see. And when one thinks further about this—when one thinks of the vast forests in other lands which the foot of man has seldom or never trod, and which, when they are entered, are found to be full of trees, flowers, birds, butterflies, so beautiful and glorious, that anything which we see in these islands is poor and plain in comparison with them; and when we remember that these beautiful creatures have been going on generation after generation, age after age, unseen and unenjoyed by any human eyes, one must ask, Why has God been creating all that beauty? simply to let it all, as it were, run to waste, till after thousands of years one traveller comes, and has a hasty glimpse of it? Impossible. Or again—and this is an example still more strange, and yet it is true. We used to think till within a very few years past, that at the bottom of the deep sea there were no living things—that miles below the surface of the ocean, in total darkness, and under such a weight of water as would crush us to a jelly, there could be nothing, except stones, and sand, and mud. But now it is found out that the bottom of the deepest seas, and the utter darkness into which no ray of light can ever pierce, are alive and swarming with millions of creatures as cunningly and exquisitely formed, and in many cases as brilliantly coloured, as those which live in the sunlight along the shallow shores.

Now, my dear friends,—surely beautiful things were made to be seen by some one, else why were they made beautiful? Common sense tells us that. But who has seen those countless tribes, which have been living down, in utter darkness, since the making of the world? Common sense, I think, can give but one answer—GOD. He, and He only, to whom the night is as clear as the day, to whom the darkness and the light are both alike. But more—God has not only made things beautiful; He has made things happy; whatever misery there may be in the world, there is no denying that. However sorrow may have come into the world, there is a great deal more happiness than misery in it. Misery is the exception; happiness is the rule. No rational man ever heard a bird sing, without feeling that that bird was happy; and, if so, his common sense ought to tell him that if God made that bird, He made it to be happy; He intended it to be happy, and He takes pleasure in its happiness, though no human ear should ever hear its song, no human heart should ever share in its joy. Yes, the world was not made for man; but man, like all the world, was made for God. Not for man's pleasure merely, not for man's use, but for God's pleasure all things are, and for God's pleasure they were created.

And now, surely, common sense will tell us why God made all things. For His own pleasure. God is pleased to make them, and pleased with what He has made, because what He has made is worth being pleased with. He has seen all things that He has made, and, behold, they are very good, and right, and wise, and beautiful, and happy, each after its kind. So that, as the Psalmist says, "The Lord shall rejoice in His works." And Scripture tells that it must be so, if we only recollect and believe one word of St. John's that "God is Love"—for it is the very essence of love, that it cannot be content to love itself. It must have something which is not itself to love that it may go out of itself, and forget itself, and spend itself in the good and in the happiness of what it loves. All true love of husband and wife, mother and child, sister and brother, friend and friend, man to his country,—what does it mean but this? Forgetting one's selfish happiness in doing good to others, and finding a deeper, higher happiness in that. The man who only loves himself knows not what Love means. In truth, he does not even love himself. He is his own worst enemy: his selfishness torments him with discontent, disgust, pride, fear, and all evil passions and lusts; and in him is fulfilled our Lord's saying, that he that will save his life shall lose it. But the man who is full of love, as God is full of love, who forgets himself in making others happy, who lives the eternal life of God, which is alone worth living, he is the only truly happy man; and in him is fulfilled that other saying of our Lord, that he who loseth his life shall save it.

And the loving, unselfish man too is the only sound theologian, for he who dwelleth in love dwelleth in God, and God in him. He alone will understand the mystery of who God is, and why He made all things. The loving man alone, I say, will understand the mystery—how because God is love He could not live alone in the abyss, but must create all things, all worlds and heavens, yea, and the heaven of heavens, that He might have something beside Himself, whereon to spend His boundless love. And why? Because love can only love what is somewhat like itself, He made all things according to the idea of His own eternal mind. Because He is unchangeable, and a God of order and of law, He made all things according to one order, and gave them a law which cannot be broken, that they might continue this day as they were at the beginning, serving Him and fulfilling His word. Because He is a God of justice, He made all things just, depending on each other, helping each other, and compelled to sacrifice themselves for each other, and minister to each other whether they will or not. Because He is a God of beauty, He made all things beautiful, of a variety and a richness unspeakable, that He might rejoice in all His works, and find a divine delight in every moss which grows upon the moor, and every gnat which dances in the sun. Because He is a God of love, He gave to every creature a power of happiness according to its kind, that He might rejoice in the happiness of His creatures. And lastly, because God is a spirit—a moral and a rational Being—therefore He created rational beings to be more like Him than any other creatures, and constituted the services of men and angels in a most wonderful order, that they might reverence law as He does, and justice as He does—that they might love to be loving as He loves, and to be useful as He is useful—that they might rejoice in the beauty of His works as He rejoices in them Himself; and, catching from time to time fuller and fuller glimpses of that Divine and wonderful order according to which He has made all things and all worlds, may see more and more clearly, as the years roll on, that all things are just, and beautiful, and good; and join more and more heartily in the hymn which goes up for ever from every sun, and star, and world, and from the tiniest creature in these worlds: "Thou art worthy, O Lord, to receive glory and honour and power; for Thou hast created all things, and for Thy pleasure they are and were created."

Now, to God the Father, who, out of His boundless love, ordains the making of all things; and to God the Son, who, out of His boundless love, performs the making of all things; and to God the Holy Spirit, who, out of His boundless love, breathes law and kind, life and growth into all things, three Persons in one, ever-blessed Trinity, be all glory, and honour, and praise, for ever and ever. Amen.

SERMON XVI

THE GLORY OF THE TRINITY

Eversley, 1868. St Mary's Chester, 1871. Trinity Sunday.

Psalm civ. 31, 33. "The glory of the Lord shall endure for ever: The Lord shall rejoice in his works. I will sing unto the Lord as long as I live: I will sing praise to my God while I have my being."

This is Trinity Sunday, on which we think especially of the name of God. A day which, to a wise man, may well be one of the most solemn, and the most humiliating days of the whole year. For is it not humiliating to look stedfastly, even for a moment, at God's greatness, and then at our own littleness; at God's strength and at our own weakness; at God's wisdom, and at our own ignorance; and, most of all, at God's righteousness, and at our own sins?

I do not say that it should not be so. Rather, I say, it should be so. For what is more wholesome for you and me, and any man, than to be humiliated—humbled—and brought to our own level—that all may see who, what, and where we are? What more wholesome than to be made holy and humble men of heart? What more wholesome for us, who are each of us tempted to behave as if we were the centre of the universe, to judge ourselves the most important personages in the world, and to judge of everything according as it is pleasant or unpleasant to us, each in our own family, our own sect, our own neighbourhood; what more wholesome than to be brought now and then face to face with God Himself, and see what poor, little, contemptible atoms we are at best, compared with Him who made heaven and earth?—to see how well God and God's world have gone on for thousands of years without our help;—how well they will go on after we are dead and gone?

Face to face with God! And how far shall we have to go to find ourselves face to face with God? Not very far, according to St Paul. God, he says, is "not far from every one of us; for in Him we live, and move, and have our being."

In God, in the ever blessed Trinity—Father, Son, and Holy Ghost—we, and not we only, but every living thing—each flower, each insect—lives, and moves, and has its being. So it is—strange as it may seem, and we cannot make it otherwise. You fancy God far off—somewhere in the skies, beyond suns and stars. Know that the heavens, and the heaven of heavens, cannot contain Him. Rather, in the very deepest sense, He contains them. In God, suns and stars, and all the host of heaven, live, and move, and have their being; and if God destroyed them all at this very moment, and the whole universe became nothing once more, as it was nothing at first, still God would remain, neither greater nor less, neither stronger nor weaker, neither richer nor poorer, than He was before. For He is the self-existent I

Am; who needs nought save Himself, and who needs nought save to assert Himself in His Word, Jesus Christ our Lord, and say "I Am," in order to create all things and beings, save Himself. He is the infinite; whom nothing, however huge, and vast, or strong, can comprehend—that is, take in and limit. He takes in and limits all things; giving to each thing, form according to its own kind, and life and growth according to its own law; appointing to all (as says St Paul) their times, and the bounds of their habitation; that if they be rational creatures, as we are, they may feel after the Lord and find Him; and if they be irrational creatures, like the animals and the plants, mountains and streams, clouds and tempests, sun and stars, they may serve God's gracious purposes in the economy of His world.

Therefore, everything which you see, is, as it were, a thought of God's, an action of God's; a message to you from God. Therefore you can look at nothing in the earth without seeing God Himself at work thereon. As our Lord said, "My Father worketh hitherto, and I work." You can look neither at the sun in the sky, nor at the grass beneath your feet, without being brought face to face with God, the ever blessed Trinity. The tiniest gnat which dances in the sun, was conceived by God the Father, in whose eternal bosom are the ideas and patterns of all things, past, present, and to come; it was created by God the Son, by whom the Father made all things, and without whom nothing is made: and it is kept alive by God the Holy Spirit, the Lord and giver of life, of whom it is written, "Thou sendest forth thy Spirit, they are created; and thou renewest the face of the earth."

Oh that we could all remember this. That when we walk across the field, or look out into the garden, we could have the wisdom to remember, Whither, O God, can I go from Thy presence? For Thou art looking down on the opening of every bud and flower, and without Thee not a sparrow falls to the ground. Whither can I flee from Thy Spirit? For Thy Spirit is giving life perpetually, alike to me and to the insect at my feet; without Thy Spirit my lungs could not breathe one breath, my heart could not beat one pulse. In Thee, I and all things live, move, and have our being. And shall I forget Thee, disobey Thee, neglect to praise, and honour, and worship Thee, and thank Thee day and night, for Thy great glory?

If we could but remember that, there would be no fear of our being ungodly, irreligious, undevout. We look too often, day after day, month after month, on the world around us just as the dumb beasts do, as a place out of which we can get something to eat, and forget that it is also a place out of which we can get, daily and hourly, something to admire, to adore, to worship, even the thought of God's wisdom, God's power, God's goodness, God's glory. Oh blind and heedless that we are. Truly said the wise man—"An undevout astronomer is mad." And truly said another wise man, an Englishman—the saintly philosopher Faraday, now with God,—"How could he be otherwise than religious; when at every step he found himself brought more closely face to face with the signs of a mind constructed like his own, with an aim and a purpose which he could understand, employing ways and means, and tending clearly to an end, and methodically following out a system which he could both perceive and grasp." Such a man's whole life is one act of reverence to that God in whose inner presence he finds himself illuminated and strengthened; and if there be revelation of divine things on earth, it is when the hidden secrets of nature are disclosed to the sincere and self-denying seeker after truth.

Yes, that is true. The more you look into the world around you, and consider every flower, and bird, and stone, the more you will see that a Mind planned them, even the mind of God; a Mind like yours and mine; but how infinitely different, how much deeper, wiser, vaster. Before that thought we shrink into the nothingness from whence He called us out at first. The difference between our minds and the Mind of God is—to what shall I liken it? Say, to the difference between a flake of soot and a mountain of pure diamond. That soot and that diamond are actually the same substance; of that there is no doubt whatsoever; but as the light, dirty, almost useless soot is to the pure, and clear, hard diamond, ay, to a mountain, a world, a whole universe made of pure diamond—if such a thing were possible—so is the mind of man compared with that Mind of the ever blessed Trinity, which made the worlds, and sustains them in life and order to this day.

My friends, it is not in great things only, but in the very smallest, that the greatest glory of the ever blessed Trinity is seen. Ay, most, perhaps, in the smallest, when one considers the utterly inconceivable wisdom, which can make the smallest animal—so made as to be almost invisible under the strongest microscope—as perfect in all its organs as the hugest elephant. Ay, more, which can not only make these tiny living things, but, more wonderful still, make them make themselves? For what is growth, but a thing making itself? What is the seed growing into a plant, the plant into a flower, the flower to a seed again, but that thing making itself, transforming itself, by an inward law of life which God's Spirit gives it. I tell you the more earnestly and carefully you examine into the creation, birth, growth of any living thing, even of the daisy on the grass outside; the more you inquire what it really is, how it came to be like what it is, how it got where it is, and so forth; you will be led away into questions which may well make you dizzy with thinking, so strange, so vast, so truly miraculous is the history of every organised creature upon earth. And when you recollect (as you are bound to do on this day), that each of these things is the work of the ever blessed Trinity; that upon every flower and every insect, generation after generation of them, since the world was made, the ever blessed Trinity has been at work, God the Father thinking and conceiving each thing, in His eternal Mind, God the Son creating it and putting it into the world, each thing according to the law of its life, God the Holy Ghost inspiring it with life and law, that it may grow and thrive after its kind—when such thoughts as these crowd upon you, and they ought to crowd upon you, this day of all the year, at sight of the meanest insect under your feet; then what can a rational man do, but bow his head and worship in awful silence, adoring humbly Him who sits upon the throne of the universe, and who says to us in all His works, even as He said to Job of old, "Where wast thou when I laid the foundations of the earth? When the morning stars sang together, and all the sons of God shouted for joy? Hast thou entered into the springs of the sea? or hast thou seen the doors of the shadow of death? Knowest thou the ordinances of heaven? Canst thou lift up thy voice to the clouds, that abundance of waters may cover thee? Canst thou send lightnings, that they may go, and say unto thee, Here we are? Wilt thou hunt the prey for the lion? or fill the appetite of the young lions? Gavest thou the goodly wings unto the peacocks? or wings and feathers unto the ostrich? Hast thou given the horse strength? hast thou clothed his neck with thunder? Doth the hawk fly by thy wisdom? doth the eagle mount up at thy command?"

When God speaks thus to us—and He does thus speak to us, by every cloud and shower, and by every lightning flash and ray of sunshine, and by every living thing which flies in air, or swims in water, or creeps upon the earth—what can we say, save what Job said—"Behold, I am vile; what shall I answer thee? I will lay mine hand upon my mouth."

But if God be so awful in the material world, of which our five senses tell us, how much more awful is He in that spiritual and moral world, of which our senses tell us nought? That unseen world of justice and truthfulness, of honour and duty, of reverence and loyalty, of love and charity, of purity and self-sacrifice; that spiritual world, I say, which can be only seen by the spiritual eye of the soul, and felt by the spiritual heart of the soul? How awful is God in that eternal world of right and wrong; wherein cherubim, seraphim, angel and archangel cry to Him for ever, not merely Mighty, mighty, mighty, but "Holy, holy, holy." How awful to poor creatures like us. For then comes in the question—not merely is God good? but, am not I bad? Is God sinless? but, am not I a sinner? Is God pure? but am not I impure? Is God wise? then am not I a fool? And when once that thought has crossed our minds, must we not tremble, must we not say with Isaiah of old, "Woe is me! for I am undone; because I am a man of unclean lips, and I dwell in the midst of a people of unclean lips: for mine eyes have seen the King, the Lord of hosts."

Yes; awful as is the thought of God's perfection in the material world about us, more awful still is the thought of His perfection in the spiritual world. So awful, that we might well be overwhelmed with dread and horror at the sight of God's righteousness and our sinfulness; were it not for the gracious message of revelation that tells us, that God, the Father of heaven, is our Father likewise, who so loved us that He gave for us His only begotten, God the Son; that for His sake our sins might be freely forgiven us; that God the Son is our Atonement, our Redeemer, our King, our Intercessor, our Example, our Saviour in life and death; and God the Holy Ghost, our Comforter, our Guide, our Inspirer, who will give to our souls the eternal life which will never perish, even as He gives to our bodies the mortal life which must perish.

On the mercy and the love of the ever blessed Trinity, shown forth in Christ upon His cross, we can cast ourselves with all our sins; we can cry to Him, and not in vain, for forgiveness and for sanctification; for a clean heart and a right spirit; and that we may become holy and humble men of heart.

We can join our feeble praises to that hymn of praise which goes up for ever to God from suns and stars, clouds and showers, beasts and birds, and every living thing, giving Him thanks for ever for His great glory. O all ye works of the Lord, bless ye the Lord; praise Him and magnify Him for ever. O ye holy and humble Men of heart, bless ye the Lord; praise Him and magnify Him for ever.

SERMON XVII

LOVE OF GOD AND MAN

FIRST SUNDAY AFTER TRINITY.
Eversley. Chester Cathedral, 1872.

1 John iv. 16, 21. "God is love; and he that dwelleth in love dwelleth
in God, and God in him. . . . And this commandment have we from Him,
That he who loveth God love his brother also."

This is the first Sunday after Trinity. On it the Church begins to teach
us morals,—that is, how to live a good life; and therefore she begins by
teaching us the foundation of all morals,—which is love,—love to God and
love to man.

But which is to come first,—love to God, or love to man?

On this point men in different ages have differed, and will differ to the
end. One party has said, You must love God first, and let love to man come
after as it can; and others have contradicted that and said, You must love
all mankind, and let love to God take its chance. But St John says, neither
of the two is before or after the other; you cannot truly love God without
loving man, or love man without loving God. St John says so, being full
of the Spirit of God: but alas! men, who are not full of the Spirit of God,
but only let themselves be taught by Him now and then and here and there,
have found it very difficult to understand St John, and still more difficult to
obey him; and therefore there always have been in God's Church these two
parties; one saying, You must love God first, and the other, You must love
your neighbour first,—and each, of course, quoting Scripture to prove that
they are in the right.

The great leader of the first party—perhaps the founder of it, as far as
I am aware—was the famous St Augustine. He first taught Christians that
they ought to love God with the same passionate affection with which they
love husband or wife, mother or child; and to use towards God the same
words of affection which those who love really utter one to each other. I will
not say much of that; still less will I mention any of the words which good
men and women who are of that way of thinking use towards God. I should
be sorry to hold up such language to blame, even if I do not agree with it;
and still more sorry to hold it up to ridicule from vulgar-minded persons if
there be any in this Church. All I say is, that all which has been written since
about this passionate and rapturous love toward God by the old monks and
nuns, and by the Protestant Pietists, both English and foreign, is all in St Augustine better said than it ever has been since. Some of the Pietist hymns, as
we know, are very beautiful; but there are things in them which one wishes
left out; which seem, or ought to seem, irreverent when used toward God;
which hurt, or ought to hurt, our plain, cool, honest English common-sense.

A true Englishman does not like to say more than he feels; and the more he feels, the more he likes to keep it to himself, instead of parading it and talking of it before men. Still waters run deep, he holds; and he is right for himself; only he must not judge others, or think that because he cannot speak to God in such passionate language as St Augustine, who was an African, a southern man, with much stronger feelings than we Englishmen usually have, that therefore St Augustine, or those who copy him now, do not really feel what they say. But, nevertheless, plain common-sense people, such as most Englishmen are, are afraid of this enthusiastical religion. They say, We do not pretend to feel this rapturous love to God, how much-soever we may reverence Him, and wish to keep His commandments; and we do not desire to feel it. For we see that people who have talked in this way about God have been almost always monks and nuns; or brain-sick, disappointed persons, who have no natural and wholesome bent for their affections. And even though this kind of religion may be very well for them, it is not the religion for a plain honest man who has a wife and family and his bread to earn in the world, and has children to provide for, and his duty to do in the State as well as in the Church. And more, they say, these enthusiastic, rapturous feelings do not seem to make people better, and more charitable, and more loving. Some really good and charitable people say that they have these feelings, but for all that we can see they would be just as good and charitable without the feelings, while most persons who take up with this sort of religion are not the better for it. They do not control their tempers; they can be full,—as they say,—of love and devotion to God one minute, but why are they the next minute peevish, proud, self-willed, harsh and cruel to those who differ from them? Their religion does not make them love their neighbours. In old times (when persecution was allowed), it made them, or at least allowed them, to persecute, torment, and kill their neighbours, and fancy that by such conduct they did God service; and now it tempts them to despise their neighbours—to look on every one who has not these strange, intense feelings which they say they have, as unconverted, and lost, and doomed to everlasting destruction. Not, says the plain man, that we are more satisfied with the mere philanthropist of modern times,—the man who professes to love the whole human race without loving God, or indeed often believing that there is a God to love. To us he seems as unloving a person as the mere fanatic. Meanwhile, plain people say, we will have nothing to do with either fanaticism or philanthropy,—we will try to do our duty where God has put us, and to behave justly and charitably by our neighbours; but beyond that we cannot go. We will not pretend to what we do not feel.

My friends, there is, as usual, truth on both sides,—both are partly right, and both are partly wrong. And both may go on arguing against each other, and quoting texts of Scripture against each other till the last day; if they will not listen to St John's message in the text. One party will say, It is written, Thou shalt love the Lord thy God with all thy heart, and soul, and strength, and mind; and if thou doest that, and thy soul is filled with love for the Creator, thou canst have no love left for the creature; or if thy heart is filled with love for the creature, there is no room left for love to God. And then thou wilt find that God is a jealous God, and will take from thee what thou lovest, because He will not have His honour given to another.

And to that the other party will answer, Has not God said, "Thou shalt love thy neighbour as thyself?" Has He not commanded us to love our wives, our children? And even if He had not, would not common sense tell us that He intended us to do so? Do you think that God is a tempter and a deceiver? He has given us feelings and powers. Has He not meant us to use them? He has given us wife and child. Did He mean us not to love them, after He has made us love them, we know not how or why? You say that God is a jealous God. Yes, jealous He may be of our worshipping false gods, and idols, saints, or anything or person save Himself,—jealous of our doing wrong, and ruining ourselves, and wandering out of the path of His commandments, in which alone is life; but jealous of our loving our fellow creature as well as Himself, never. That sort of jealousy is a base and wicked passion in man, and dare we attribute it to God? What a thing to say of the loving God, that He takes away people's children, husbands, and friends, because they love them too much!

Then the first party will say, But is it not written, "Love not the world, neither the things that are in the world. If any man love the world, the love of the Father is not in him?" And to that, the second party will answer, And do you say that we are not to love this fair and wonderful earth which God has made for our use, and put us into it? Why did He make it lovely? Why did He put us into it, if He did not mean us to enjoy it? That is contrary to common sense, and contrary to the whole teaching of the Old Testament. But if by the world you mean the world of man, the society in which we live—dare you compare a Christian and civilized country like England with that detestable Roman world, sunk in all abominable vices, against which St John and St Paul prophesied? Are not such thoughts unjust and uncharitable to your neighbours, to your country, to all mankind? Then the first party will say, But you do away with all devoutness; and the second party will answer, And you do away with all morality, for you tell people that the only way to please God is to feel about Him in a way which not one person in a thousand can feel; and therefore what will come, and does come, of your binding heavy burdens and grievous to be borne and laying them on men's shoulders is this,—that the generality of people will care nothing about being good or doing right, because you teach them that it will not please God, and will leave all religion to a few who have these peculiar fancies and feelings.

And so they may argue on for ever, unless they will take honestly the plain words of St John, and see that to love their neighbour is to love God, and to love God is to love their neighbour. So says St John clearly enough twice over. "God is love; and he that dwelleth in love dwelleth in God, and God in him." The two things are one, and the one cannot be without the other.

Does this seem strange to you? Oh, my friends, it need not seem strange, if you will but consider who God is, and who man is. Thou lovest God?

Then, if thou lovest Him, thou must needs love all that He has made. And what has He made? All things, except sin; and what sin is He has told thee. He has given thee ten commandments, and let no man give thee an eleventh commandment out of his own conceit and will worship; calling unclean what God hath made clean, and cursing what God hath blessed. Thou lovest God? Then thou lovest all that is good; for God is good, and from Him all good things come. But what is good? All is good except sin; for it is written, "God saw every thing that He had made, and, behold, it was very good." Therefore, if thou lovest God, thou must love all things, for all things are of Him, and by Him, and through Him; and in Him all live and move and have their being. Then thou wilt truly love God. Thou wilt be content with God; and so thy love will cast out fear. Thou wilt trust God; thou wilt have the mind of God; thou wilt be satisfied with God's working, from the rise and fall of great nations to the life and death of the smallest gnat which dances in the sun; thou wilt say for ever, and concerning all things, I know in whom I have believed. It is the good Lord, let Him do what seemeth Him good.

Again. Thou lovest thy neighbour; thou lovest wife and child; thou lovest thy friends; thou lovest or wishest to love all men, and to do them good. Then thou lovest God. For what is it that thou lovest in thy neighbour? Not that which is bad in him? No, but that which is good. Thou lovest him for his kindliness, his honesty, his helpfulness,—for some good quality in him. But from whom does that good come, save from Christ and from the Spirit of Christ, from whom alone come all good gifts? Yes, if you will receive it;—when we love our neighbours, it is God in them, Christ in them, whom we love,—Christ in them, the hope of glory.

What, some one will ask, when a man loves a fair face, does he love Christ then? Ah! my friends, that is not true love, as all know well enough if they will let their own hearts tell them truth. True love is when two people love each other for the goodness which is in them. True love is the love which endures after beauty has faded, and youth, and health, and all that seems to make life worth having is gone. Have we not seen ere now two old people, worn, crippled, diseased, yet living on together, helping each other, nursing each other, tottering on hand in hand to the grave, dying, perhaps, almost together,—because neither cared to live when the other is gone before, and loving all the while as truly and tenderly as in the days of youth? They know not why. No; but God knows why. It is Christ in each other whom they love;—Christ, the hope of glory. Yes, we have seen that, surely; and seen in it one of the most beautiful, the most divine sights upon earth,—one which should teach us, if we will look at it aright, that when we love our neighbour truly, it is the divine part in him, the spark of eternal goodness in him,—what St Paul says is Christ in him,—which we admire, and cling to, and love.

But by that rule we cannot love every one, for every one is not good. Be not too sure of that. All are not good, alas! but in all there is some good. It may be a very little,—a hope of glory in them, even though that hope be very faint. It may be dying out; it may die altogether, and their souls may become utterly base and evil, and be lost for ever. Still, while there is life there is hope, even for the worst; and just as far as our hearts are full of the Spirit of God, we shall see the Spirit of God striving with the souls even of the worst men, and love them for that. Just as far as we have the likeness of Christ in us, we shall be quick to catch the least gleam of His likeness in our neighbours, and love them for that. Just as far as our hearts are full of love we shall see something worth loving in every human being we meet, and love them for that. I know it is difficult. It is not gotten in a day, that wide and deep spirit of love to all mankind which St Paul had; which made him weep with those who wept and rejoice with those who rejoiced, and become all things to all men, if by any means he might save some. Before our eyes are cleansed and purged to see some trace of good in every man, our hearts must be cleansed and purged from all selfishness, and bigotry, and pride, and fancifulness, and anger, so that they may be filled with the loving Spirit of God. As long as a taint of selfishness or pride remains in us, we shall be in continual danger of hating those whom God does not hate, despising those whom God does not despise, and condemning those whom God does not condemn. But if self is cast out of us, and the Spirit of God and of Christ enthroned in our hearts, then we shall love our brother, and in loving him love God, who made him; and so, dwelling in love, we shall dwell in God, and God in us:—to which true and only everlasting life may He of His mercy bring us, either in this world or in the world to come. Amen.

SERMON XVIII

COURAGE

Chester Cathedral, 1871.

Acts iv. 13, 18-20. "Now when they saw the boldness of Peter and John, and perceived that they were unlearned and ignorant men, they marvelled; and they took knowledge of them, that they had been with Jesus. . . . And they called them, and commanded them not to speak at all nor teach in the name of Jesus. But Peter and John answered and said unto them, Whether it be right in the sight of God to hearken unto you more than unto God, judge ye. For we cannot but speak the things which we have seen and heard."

Last Thursday was St Peter's Day. The congregation on that day was, as far as I could perceive, no larger than usual; and this is not a matter of surprise. Since we gave up at the Reformation the superstitious practice of praying to the saints, saints' days have sunk—and indeed sunk too much—into neglect. For most men's religion has a touch of self-interest in it; and therefore when people discovered that they could get nothing out of St Peter or St John by praying to them, they began to forget the very memory, many of them, of St Peter, St John, and other saints and apostles. They forget, too, often, still, that though praying to any saint, or angel, or other created being, is contrary both to reason and to Scripture; yet it is according to reason and to Scripture to commemorate them. That is to remember them, to study their characters, and to thank God for them—both for the virtues which He bestowed on them, and the example which He has given us in them.

For these old saints lived and died for our example. They are, next of course to the Lord Himself, the ideals, the patterns, of Christian life—the primeval heroes of our holy faith. They shew to us of what stuff the early Christians were made; what sort of stone—to use St Paul's own figure,—the Lord chose wherewith to build up His Church. They are our spiritual ancestors, for they spread the Gospel into all lands; and they spread it, remember always, not only by preaching what they knew, but by being what they were. Their characters, their personal histories, are as important to us as their writings; nay, in the case of St Peter, even more important. For if these two epistles of his had been lost, and never handed down to us, St Peter himself would have remained, as he is drawn in the Gospels and the Acts, a grand and colossal human figure, every line and feature of which is full of meaning and full of teaching to us.

Now I think that the quality—the grace of God—which St Peter's character and story specially force on our notice, is, the true courage which comes by faith. I say, the courage which comes by faith. There is a courage which does not come by faith. There is brute courage, which comes from hardness of heart, from stupidity, obstinacy, or anger, which does not see danger, or does not feel pain. That is the courage of the brute. One does not blame it, or call it wrong. It is good in its place, as all natural things are, which God has made. It is good enough for the brutes, but it is not good enough for man. You cannot trust it in man. And the more a man is what a man should be, the less he can trust it. The more mind and understanding a man has, so as to be able to foresee danger, and measure it, the more chance there is of his brute courage giving way. The more feeling a man has, the more keenly he feels pain of body, or pain of mind, such as shame, loneliness, the dislike, ridicule, and contempt of his fellow men; in a word, the more of a man he is, and the less of a mere brute, the more chance there is of his brute courage breaking down, just when he wants it most to keep him up, by leaving him to play the coward and come to shame. Yes. To go through with a difficult and dangerous undertaking, a man wants more than brute courage. He wants spiritual courage—the courage which comes by faith. He needs to have faith in what he is doing; to be certain that he is doing his duty, to be certain that he is in the right. Certain that right will conquer, certain that God will make it conquer, by him or by some one else; certain that he will either conquer honourably, or fail honourably, for God is with him. In a word, to have true courage, man needs faith in God.

To give one example. Look at the class of men who, in all England, undergo the most fearful dangers; who know not at what hour of any night they may not be called up to the most serious labour and responsibility, with the chance of a horrible and torturing death. I mean the firemen of our great cities, than whom there are no steadier, braver, nobler-hearted men. Not a week passes without one or more of these firemen, in trying to save life and property, doing things which are altogether heroic. What do you fancy keeps them up to their work? High pay? The amusement and excitement of fires? The vanity of being praised for their courage? My friends, those would be but paltry weak motives, which would not keep a man's heart calm and his head clear under such responsibility and danger as theirs. No. It is the sense of duty,—the knowledge that they are doing a good and a noble work in saving the lives of human beings and the wealth of the nation,—the knowledge that they are in God's hands, and that no real evil can happen to him who is doing right,—that to him even death at his post is not a loss, but a gain. In short, faith in God, more or less clear, is what gives those men their strong and quiet courage. God grant that you and I, if ever we have dangerous work to do, may get true courage from the same fountain of ghostly strength.

Now, St Peter's history is, I think, a special example of this. He was naturally, it seems, a daring man,—a man of great brute courage. So far so good; but he had to be taught, by severe lessons, that his brute courage was not enough,—that he wanted spiritual courage, the courage which came by faith, and that if that failed him, the brute courage would fail too.

He throws himself into the lake, to walk upon the water to Christ; and as soon as he is afraid he begins to sink. The Lord saves him, and tells him why he had sank. Because he had doubted, his faith had failed him. So he found out the weakness of courage without faith. Then, again, he tells our Lord, "Though all men shall be offended of Thee, yet will I never be offended. I am ready to go with Thee both into prison, and to death." And shortly after, his mere animal courage breaks out again, and does what little it can do, and little enough. He draws sword, single-handed, on the soldiers in the garden, and cuts down a servant of the high priest's, and perhaps would have flung his life away, desperately and uselessly, had not our Lord restrained him. But when the fit of excitement is past, his animal courage deserts him, and his moral courage too, and he denies his Lord. So he found out that he was like too many,—full of bodily courage, perhaps, but morally weak. He had to undergo a great change. He had to be converted by the Holy Spirit of God, and strengthened by that Spirit, to have a boldness which no worldly courage can give. Then, when he was strong himself, he was able to strengthen his brethren. Then he was able, ignorant and unlearned man as he was, to stand up before the high priests and rulers of his nation, and to say, simply and firmly, without boasting, without defiance, "Whether it be right in the sight of God to hearken unto you more than unto God, judge ye. For we cannot but speak the things which we have seen and heard." Yes, my friends, it is the courage which comes by faith which makes truly brave men,—men like St Peter and St John. He who can say, I am right, can say likewise, God is on my side, and I will not fear what man can do to me.

"We will not fear," said the Psalmist, "though the earth be removed, and though the hills be carried into the midst of the sea." "The just man, who holds firm to his purpose," says a wise old heathen, "he will not be shaken from his solid mind by the rage of the mob bidding him do base things or the frowns of the tyrant who persecutes him. Though the world were to crumble to pieces round him, its ruins would strike him without making him tremble." "Whether it be right," said Peter and John to the great men and judges of the Jews, "to hearken to God more than to you, judge ye. We cannot but speak the things which we have seen and heard." We cannot but speak what we know to be true.

It was that courage which enabled our forefathers,—and not the great men among them, not the rich, not even the learned, save a few valiant bishops and clergy, but for the most part poor, unlearned, labouring men and women,—to throw off the yoke of Popery, and say, "Reason and Scripture tell us that it is absurd and wrong to worship images and pray to saints,— tell us that your doctrines are not true. And we will say so in spite of the Pope and all his power,—in spite of torture and a fiery death. We cannot palter; we cannot dissemble; we cannot shelter ourselves under half-truths, and make a covenant with lies. 'Whether it be right in the sight of God to hearken unto you more than to God, judge ye. We cannot but speak the things which we know to be true.'"

So it has been in all ages, and so it will be for ever. Faith, the certainty that a man is right, will give him a courage which will enable him to resist, if need be, the rich ones, the strong ones, the learned ones of the earth. It has made poor unlearned men heroes and deliverers of their countrymen from slavery and ignorance. It has made weak women martyrs and saints. It has enabled men who made great discoveries to face unbelief, ridicule, neglect, poverty; knowing that their worth would be acknowledged at last, their names honoured at last as benefactors by the very men who laughed at them and reviled them. It has made men, shut up in prison for long weary years for doing what was right and saying what was true, endure manfully for the sake of some good cause, and say,—

> "Stone walls do not a prison make,
>   Nor iron bars a cage;
> Minds innocent and quiet take
>   That for an hermitage.
> If I have freedom in my thought,
>   And in my love am free,
> Angels alone, that soar above,
>   Enjoy such liberty."

Yes; settle it in your hearts, all of you. There is but one thing which you have to fear in earth or heaven,—being untrue to your better selves, and therefore untrue to God. If you will not do the thing you know to be right, and say the thing you know to be true, then indeed you are weak. You are a coward, and sin against God, and suffer the penalty of your cowardice. You desert God, and therefore you cannot expect Him to stand by you.

But if you will do the thing you know to be right, and say the thing you know to be true, then what can harm you? Who will harm you, asks St Peter himself, "if you be followers of that which is good? For the eyes of the Lord are over the righteous, and His ears are open to their prayers. But if ye suffer for righteousness' sake, happy are ye; and be not afraid of those who try to terrify you, neither be troubled, but sanctify the Lord God in your hearts. Remember that He is just and holy, and a rewarder of all who diligently seek Him. Worship Him in your hearts, and all will be well. For says David again, "Lord, who shall dwell in Thy tabernacle, or who shall rest upon Thy holy hill? Even he that leadeth an uncorrupt life, and doeth the thing which is right, and speaketh the truth from his heart. Whoso doeth these things shall never fall."

Yes, my friends; there is a tabernacle of God in which, even in this life, He will hide us from the strife of tongues. There is a hill of God on which, even in the midst of labour and anxiety, we may rest both day and night. Even Jesus Christ, the Rock of Ages,—He who is the Righteousness itself, the Truth itself; and whosoever does righteousness and speaks truth dwells in Christ in this life, as well as in the life to come; and Christ will strengthen him by His Holy Spirit to stand in the evil day, if it shall come, and having done all, to stand. My dear friends, if any of you are minded to be good men and women, pray for the Holy Spirit of God. First for the spirit of love to give you good desires; then the spirit of faith, to make you believe deeply in the living God, who rewards every man according to his work; and then for the spirit of strength, to enable you to bring these desires to good effect.

Pray for that spirit, I say; for we all need help. There are too many people in the world—too many, perhaps, among us here—who are not what they ought to be, and what they really wish to be, because they are weak. They see what is right, and admire it; but they have not courage or determination to do it. Most sad and pitiable it is to see how much weakness of heart there is in the world—how little true moral courage. I suppose that the reason is, that there is so little faith; that people do not believe heartily and deeply enough in the absolute necessity of doing right and being honest. They do not believe heartily and deeply enough in God to trust Him to defend and reward them, if they will but be true to Him, and to themselves. And therefore they have no moral courage. They are weak. They are kind, perhaps, and easy; easily led right; but, alas! just as easily led wrong. Their good resolutions are not carried out; their right doctrines not acted up to; and they live pitiful, confused, useless, inconsistent lives; talking about religion, and yet denying the power of religion in their daily lives; playing with holy and noble thoughts and feelings, without giving themselves up to them in earnest, to be led by the Spirit of God, to do all the good works which God has prepared for them to walk in. Pray all of you, then, for the spirit of faith, to believe really in God; and for the spirit of ghostly strength, to obey God honestly. No man ever asked earnestly for that spirit but what he gained it at last. And no man ever gained it but what he found the truth of St Peter's own words, "Who will harm you if ye be followers of that which is good?"

SERMON XIX

GOOD DAYS

Eversley, 1867. Westminster, Sept. 27, 1872.

1 Peter iii. 8-12. "Be ye all of one mind, having compassion one of another, love as brethren, be pitiful, be courteous: Not rendering evil for evil, or railing for railing: but contrariwise blessing; knowing that ye are thereunto called, that ye should inherit a blessing. For he that will love life and see good days, let him refrain his tongue from evil, and his lips that they speak no guile: Let him eschew evil, and do good; let him seek peace, and ensue it. For the eyes of the Lord are over the righteous, and His ears are open unto their prayers: but the face of the Lord is against them that do evil."

This is one of the texts which is apt to puzzle people who do not read their Bibles carefully enough. They cannot see what the latter part of it has to do with the former.

St. Peter says that we Christians are called that we should inherit a blessing. That means, of course, they say, the blessing of salvation, everlasting life in heaven. But then St. Peter quotes from the 34th Psalm. "For he that will love life, and see good days, let him refrain his tongue from evil, and his lips that they speak no guile." Now that Psalm, they say, speaks of blessing and happiness in this life. Then why does St. Peter give it as a reason for expecting blessing and happiness in the life to come? And then, they say, to make it fit in, it must be understood spiritually; and what they mean by that, I do not clearly know.

Their notion is, that the promises of the Old Testament are more or less carnal, because they speak of God's rewarding men in this life; and that the promises of the New Testament are spiritual, because they speak of God's rewarding men in the next life; and what they mean by that, again, I do not clearly know.

For is not the Old Testament spiritual as well as the New? I trust so, my friends. Is not the Old Testament inspired, and that by the Spirit of God? and if it be inspired by the Spirit, what can it be but spiritual? Therefore, if we want to find the spiritual meaning of Old Testament promises, we need not to alter them to suit any fancies of our own; like those monks of the fourth and succeeding centuries, who saw no sanctity in family or national life; no sanctity in the natural world, and, therefore, were forced to travesty the Hebrew historians, psalmists, and prophets, with all their simple, healthy objective humanity, and politics, and poetry, into metaphorical and subjective, or, as they miscalled them, spiritual meanings, to make the Old Testament mean anything at all. No; if we have any real reverence for the Holy Scriptures, we must take them word for word in their plain meaning, and find the message of God's Spirit in that plain meaning, instead of trying to put it in for ourselves. Therefore it is that the VII. Article bids us beware of playing with Scripture in this way. It says the Old Testament is not contrary to the New, for both in the Old and New Testament everlasting life is offered to mankind by Christ. Wherefore they are not to be heard who feign that the old fathers did look only for transitory promises, that is temporary promises, promises which would be fulfilled only in this life, and end and pass away when they died.

But some one will say, how can that be, when so many of the old Hebrews seem to have known nothing about the next life? Moses, for instance, always promises the Children of Israel that if they do right, and obey God, they shall be rewarded in this life, with peace and prosperity, fruitfulness and wealth; but of their being rewarded in the next life he never says one word—which last statement is undeniably true.

Is not then the Old Testament contrary to the New, if the Old Testament teaches men to look for their reward in this life, and the New Testament in the next? No, it is not, my friends. And I think we shall see that it is not, and why it is not, if we will look honestly at this very important text. If we do that we shall see that what St. Peter meant—what the VII. Article means is the only meaning which will make sense of either one or the other; is simply this—that what causes a man to enjoy this life, is the same that will cause him to enjoy the life to come. That what will bring a blessing on him in this life, will bring a blessing on him in the life to come. That what blessed the old Jews, will bless us Christians. That if we refrain our tongue from evil, and our lips from speaking deceit; it we avoid evil and do good; if we seek peace and follow earnestly after it; then shall we enjoy life, and see good days, and inherit a blessing; whether in this life or in the life to come.

And why? Because then we shall be living the one and only everlasting life of goodness, which alone brings blessings; alone gives good days; and is the only life worth living, whether in earth or heaven.

My dear friends, lay this seriously to heart, in these days especially, when people and preachers alike have taken to part earth and heaven, in a fashion which we never find in Holy Scripture. Lay it to heart, I say, and believe that what is right, and therefore good, for the next life, is right, and therefore good, for this. That the next life is not contrary to this life. That the same moral laws hold good in heaven, as on earth. Mark this well; for it must be so, if morality, that is right and goodness, is of the eternal and immutable essence of God. And therefore, mark this well again, there is but one true, real, and right life for rational beings, one only life worth living, and worth living in this world or in any other life, past, present, or to come. And that is the eternal life which was before all worlds, and will be after all are passed away—and that is neither more nor less than a good life; a life of good feelings, good thoughts, good words, good deeds, the life of Christ and of God.

It is needful, I say, to bear this in mind just now. People are, as I told you, too apt to say that the Old Testament saints got their rewards in this life, while we shall get them in the next. Do they find that in Scripture? If they will read their Bible they will find that the Old Testament saints were men whom God was training and educating, as He does us, by experience and by suffering. That David, so far from having his reward at once in this life, had his bitter sorrows and trials; that Moses, Isaiah, Jeremiah, Job, all, indeed, of the old prophets, had to be made perfect by suffering, and (as St. Paul says) died in faith not having received the promises. So that if they had their reward in this life, it must have been a spiritual reward, the reward of a good conscience, and of the favour of Almighty God. And that is no transitory or passing reward, but enduring as immortality itself. But people do not usually care for that spiritual reward. Their notion of reward and happiness is that they are to have all sorts of pleasures, they know not what, and know not really why. And because they cannot get pleasant things enough to satisfy them in this life, they look forward greedily to getting them in the next life; and meanwhile are discontented with God's Providence, and talk of God's good world as if some fiend and not the Lord Jesus Christ was the maker and ruler thereof. Do not misunderstand me. I am no optimist. I know well that things happen in this world which must, which ought to make us sad—so sad that at moments we envy the dead, who are gone home to their rest; real tragedies, real griefs, divine and Christlike griefs, which only loving hearts know—the suffering of those we love, the loss of those we love, and, last and worst, the sin of those we love. Ah! if any of those swords have pierced the heart of any soul here, shall I blame that man, that woman, if they cry at times, "Father, take me home, this earth is no place for me." Shall I bid them do aught but cling to the feet of Christ and cry, "If it be possible, let this cup pass from me; nevertheless, not as I will, but as Thou wilt." Oh, not of such do I speak; not of such sharers of Christ's unselfish suffering here, that they may be sharers of His unselfish joy hereafter. Not of them do I speak; but of those who only wish to make up for selfish discomforts and disappointments in this life by selfish comforts and satisfaction in the next; and who therefore take up (let me use the honest English word) some maundering form of religion, which, to judge from their own conduct, they usually only half believe; those who seem, on six days of the week, as fond of finery and frivolity as any other gay worldlings, and on the seventh join eagerly in hymns in which (in one case at least) they inform the Almighty God of truth, who will not be mocked, that they lie awake at night, weeping because they cannot die and see "Jerusalem the golden," and so forth. Or those, again, who for six days in the week are absorbed in making money—honestly if they can, no doubt, but still making money, and living luxuriously on their profits—and on the seventh listen with satisfaction to preachers and hymns which tell them that this world is all a howling wilderness, full of snares and pitfalls; and that in this wretched place the Christian can expect nothing but tribulation and persecution till he "crosses Jordan, and is landed safe on Canaan's store," and so forth.

My friends, my friends, as long as a man talks so, blaspheming God's world—which, when He made it, behold it was all very good—and laying the blame of their own ignorance and peevishness on God who made them, they must expect nothing but tribulation and sorrow. But the tribulation and the sorrow will be their own fault, and not God's. If religious professors will not take St. Peter's advice and the Psalmist's advice; if they will go on coveting and scheming about money, and how they may get money; if they will go on being neither pitiful, courteous, nor forgiving, and hating and maligning whether it be those who differ from them in doctrine, or those who they fancy have injured them, or those who merely are their rivals in the race of life; then they are but too likely to find this world a thorny place, because they themselves raise the thorns; and a disorderly place, because their own tempers and desires are disorderly; and a wilderness, because they themselves have run wild, barbarians at heart, however civilised in dress and outward manners. St. James tells them that of old. "From whence," he says, "come wars and quarrels among you? Come they not hence, even of the lusts which war in your members? You long, and have not. You fight and war, yet you have not, because you ask not. You ask, and have not. You pray for this and that, and God does not give it you. Because you ask amiss, selfishly to consume it on your lusts." And then you say, This world is an evil place, full of temptations. What says St. James to that? "Let no man say when he is tempted, I am tempted of God: for God cannot be tempted with evil, neither tempteth He any man. But every man is tempted, when he is drawn away of his own lust, and enticed."

So it was in the Old Testament times, and so it is in these Christian times. God is good, and God's world is good; and the evil is not in the world around us, but in our own foolish hearts. If we follow our own foolish hearts, we shall find this world a bad place, as the old Jews found it—whenever they went wrong and sinned against God—because we are breaking its laws, and they will punish us. If we follow the commandments of God, we shall find this world a good place, as the old Jews found it—whenever they went right, and obeyed God—because we shall be obeying its laws, and they will reward us. This is God's promise alike to the old Jewish fathers and to us Christian men. And this is no transitory or passing promise, but is founded on the eternal and everlasting law of right, by which God has made all worlds, and which He Himself cannot alter, for it springs out of His own essence and His own eternal being. Hear, then, the conclusion of the whole matter: God hath called you that you might inherit a blessing.

He hath made you of a blessed race, created in His own likeness, to whom He hath put all things in subjection, making man a little lower than the angels, that He might crown him with glory and worship: a race so precious in God's eyes—we know not why—that when mankind had fallen, and seemed ready to perish from their own sin and ignorance, God spared not His only begotten Son, but freely gave Him for us, that the world by Him might be saved. And God hath put you in a blessed place, even His wondrous and fruitful world, which praises God day and night, fulfilling His word; for it continues this day as in the beginning, and He has given it a law which cannot be broken. He has made you citizens of a blessed kingdom, even the kingdom of heaven, into which you were baptised; and has given you the Holy Bible, that you might learn the laws of the kingdom, and live for ever, blessing and blest.

And the Head of this blessed race, the Maker of this blessed world, the King of this blessed kingdom, is the most blessed of all beings, Jesus Christ, the only-begotten Son, both God and man. He has washed you freely from your sins in His own blood; He has poured out on you freely His renewing Spirit. And He asks you to enter into your inheritance; that you may love your life, and see good days, by living the blessed life, which is the life of self-sacrifice. But not such self-sacrifices as too many have fancied who did not believe that mankind was a blessed race, and this earth a blessed place. He does not ask you to give up wife, child, property, or any of the good things of this life. He only asks you to give up that selfishness which will prevent you enjoying wife, child, or property, or anything else in earth, or in heaven either. He asks you not to give up anything which is around you, for that which cometh from without defileth not a man; but to give up something which is within you, for that which cometh from within, that defileth a man.

He asks you to give up selfishness and all the evil tempers which that selfishness breeds. To give up the tongue which speaks evil of your fellow-men; and the lips which utter deceit; and the brain which imagines cunning; and the heart which quarrels with your neighbour. To give these up and to seek peace, and pursue it by all means reasonable or honourable; peace with all around you, which comes by having first peace with God; next, peace with your own conscience. This is the peace which passeth understanding; for if you have it, men will not be able to understand why you have it. They will see you at peace when men admire you and praise you, and at peace also when they insult you and injure you; at peace when you are prosperous and thriving, and at peace also when you are poor and desolate. And that inward peace of yours will pass their understanding as it will pass your own understanding also. You will know that God sends you the peace, and sends it you the more the more you pray for it: but how He sends it you will not understand; for it springs out of those inner depths of your being which are beyond the narrow range of consciousness, and is spiritual and a mystery, and comes by the inspiration of the holy Spirit of God.

But remember that all your prayers will not get that peace if your heart be tainted with malice and selfishness and covetousness, falsehood and pride and vanity. You must ask God first to root those foul seeds out of your heart, or the seed of His Spirit will not spring up and bear fruit in you to the everlasting life of love and peace and joy in the holy Spirit. But if your heart be purged and cleansed of self, then indeed will the holy Spirit enter in and dwell there; and you will abide in peace, through all the chances and changes of this mortal life, for you will abide in God, who is for ever at peace. And you will inherit a blessing; for you will inherit Christ, your light and your life, who is blessed for ever. And you will love life; for life will be full to you of hope, of work, of duty, of interest, of lessons without number. And you will see good days; for all days will seem good to you, even those which seem to the world bad days of affliction and distress. And so the peace of God will keep you in Jesus Christ, in this life, and in the life to come. Amen.

SERMON XX

GRACE

Eversley. 1856.

St. John i. 16, 17. "Of His fulness have all we received, and grace for grace. For the law was given by Moses, but grace and truth came by Jesus Christ."

I wish you to mind particularly this word grace. You meet it very often in the Bible. You hear often said, The grace of our Lord Jesus Christ be with you all. Now, what does this word grace mean? It is really worth your while to know; for if a man or a woman has not grace, they will be very unhappy people, and very disagreeable people also; a torment to themselves, and a torment to their neighbours also; and if they live without grace, they will live but a poor life; if they die without grace, they will come to a very bad end indeed. What, then, does this word mean? Some of you will answer that grace means God's Holy Spirit, or that it means what God gives to our souls by His Spirit. But what does that mean? What does God's Spirit give us? What is the grace of Jesus Christ like, and how is it the same as the grace of God's Spirit?

Now, to know what grace means, we must know what St John and St Paul meant by it, and what the word meant in their time, and what the Ephesians, and Corinthians, and Romans, to whom they wrote, would have understood by this word grace.

Now these heathens, to whom the apostles preached, before they heard the gospel, knew that word grace very well indeed, often used it; and saw it written up in their heathen temples all about them. And they meant by it just what we mean, when we talk of a graceful person, or a graceful tree or flower; and what we mean, too, when we say that any one is gracious; that they do things gracefully, and have a great deal of grace in their way of speaking and behaving. We mean by that that they are handsome, agreeable, amiable, pleasant to look at, and talk to, and deal with. And so these heathens meant, before they were Christians. The Romans used to talk about some one called a Grace. The Greeks called her Charis; which is exactly the word which St John and St Paul use, and from it come our words charity and charitable. But more; they used to talk of three Graces: they fancied that they were goddesses—spirits of some kind in the shape of beautiful, and amiable, and innocent maidens, who took delight in going about the world and making people happy and amiable like themselves; and they used to make images of these graces, and pray to them to make them lovely, and happy, and agreeable. And painters and statuaries, too, used to pray to these graces, and ask them to put beautiful fancies into their minds, that they might be able to paint beautiful pictures, and carve beautiful statues. So when St Paul or St John talked to these heathens about grace, or Charis (as the Testament calls it), they knew quite well what the apostles meant.

Did the apostles, then, believe in these three goddesses? Heaven forbid. They came to teach these heathens to turn from those very vanities, and worship the living-God. And so they told them,—You are quite right in thinking that grace comes from heaven, and is God's gift; that it is God who makes people amiable, cheerful, lovely, and honourable; that it is God who gives happiness and all the joys of life: but which god? Not those three maidens; they are but a dream and fancy. All that is lovely and pleasant in men and women—and our life here, and our everlasting life after death, in this world and in all worlds to come—all comes from Jesus Christ and from Him alone. God has gathered together all things in Him, whether things in heaven or things on earth; and He bestows blessings and graces on all who will ask Him, to each as much as is good for him. He is full of grace—more full of it than all the human beings in the world put together. All the goodness and sweetness, and all the graciousness which you ever saw in all the men and women whom you ever met; all the goodness and sweetness which you ever fancied for yourselves, all put together is not to be compared to Him. For He is the perfect brightness of God's glory, and the express image of God's person; and in Him is gathered together all grace, all goodness, all which makes men or angels good, and lovely, and loving. All is in Him, and He gives it freely to all, said the apostles; we know that He speaks truth, we have seen Him; our eyes saw Him, our hands touched Him, and there was a glory about Him such as there never could be about any other person. A glory as of the only begotten of the Father, full of grace and truth. A person whom we could not help loving; could not help admiring; could not help trusting; could not help giving ourselves up to—to live for Him, and if need be, die for Him.

And, said the apostles, there was a grace of truth in another of your heathen fancies. You thought that these goddesses, because they were amiable and innocent themselves, liked to make every one amiable, innocent, and happy also. Your conscience, your reason were right there. That is the very nature of grace, not to keep itself to itself, but to spend itself on every one round it, and try to make every one like itself. If a man be good, he will long to make others good; if tender, he will long to make others tender; if gentle, he will long to make others gentle; if cheerful, he will long to make others cheerful; if forgiving, he will long to make others forgiving; if happy, he will long to make others happy. Then said the apostles, only believe that the Lord Jesus Christ, just because He is full of grace, wishes to fill you with grace, ten thousand times better grace than you ever fancied those false goddesses could give you—of His fulness you may all receive, and grace for grace. All the grace of this world comes from Him—health, and youth, and happiness, and all the innocent pleasures of life, and He delights in giving you them. But, over and above that, comes a deeper and nobler grace—spiritual grace, the grace of the immortal soul, which will last on, and make you loving and loveable, pure and true, gracious and generous, honourable and worthy of respect, when the grace of the body is gone, and the eye is grown dim, and the hair is grey, and the limbs, feeble; a grace which will make you gracious in old age, gracious in death, gracious for ever and ever, after the body has crumbled again to its dust. Whatsoever things are honourable, lovely, and of good report; whatsoever tempers of mind make you a comfort to yourselves and all around you; Christ has them all, and He can give you them all, one after the other, till Christ be formed in you, till you come to be perfect men and women, to the measure of the stature of the fulness of Christ. Come, then, boldly to His throne of grace, to find mercy, and grace to help you in the time of need.

This was what the apostles taught the heathen, and their words were true. You may see them come true round you every day. For, my friends, just as far as people pray for Christ's grace, and give themselves up to be led by God's Spirit, they become full of grace themselves, courteous and civil, loving and amiable, true and honourable—a pleasure to themselves and to all round them. While, on the other hand; all rudeness, all ill-temper, all selfishness, all greediness are just so many sins against the grace of Christ, which grieve the Spirit of God, at the same time that they grieve our neighbours for whom Christ died, and cut us off, as long as we give way to them, from the communion of saints.

Well would it be for married people, if they would but remember this. Well for them, for their own sake and for their children's. "Heirs together," St Peter says they are, "of the grace of life." Think of those words; for in them lies the true secret of happiness. Not in the mere grace of youth, which pleases the fancy at first; that must soon fade; and then comes, too often, coldness between man and wife; neglect, rudeness, ill-temper, because the grace of life is not there—the grace of the inner life, of the immortal soul, which alone makes life pleasant, even tolerable, to two people who are bound together for better or for worse. But yet, unless St Peter be mistaken, the fault in such sad case is on the man's side. Yes, we must face that truth, we men; and face it like men. If we are unhappy in our marriage it is our own fault. It is the woman who is the weaker, says St Peter, and selfish men are apt to say, "Then it is the woman's fault, if we are not happy." St Peter says exactly the opposite. He says,—Because she is the weaker you are the stronger; and therefore it is your fault if she is not what she should be; for you are able to help her, and lead her; you took her to your heart for that very purpose, you swore to cherish her. Because she is the weaker, you can teach her, help her, improve her character, if you will. You have more knowledge of life and the world than she has. Dwell with her according to knowledge, says St Peter; use your experience to set her right if she be wrong; and use your experience and your strength, too, to keep down your own temper and your own selfishness toward her, to bear and forbear, to give and forgive, live and let live. Remember that you are heirs together of the grace of life; and if the grace of life is not in you, you cannot expect it to be in her. And what is the grace of life? It must be the grace of Christ. St John says that Christ is the Life. And what is the grace of Christ? Christ's grace, Christ's gracefulness, Christ's beautiful and noble and loving character—the grace of Christ is Christ's likeness. Do you ask what will Christ give me? He will give you Himself. He will make you like Himself, partaker of His grace; and what is that? It is this—to be loving, gentle, temperate, courteous, condescending, self-sacrificing. Giving honour to those who are weaker than yourself, just because they are weaker; ready and willing, ay, and counting it an honour to take trouble for other people, to be of use to other people, to give way to other people; and, above all, to the woman who has given herself to you, body and soul. That is the grace of Christ; that is the grace of life; that is what makes life worth having: ay, makes it a foretaste of heaven upon earth; when man and wife are heirs together of the grace of life, of all those tempers which make life graceful and pleasant, giving way to each other in everything which is not wrong; studying each other's comfort, taking each other's advice, shutting their eyes to each other's little failings, and correcting each other's great failings, not by harsh words, but silently and kindly, by example. And if the man will do that, there is little fear but that the woman will do it also. And so, their prayers are not hindered.

Married people cannot pray, they have no heart to pray, while they are discontented with each other. They feel themselves wrong, and because they are parted from each other, they feel parted from God too; and their selfishness or anger rises as a black wall, not merely between them, but between each of them and God. And so the grace of life is indeed gone away from them, and the whole world looks dark and ugly to them, because it is not bright and cheerful in the light of Christ's grace, which makes all the world full of sunshine and joy. But it need not be so, friends. It would not be so, if married people would take the advice which the Prayer Book gives them, and come to Holy communion. Would to God, my friends, that all married people would understand what that Holy communion says to them; and come together Sunday after Sunday to that throne of grace, there to receive of Christ's fulness, and grace upon grace. For that Table says to you: You are heirs together of the grace of life; you are not meant merely to feed together for a few short years, at the same table, on the bread which perishes, but to feed for ever together on the bread which comes down from heaven, even on Christ Himself, the life of the world; to receive life from His life, that you may live together such a life as He lived, and lives still; to receive grace from the fulness of His grace, that you may be full of grace as He is. That Table tells you that because you both must live by the same life of Christ, you must live the same life as each other, and grow more and more like each other year by year; that as you both receive the same grace of Christ, you will become more and more gracious to each other year by year, and both grow together, nearer and dearer to each other, more worthy of each other's respect, more worthy of each other's trust, more worthy of each other's love. And then "till death us do part" may mean what it will. Let death part what of them he can part, the perishing mortal body; he has no power over the soul, or over the body which shall rise to life eternal. Let death do his worst. They belong to Christ who conquered death, and they live by His everlasting life, and their life is hid with Christ in God, where death cannot reach it or find it; and therefore their life and their love, and the grace of it, will last as long as Christ's life and Christ's love, and Christ's grace last—and that will be for ever and ever.

SERMON XXI

FATHER AND CHILD

Eversley. 1861.

1 Cor. i. 4, 5, 7. "I thank my God always on your behalf, for the grace of God which is given you by Jesus Christ. That in every thing ye are enriched by Him, in all utterance, and in all knowledge . . . So that ye come behind in no gift; waiting for the coming of our Lord Jesus Christ. Who shall also confirm you unto the end, that ye may be blameless in the day of our Lord Jesus Christ."

This text is a very important one. It ought to teach me how I should treat you. It ought to teach you how you should treat your children. It ought to teach you how God, your heavenly Father, treats you. You see at the first glance how cheerful and hopeful St Paul is about these Corinthians. He is always thanking God, he says, about them, for the grace of God which was given them by Jesus Christ, that in everything they were enriched by Him, in all utterance and in all knowledge. And he has good hope for them. Nay, he seems to be certain about them, that they will persevere, and conquer, and be saved; for Christ Himself will confirm them (that is strengthen them) to the end, that they may be blameless in the way of our Lord Jesus Christ.

If we knew no more of these Corinthians than what these words tell us, we should suppose that they were very great saints, leading holy and irreproachable lives before God and man. But we know that it was not so. That they were going on very ill. That this is the beginning of an epistle in which St Paul is going to rebuke them very severely; and to tell them, that unless they mend, they will surely become reprobates, and be lost after all. He is going to rebuke them for having heresies among them, that is religious parties and religious quarrels—very much as we have now; for being puffed up with spiritual self-conceit; for despising and disparaging him; for loose lives, allowing (in one case) such a crime among them as even the heathen did not allow; for profaning the Lord's Supper, to such an extent that some seem even to have got drunk at it; for want of charity to each other; for indulging in fanatical excitement; for denying, some of them, the resurrection of the dead; on the whole, for being in so unwholesome a state of mind that he has to warn them solemnly of the fearful example of the old Israelites, who perished in the wilderness for their sins—as they will perish, he hints, unless they mend.

And yet he begins by thanking God for them, by speaking of them, and to them, in this cheerful and hopeful tone.

Does that seem strange? Why should it seem strange, my friends, to us, if we are in the habit of training our children, and rebuking our children, as we ought? If we have to rebuke our children for doing wrong, do we begin by trying to break their hearts? by raking up old offences, by reproaching them with all the wrong they ever did in their lives, and giving them to understand that they are thoroughly bad, and have altogether lost our love, so that we will have nothing more to do with them unless they mend? Or do we begin by making them feel that however grieved we are with them, we love them still; that however wrong they have been, there is right feeling left in them still; and by giving them credit for whatever good there is in them—by appealing to that; calling on them to act up to that; to be true to themselves, and to their better nature; saying, You can do right in one thing—then do right in another—and do right in all? If we do not do this we do wrong; we destroy our children's self-respect, we make them despair of improving, we make them fancy themselves bad children: that is the very surest plan we can take to make them bad children, by making them reckless.

But if we be wise parents—such parents to our children as St Paul was to his spiritual children, the Corinthians—we shall do by them just what St Paul did by these Corinthians. Before he says one harsh word to them, he will awaken in them faith and love. He will make them trust him and love him, all the more because he knows that through false teaching they do not trust and love him as they used to do. But till they do, he knows that there is no use in rebuking them. Till they trust him and love him, they will not listen to him. And how does he try to bring them round to him? By praising them:—by telling them that he trusts them and loves them, because in spite of all their faults there is something in them worthy to be loved and trusted. He begins by giving them credit for whatever good there is in them. They are rich in all utterance and all knowledge; that is, they are very brilliant and eloquent talkers about spiritual things, and also very deep and subtle thinkers about spiritual things. So far so good. These are great gifts—gifts of Christ, too,—tokens that God's spirit is with them, and that all they need is to be true to His gracious inspirations. Then, when he has told them that, or rather made them understand that he knows that, and is delighted at it, then he can go on safely and boldly to tell them of their sins also in the plainest and sternest and yet the most tender and fatherly language.

This is very important, my friends. I cannot tell you fully how important I think it, in more ways than one. I am sure that if we took St Paul's method with our children we should succeed with them far better than we do. And I think, I have thought long, that if we could see that St Paul's method with those Corinthians was actually the same as God's method with us, we should have far truer notions of God, and God's dealings with us; and should reverence and value far more that Holy Catholic Church into which we have been, by God's infinite mercy, baptized, and wherein we have been educated.

For, and now I entreat you to listen to me carefully, you who have sound heads and earnest hearts, ready and willing to know the truth about God and yourselves, if St Paul looked at the Corinthians in this light, may not God have looked at them in the same light? If St Paul accepted them for the sake of the good which was in them, in spite of all their faults, may not God have accepted them for the sake of the good which was in them, in spite of all their faults? and may not He accept us likewise? I think it must be so. For was not St Paul an inspired apostle? and are not these words of his inspired by the Holy Spirit of God? But if so, then the Spirit of God must have looked at these Corinthians in the same light as St Paul, and therefore God must do likewise, because the Holy Spirit is God. Must it not be so? Can we suppose that God would take one view of these Corinthians, and then inspire St Paul to take another view? What does being inspired mean at all, save having the mind of Christ and of God,—being taught to see men and things as God sees them, to feel for them and think of them as God does? If inspiration does not mean that, what does it mean? Therefore, I think, we have a right to believe that St Paul's words express the mind of God concerning these Corinthians; that God was pleased with their utterance and their knowledge, and accepted them for that; and that in the same way God is pleased with whatsoever He sees good in us, and accepts us for that. But, remember, not for our own works or deservings any more than these Corinthians. They were, and we are accepted in Christ, and for the merits of Christ. And any good points in us, or in these Corinthians, as St Paul says expressly (here and elsewhere), are not our own, but come from Christ, by the inspiration of His Holy Spirit.

I know many people do not think thus. They think of God as looking only at our faults; as extreme to mark what is done amiss; as never content with us; as always crying to men, Yes, you have done this and that well, and yet not quite well, for even in what you have done there are blots and mistakes; but this and that you have not done, and therefore you are still guilty, still under infinite displeasure. And they think that they exalt God's holiness by such thoughts, and magnify His hatred of sin thereby. And they invent arguments to prove themselves right, such as this: That because God is an infinite being, every sin committed against Him is infinite; and therefore deserves an infinite punishment; which is a juggle of words of which any educated man ought to be ashamed.

I do not know where, in the Bible, they find all this. Certainly not in the writings of St Paul. They seem to me to find it, not in the Bible at all, but in their own hearts, judging that God must be as hard upon His children as they are apt to be upon their own. I know that God is never content with us, or with any man. How can He be? But in what sense is He not content? In the sense in which a hard task-master is not content with his slave, when he flogs him cruelly for the slightest fault? Or in the sense in which a loving father is not content with his child, grieving over him, counselling him, as long as he sees him, even in the slightest matter, doing less well than he might do? Think of that, and when you have thought of it, believe that in this grand text St Paul speaks really by the Spirit of God, and according to the mind of God, and teaches not these old Corinthians merely, but you and your children after you, what is the mind of God concerning you, what is the light in which God looks upon you. For, if you will but think over your own lives, and over the Catechism which you learned in your youth, has not God's way of dealing with you been just the same as St Paul's with those

Corinthians, teaching you to love and trust Him almost before He taught you the difference between right and wrong? I know that some think otherwise. Many who do not belong to the Church, and many, alas! who profess to belong to the Church, will tell you that God's method is, first to terrify men by the threats of the law and the sight of their sins and the fear of damnation, and afterwards to reveal to them the gospel and His mercy and salvation in Christ. Now I can only answer that it is not so. Not so in fact. These preachers themselves may do it; but that is no proof that God does it. What God's plan is can only be known from facts, from experience, from what actually happens; first in God's kingdom of nature, and next in God's kingdom of grace, which is the Church. And in the kingdom of nature how does God begin with mankind? What are a child's first impressions of this life? Does he hear voices from heaven telling little children that they are lost sinners? Does he see lightning come from heaven to strike sinners dead, or earthquakes rise and swallow them up? Nothing of the kind. A child's first impressions of this life, what are they but pleasure? His mother's breast, warmth, light, food, play, flowers, and all pleasant things,—by these God educates the child, even of the heathen and the savage:—and why? If haply he may feel after God and find Him, and find that He is a God of love and mercy, a giver of good things, who knows men's necessities before they ask,—a good and loving God, and not a being such as I will not, I dare not speak of.

I say with the very heathen God deals thus. We have plain Scripture for that. For we have, and thanks be to God that we have, in such times as these, a missionary sermon preached by St Paul to the heathen at Lystra. And in that is not one word concerning these terrors of the law. He says, I preach to you God, whom you ought to have known of yourselves, because He has not left Himself without witness. And what is this witness of which the apostle speaks? Wrath and terror and destruction? Not so, says St Paul. This is His witness, that He has sent you rain and fruitful seasons, filling your heart with food and gladness. His goodness, His bounty,—it is the witness of God and of the character of God. There is wrath and terror enough, says St Paul elsewhere, awaiting those who go on in sin. But then what does he say is their sin? Despising the goodness of God, by which He has been trying to win mankind to love and trust Him, before He threatens and before He punishes at all. So much for the terrors of the law coming before the good news of the gospel in God's kingdom of nature.

And still less do the terrors of the law come first in God's kingdom of grace, which is the Church. They did not come first to you or to me, or to any one in His Church who has been taught, as churchmen should be, their Catechism. If any have been, unhappily for them, brought up to learn Catechisms and hymns which do not belong to the Church, and which terrify little children with horrible notions of God's wrath, and the torments prepared not merely for wicked men, but for unconverted children, and then teach them to say,—

"Can such a wretch as I
Escape this dreadful end?"

so much the worse for them. We, who are Church people, are bound to believe that God speaks to us through the Church books, and that it was His will that we should have been brought up to believe the Catechism. And in that Catechism we heard not one word of these terrors of the law or of God's wrath hanging over us. We were taught that before we even knew right from wrong, God adopted us freely as His children, freely forgave us our original sin for the sake of Christ's blood, freely renewed us by His Holy Spirit, freely placed us in His Church;—that we might love Him, because He first loved us; trust Him because He has done all that even God could do to win our trust; and obey Him, because we are boundlessly in debt to Him for boundless mercies. This is God's method with us in His Church, and what is it but St Paul's method with these Corinthians?

Believe this, then, you who wish to be Churchmen in spirit and in truth. Believe that St Paul's conduct is to you a type and pattern of what God does, and what you ought to do. That God's method of winning you to do right is to make you love Him and trust Him; and that your method of winning your children to do right is to make them love and trust you. Let us remember that if our children are not perfect, they at least inherited their imperfections from us; and if our Father in heaven, from whom we inherit no sin, but only good, have patience with us, shall we not have patience with our children, who owe to us their fallen nature?

Ah! cast thy bread upon the waters,—the bread which even the poorest can give to their children abundantly and without stint,—the bread of charity,—human tenderness, forbearance, hopefulness,—cast that bread upon the waters, and thou shalt find it after many days.

SERMON XXII

GOD IS OUR REFUGE

Westminster Abbey, 1873.

Psalm xlvi. 1. "God is our refuge and strength, a very present help in trouble."

This is a noble psalm, full of hope and comfort; and it will be more and more full of hope and comfort, the more faithfully we believe in the incarnation, the passion, the resurrection, and the ascension of our Lord Jesus Christ. For if we are to give credit to His express words, and to those of every book of the New Testament, and to the opinion of that Church into which we are baptised, then Jesus Christ is none other than the same Jehovah, Lord, and God who brought the Jews out of Egypt, who guided them and governed them through all their history—teaching, judging, rewarding, punishing them and all the nations of the earth. This psalm, therefore, is concerning our Lord Jesus Christ, to whom all power is given in heaven and earth, and who ascended up on high; that He might be as He had been from the beginning, King of kings and Lord of lords, the Master of this world and all the nations in it. This psalm, therefore, is a hymn concerning the kingdom of Christ and of God. It tells us something of the government which Christ has been exercising over the world ever since the beginning of it, and which He is exercising over this world now. It bids us be still, and know that He is God—that He will be exalted among the nations, and will be exalted in the earth, whether men like it or not; but that they ought to like it and rejoice in it, and find comfort in the thought that Christ Jesus is their refuge and their strength—a very present help in trouble—as the old Jew who wrote this psalm found comfort.

When this psalm was written, or what particular events it speaks of, I cannot tell, for I do not think we have any means of finding out. It may have been written in the time of David, or of Solomon, or of Hezekiah. It may possibly have been written much later. It seems to mo probably to refer—but I speak with extreme diffidence—to that Assyrian invasion, and that preservation of Jerusalem, of which we heard in the magnificent first lesson for this morning and this afternoon; when, at the same time that the Assyrians were crushing, one by one, every nation in the East, there was, as the elder Isaiah and Micah tell us plainly, a great volcanic outbreak in the Holy Land. But all this matters very little to us; because events analogous to those of which it speaks have happened not once only, but many times, and will happen often again. And this psalm lays down a rule for judging of such startling and terrible events whenever they happen, and for saying of them, "God is our refuge and strength, a very present help in trouble." It seems from the beginning of the psalm that there had been earthquakes or hurricanes in Judea—more probably earthquakes, which were and are now frequent there. It seems as if the land had been shaken, and cliffs thrown into the sea, which had rolled back in a mighty wave, such as only too often accompanies an earthquake. But the Psalmist knew that that was God's doing; and therefore he would not fear, though the earth was moved, and though the hills were earned into the very midst of the sea. It seems, moreover, that Jerusalem itself had, as in Hezekiah's time, not been shaken, or at least seriously injured, by the earthquake. But why? "God is in the midst of her, therefore shall she not be removed." It seems, also, as if the earthquake or hurricane had been actually a benefit to Jerusalem—which was often then, and has been often since, in want of water—that either fresh springs had broken out, or abundant rain had fallen, as occurs at times in such convulsions of nature. But that, too, was God's doing on behalf of His chosen city. "The rivers of the flood" had made "glad the city of God, the holy place of the tabernacle of the most highest."

Moreover, there seem to have been great disturbances and wars among the nations round. The heathen had made much ado, and the kingdoms had been moved. But whatever their plans were, it was God who had brought them to naught. God had shewed His voice, and the earth melted away; and (we know not how) discomfiture had fallen upon them, and a general peace had followed. "O come hither," says the Psalmist, "and behold the works of the Lord, what desolations He has made in the earth." Not a desolation of cruelty and tyranny: but a desolation of mercy and justice; putting down the proud, the aggressive, the ruthless, and helping the meek, the simple, the industrious, and the innocent. It is He, says the Psalmist, who has made wars to cease in all the world, who has broken the bow and snapped the spear in sunder, and burned the chariots in the fire; and so, by the voice of fact, said to these kings and to their armies, if they would but understand it, "Be still, and know that I am God"—that I, not you, will be exalted among the nations—that I, not you, will be exalted in the earth.

Such is the 46th Psalm, one of the noblest utterances of the whole Old Testament. And is it not as true for us now, ay, for all nations and all mankind now, as it was when it was uttered? Is not Jesus Christ the same yesterday, to-day, and for ever? Have His words passed away? Did He say in vain, "All power is given unto me in heaven and earth?" Did He say in vain, "Lo, I am with you alway, even unto the end of the world?" I trust not. I trust and I hope that you, or at least some here, believe that Christ is ruling and guiding the world, the church, and every individual soul who trusts in Him toward—

> "One far off divine event,
> To which the whole creation moves."

I hope you do have that trust, for your own sakes, for the sake of your own happiness, your own sound peace of mind; for then, and then only, you can afford to be hopeful concerning yourselves, your families, your country, and the whole human race. It must be so. If you believe that He who hung upon the cross for all mankind is your refuge and strength, and the refuge and strength of all mankind, then, amid all the changes and chances of this mortal life, you can afford to be still calm in sudden calamity, patient in long afflictions; for you know that He is God, He is the Lord, He is the Redeemer, He is the King. He knows best. He must be right, whosoever else is wrong. Let Him do what seemeth Him good.

Now I cannot but feel (what wiser and better men than I am feel more deeply), that this old-fashioned faith in the living Christ is dying out among us. That men do not believe as they used to do in the living Lord and in His government, in that perpetual divine providence which the Scriptures call "the kingdom of God." They have lost faith in Christ's immediate and personal government of the world and its nations; and, therefore, they are tempted more and more, either to try to misgovern the world themselves, or to fancy that Christ has entrusted His government, as to a substitute and vicar, to an aged priest at Rome. They have lost faith, likewise, in Christ's immediate government of themselves; their own fortunes, their own characters, and inmost souls; and, therefore, they are tempted either to follow no rule or guidance save their own instincts, passions, fancies; or else, in despair at their own inward anarchy, to commit the keeping of their souls to directors and confessors, instead of to Christ Himself, the Lord of the spirits of all flesh.

Yes, the faith which keeps a man ever face to face with God and with Christ, in the least as well as in the greatest events of life; which says in prosperity and in adversity, in plenty and scarcity, in joy and sorrow, in peace and war,—It is the Lord's doing, it is the Lord's sending, and therefore we can trust in the Lord—that faith is growing, I fear, very rare. That faith was more common, I think, a generation or two back, in old-fashioned church people than in any other. It could not help being so; for the good old Prayer-Book upon which they were brought up is more full of that simple and living faith in the Lord, from beginning to end, than any other book on earth except the Bible. It was more common, too, and I suppose always will be, among the poor than among the rich; for the poor soon find out how little they have to depend upon except the Lord and His good providence; while the rich are tempted, and always will be, to depend upon their own wealth and their own power, to trust in uncertain riches, and say, "Soul, take thine ease, thou hast much goods laid up for many years." It was more common, too, and I suppose always will be, among the old than among the young; for the young are tempted to trust not in the Lord, but in their own health, strength, wit, courage, and to put their hopes, not on God's Providence, but on the unknown chapter of accidents in the future, most of which will never come to pass; while the old have learned by experience and disappointment the vanity of human riches, the helplessness of human endeavour, the blindness of human foresight, and are content to go where God leads them, and say, "I will go forth in the strength of the Lord God, and will make mention of Thy righteousness only. Thou, O God, hast taught me from my youth up until now: therefore will I tell of Thy wondrous works. Forsake me not, O God, in mine old age, when I am grey-headed; until I have showed Thy strength unto this generation, and Thy power to all them which are yet for to come."

But, for some reason or other, this generation does not seem to care to see God's strength; and those that are yet for to come seem likely to believe less and less in God's power—believe less and less that they are in Christ's kingdom, and that Christ is ruling over them and all the world. They have not faith in the Living Lord. But they must get back that faith, if they wish to keep that wealth and prosperity after which every one scrambles so greedily now-a-days; for those who forget God are treading, they and their children after them, not, as they fancy, the road to riches—they are treading the road to ruin. So it always was, so it always will be. Yet the majority of mankind will not see it, and the preacher must not expect to be believed when he says it. Nevertheless it is true. Those who forget that they are in Christ's kingdom, Christ does not go out of His way to punish them. They simply punish themselves. They earn their own ruin by the very laws of human nature. They must find hope in something and strength in something; and if they will not see that God is their hope, they will hope to get rich as fast as possible, and make themselves safe so. If they will not see that God is their strength, they will find strength in cunning, in intrigue, in flattery of the strong and tyranny over the weak, and in making themselves strong so. They want a present help in trouble; and if they will not believe that God is a present help in trouble, they will try to help themselves out of their trouble by begging, lying, swindling, forging, and all those meannesses which fill our newspapers with shameful stories day by day, and which all arise simply out of want of faith in God.

Moreover, it is written, "Be still, and know that I am God." And if men will not be still, they will not know that He is God. And if they do not know that the gracious Christ is God, they will not be still; and therefore they will grow more and more restless, discontented, envious, violent, irreverent, full of passions which injure their own souls, and sap the very foundations of order and society and civilised life. And what can come out of all these selfish passions, when they are let loose, but that in which selfishness must always end, but that same mistrust and anarchy, ending in that same poverty and wretchedness, under which so many countries of the world now lie, as it were, weltering in the mire. Alas! say rather weltering in their own life-blood—and all because they have forgotten the living God?

Oh, my dear friends, take these words solemnly to heart—for yourselves, and for your children after you. If you wish to prosper on the earth, let God be in all your thoughts. Remember that the Lord is on your right hand; and then, and then alone, will you not be moved, either to terror or to sin, by any of the chances and changes of this mortal life. "Fret not thyself," says the Psalmist, "else shalt thou be moved to do evil." And the only way not to fret yourselves is to remember that God is your refuge and strength, a very present help in trouble. "He that believeth," saith the Prophet, "shall not make haste"—not hurry himself into folly and disappointment and shame. Why should you hurry, if you remember that you are in the kingdom of Christ and of God? You cannot hurry God's Providence, if you would; you ought not, if you could. God must know best; God's Laws must work at the right pace, and fulfil His Will in the right way and at the right time. As for what that Will is, we can know from the angels' song on Christmas Eve, which told us how God's Will was a good will towards men.

For who is our Lord? Who is our King? Who is our Governor? Who is our Lawgiver? Who is our Guide? Christ, who died for us on Calvary; who rose again for us; who ascended into heaven for us; who sits at God's right hand for us; who sent down His Holy Spirit at the first Whitsuntide; and sends Him down for ever to us; that by His gracious inspiration we may both perceive and know what we ought to do, and also may have grace and power faithfully to fulfil the same. With such a King over us, how can the world but go right? With such a King over us, what refuge or strength or help in trouble do we need but Him Himself?—His Providence, which is Love, and His Laws, which are Life.

SERMON XXIII

PRIDE AND HUMILITY

Eversley, 1869. Chester Cathedral, 1870.

1st. Peter v. 5. "God resisteth the proud, and giveth grace to the humble."

Let me, this evening, say a few words to you on theology, that is, on the being and character of God. You need not be afraid that I shall use long or difficult words. Sound theology is simple enough, and I hope that my words about it will be simple enough for the worst scholar here to understand.

"God resisteth the proud, and giveth grace to the humble." Now, this saying is an old one. It had been said, in different words, centuries before St Peter said it. The old prophets and psalmists say it again and again. The idea of it runs through the whole of the Old Testament, as anyone must know who has read his Bible with common care. But why should it be true? What reason is there for it? What is there in the character of God which makes it reasonable, probable, likely to be true? That God would give grace to the humble, and reward men for bowing down before His Majesty, seems not so difficult to understand. But why should God resist the proud? How does a man's being proud injure God, who is "I AM THAT I AM;" perfectly self-sufficient, having neither parts nor passions, who tempteth no man, neither is tempted of any? "Why should God go out of His way, as it were, to care for such a paltry folly as the pride of an ignorant, weak, short-sighted creature like man?

Now, let us take care that we do not give a wrong answer to this question—an answer which too many have given, in their hearts and minds, though not perhaps in words, and so have fallen into abject and cruel superstitions, from which may God keep us, and our children after us. They have said to themselves, God is proud, and has a right to be proud: and therefore He chooses no one to be proud but Himself. Pride in man calls out His pride, and makes Him angry. They have thought of God as some despotic Sultan of the Indies, who is surrounded, not by free men, but by slaves; who will have those slaves at his beck and nod. In one word, they have thought of God as a tyrant. They have thought of God, and, may God forgive them, have talked of God as if He were like Nebuchadnezzar of old, who, when the three young men refused to obey him, was filled with rage and fury, and cast them into a burning fiery furnace. That is some men's God—a God who must be propitiated by crouching and flattery, lest he should destroy them—a God who holds all men as his slaves, and therefore hates pride in them. For what has a slave to do with pride?

But that is not the God of the Bible, my friends, nor the God of Nature either, the God who made the world and man. For He is not a tyrant, but a Father. He wishes men not to be His slaves, but His children. And if He resists the proud, it is because children have no right to be proud. If He resists the proud, it is in fatherly love, because it is bad for them to be proud. Not because the proud are injuring God, but because they are injuring themselves, does God resist them, and bring them low, and show them what they are, and where they are, that they may repent, and be converted, and turned back into the right way.

Remember always that God is your Father. This question, like all questions between God and man, is a question between a father and a child; and if you see it in any other light, and judge it by any other rule, you see it and judge it wrongly, and learn nothing about it, or worse than nothing. If God were really angry with, really hated, the proud man, or any other man, would He need only to resist him? would He have to wait till the next life to punish him? My dear friends, if God really hated you or me, do you not suppose that He would simply destroy us—get rid of us—abolish us and annihilate us off the face of the earth, just as we crush a gnat when it bites us?

That God can do; and more—He does it now and then. He will endure with much long suffering vessels of wrath, fitted to destruction: but a moment sometimes comes when He will endure them no longer, and He destroys them with the destruction for which they have fitted themselves. In them is fulfilled the parable of the rich man, who said to himself, "Soul, thou hast much good laid up for many years; take thine ease, eat, drink, and be merry. But God said unto him, Thou fool, this night thy soul shall be required of thee."

But for the most part, thanks to the mercy of our Heavenly Father, we are not destroyed by our pride and for our pride. We are only chastened, as a father chastens his child. And that we are chastised for pride, who does not know? What proverb more common, what proverb more true, than that after pride comes a fall? Do we not know (if we do not, we shall know sooner or later) that the surest way to fail in any undertaking is to set about it in self-will and self-conceit; that the surest way to do a foolish thing, is to fancy that we are going to do a very wise one; that the surest way to make ourselves ridiculous in the eyes of our fellow-men, is to assume airs, and boast, shew ourselves off, and end by shewing off only our own folly?

Why is it so? Why has God so ordered the world and human nature, that pride punishes itself? Because, I presume, pride is begotten and born of a lie, and God hates a lie, because all lies lead to ruin, and this lie of pride above all. It is as it were the root lie of all lies. The very lie by which, as old tales tell, Satan fell from heaven, and when he tried to become a god in his own right, found himself, to his surprise and disappointment, only a devil. For pride and self-conceit contradict the original constitution of man and the universe, which is this—that of God are all things, and in God are all things, and for God are all things. Man depends on God. Self tells him that he depends on himself. Man has nothing but what he receives from God. Self tells him that what he has is his own, and that he has a right to do with it what he likes. Man knows nothing but what God teaches him. Self tells him that he has found out everything for himself, and can say what he thinks fit without fear of God or man. Therefore the proud, self-willed, self-conceited man must come to harm, like Malvolio in the famous play, merely because he is in the blackest night of ignorance. He has mistaken who he is, what he is, where he is. He is fancying himself, as many mad men do, the centre of the universe; while God is the centre of the universe. He is just as certain to come to harm as a man would be on board a ship, who should fancy that he himself, and not the ship, was keeping him afloat, and step overboard to walk upon the sea. We all know what would happen to that man. Let us thank God our Father that He not only knows what would happen to such men: but desires to save them from the consequences of their own folly, by letting them feel the consequences of their own folly.

Oh my friends, let us search our hearts, and pray to our Father in Heaven to take out of them, by whatever painful means, the poisonous root of pride, self-conceit, self-will. So only shall we be truly strong—truly wise. So only shall we see what and where we are.

Do we pride ourselves on being something? Shall we pride ourselves on health and strength? A tile falling off the roof, a little powder and lead in the hands of a careless child, can blast us out of this world in a moment—whither, who can tell? What is our cleverness—our strength of mind? A tiny blood vessel bursting on the brain, will make us in one moment paralytic, helpless, babblers, and idiots. What is our knowledge of the world? That of a man, who is forcing his way alone through a thick and pathless wood, where he has never been before, to a place which he has never seen. What is our wisdom—What does a wise man say of his?

"So runs my dream; but what am I?
An infant crying in the night;
An infant crying for the light;
And with no language but a cry."

Yes. Our true knowledge is to know our own ignorance. Our true strength is to know our own weakness. Our true dignity is to confess that we have no dignity, and are nobody, and nothing in ourselves, and to cast ourselves down before the Dignity of God, under the shadow of whose wings, and in the smile of whose countenance, alone, is any created being safe. Let us cling to our Father in Heaven, as a child, walking in the night, clings to his father's hand. Let us take refuge on the lowest step of the throne of Christ our Lord, and humble ourselves under His mighty hand; and, instead of exalting ourselves in undue time, leave Him to exalt us again in due time, when the chastisement has told on us, and patience had her perfect work; casting all our care on Him, who surely cares for us still, if He cared for us once, enough to die for us on the cross; caring for God's opinion and not for the opinion of the world. And then we shall be among the truly humble, to whom God gives grace—first grace in their own hearts, that they may live gracious lives, modest and contented, dignified and independent, trusting in God and not in man; and then, grace in the eyes of their fellow-men, for what is more graceful, what is more gracious, pleasant to see, pleasant to deal with, than the humble man, the modest man? I do not mean the cringing man, the flattering man, the man who apes humility for his own ends, because he wants to climb high, by pretending to be lowly. He is neither graceful or gracious. He is only contemptible, and he punishes himself. He spoils his own game. He defeats his own purpose. For men despise him, and use him, and throw him away when they have done with him, as they throw away a dirty worn-out tool.

Not him do I mean by the humble man, the modest man. I mean the man who, like a good soldier, knows his place and keeps it, knows his duty, and does it; who expects to be treated as a man should be, with fairness, consideration, respect, kindness—and God will always treat him so, whether man does or not: but who, beyond that, does not trouble his mind with whether he be private or sergeant, lieutenant or colonel, but with whether he can do his duty as private, his duty as sergeant, his duty as lieutenant, his duty as colonel; who has learnt the golden lesson, which so few learn in these struggling, envious, covetous, ambitious days, namely, to abide in the calling to which he is called, and in whatsoever state he is, therewith to be content. To be sure that in God's world, the only safe way to become ruler over many things is to be a good ruler over a few things; that if he is fit for better work than he is doing now, God will find that out, sooner and more surely than he, or any man will, and will set him about it; and that, meanwhile, God has set him about work which he can do, and that the true wisdom is to do that and do it well, and so approve himself alike to man and God, humbling himself under the mighty hand of God, that He may exalt him in good time, by giving him grace and strength to do great things, as He has given him grace and strength to do small things.

Am I speaking almost to deaf ears? I fear that few here will take my advice. I fear that many here will have excellent excuses and plain reasons, why they should not take it. Be it so. They cannot alter eternal fact. In one word, they cannot alter Theology. They cannot alter the laws of God. They cannot alter the character of God. And sooner or later, in this world or in the next, they will find out that Theology is right: and St Peter is right: that God does resist the proud, that God does give grace to the humble.

SERMON XXIV

WORSHIP

Eversley, September 4, 1870.

Revelation xi. 16, 17. "And the four and twenty elders, which sat before God on their seats, fell upon their faces, and worshipped God, saying, We give thee thanks, O Lord God Almighty, which art, and wast, and art to come; because thou hast taken to thee thy great power, and hast reigned."

My dear friends,—I wish to speak a few plain words to you this morning, on a matter which has been on my mind ever since I returned from Chester, namely,—The duty of the congregation to make the responses in Church.

Now I am not going to scold—even to blame. To do so would be not only unjust, but ungrateful in me, to a congregation which is as attentive and as reverent as you are. Indeed, I am the only person to blame, for I ought to have spoken on the subject long ago.

As it is, coming fresh from Chester, and accustomed to hear congregations, in that city and in the country round, reading the responses aloud throughout the service with earnestness, and reverence, I was painfully struck by the silence in this church. I had before grown so accustomed to it that I did not perceive it, just as one grows accustomed to a great many things which ought not to be, till one forgets that, however usual they may be, wrong they are, and ought to be amended.

Now, it is always best to begin at the root of a matter. So to begin at the root of this. Why do we come to church at all?

Some will say, to hear the sermon. That is often too true. Some folks do come to church to hear a man get up and preach, just as they go to a concert to hear a man get up and sing, to amuse and interest them for half-an-hour. Some go to hear sermons, doubtless, in order that they may learn from them. But are there not, especially in these days of cheap printing, books of devotion, tracts, sermons, printed, which contain better preaching than any which they are likely to hear in church? If teaching is all that they come to church for, they can get that in plenty at home. Moreover, nine people out of ten who come to church need no teaching at all. They know already, just as well as the preacher, what is right and what is wrong; they know their duty; they know how to do it. And if they do not intend to do it, all the talking in the world (as far as I have seen) will not make them do it. Moreover, if the teaching in the sermon be what we come to church for, why have we prayer-books full of prayers, thanksgivings, psalms, and so forth, which are not sermons at all? What is the use of the service, as we call it, if the sermon is the only or even the principal object for which we come? I trust there are many of you here who agree with me so fully, that you would come regularly to church, as I should, even if there were no sermon, knowing that God preaches to every man, in the depths of his own heart and conscience, far more solemn and startling sermons than any mortal man can utter.

Others will answer that they come to church to say their prayers. Well: that is a wiser answer than the last. But if that be all, why can they not say their prayers at home? God is everywhere. God is all-seeing, all-hearing, about our path and about our bed, and spying out all our ways. Is He not as ready to hear in the field, and in the workshop and in the bed-chamber, as in the church? "When thou prayest," says our Lord, "enter into thy closet, and when thou hast shut thy door, pray to thy Father which is in secret; and thy Father which seeth in secret shall reward thee openly." Those are not my words, they are the words of our Lord Jesus Christ Himself; and none can gainsay them. None dare take from them or add to them; and our coming to church, therefore, must be for more reasons than for the mere saying of our prayers.

Others will answer—very many, indeed, will answer—we come to church because—because, we hardly know why, but because we ought to come to church.

Some may call that a silly answer, only fit for children: but I do not think so. It seems to me a very rational answer: perhaps a very reverent and godly answer. A man comes to church for reasons which he cannot explain to himself: just so—and many of the deepest and best feelings of our hearts, are just those that we cannot explain to ourselves, though we believe in them, would fight for them, die for them. The man who frankly confesses that he does not quite know why he comes to church is most likely to know at last why he does come; most likely to understand the answer which Scripture gives to the question why we come to church. And what answer is that? Strange to say, one which people now-a-days, with their Bibles in their hands, have almost forgotten. We come to church, according to the Bible, to worship God.

To worship. Think awhile what that ancient and deep and noble word signifies. So ancient is it, that man learnt to worship even before he learnt to till the ground. So deep, that even to this day no man altogether understands what worshipping means. So noble, that the noblest souls on earth delight most in worshipping; that the angels, and archangels, and the spirits of just men made perfect, find no nobler occupation, no higher enjoyment, in the heavenly world than worshipping for ever Him whose glory fills all earth and heaven. To worship. That power of worship, that longing to worship, that instinct that it is his duty to worship something, is—if you will receive it—the true distinction between men and brutes. Philosophers have tried to define man as this sort of animal and that sort of animal. The only sound definition is this: man is the one animal who worships; and he worships, just because he is not merely an animal, but a man, with an immortal soul within him. Just in as far as man sinks down again to the level of the brute— whether in some savage island of the South Seas, or in some equally savage alley of our own great cities—God forgive us that such human brutes should exist here in Christian England—just so far he feels no need to worship. He thinks of no unseen God or powers above him. He cares for nothing but what his five senses tell him of; he feels no need to go to church and worship. Just in as far as a man rises to the true standard of a man; just in as far as his heart and his mind are truly cultivated, truly developed, just so far does he become more and more aware of an unseen world about him; more and more aware that in God he lives and moves and has his being—and so much the more he feels the longing and the duty to worship that unseen God on whom he and the whole universe depend.

I know what seeming exceptions there are to this rule, especially in these days. But I say that they are only seeming exceptions. I never knew yet (and I have known many of them) a virtuous and high-minded unbeliever: but what there was in him the instinct of worshipping—the longing to worship—he knew not what, the spirit of reverence, which confesses its own ignorance and weakness, and is ready to set up, like the Athenians of old, an altar—in the heart at least—to the unknown God.

But how to worship Him? The word itself, if we consider what it means, will tell us that. Worship, without doubt, is the same word as worth-ship. It signifies the worth of Him whom we worship, that He is worthy,—a worthy God, not merely because of what He has done, but because of what He is worth in Himself. Good, excellent, and perfect in Himself, and therefore to be admired, praised, reverenced, adored, worshipped—even if He had never done a kindness to you or to any human being. Remember this last truth. For true it is; and we remember it too little. Of course we know that God is good; first and mainly by His goodness to us. Because He is good enough to give us life and breath and all things, we conclude that He is a good being. Because He is good enough to have not spared His only begotten Son, but freely given Him for us, when we were still sinners and rebels, we conclude Him to be the best of all beings, a being of boundless goodness. But it is because God is so perfectly and gloriously good in Himself, and not merely because He has done us kindnesses, yea, heaped us with undeserved benefits, that we are to worship Him. For His kindnesses we owe Him gratitude, and gratitude without end. But for His excellent and glorious goodness, we owe Him worship, and worship without end.

There are some hearts, surely, among you here who know what I mean: some here who have felt reverence and admiration for some great and good human being, and who have felt, too, that that reverence and admiration is one of the most elevating and unselfish of all feelings, and quite distinct from any gratitude, however just, for favours done; who can say, in their hearts, of some noble human being: "If he never did me a kindness, never spoke to me, never knew of my existence, I should honour him and love him just the same, for the noble and good personage that he is, irrespective of little me, and my paltry wants." Then, even such ought to be our feeling toward God, our worship of God. Even so should we adore Him who alone is worthy of glory, and honour, and praise, and thanksgiving, because He is good, and beautiful, and wise Himself, and the cause and source of all goodness, and beauty, and wisdom, in all created beings, and in the whole universe, past, present, and to come. Consider, I beseech you, those glimpses of the Eternal Worship in heaven which St John gives us in the Book of Revelation—How he saw the elders fall down before Him who sat upon the throne, and worship Him that liveth for ever, and cast their crowns before the throne, saying: "Thou art worthy, O Lord, to receive glory, and honour, and power; for Thou hast created all things, and for Thy pleasure they are and were created."

Consider that—Those blessed spirits of just men made perfect, confessing that they are nothing, but that Christ is all; that they have nothing, but that they owe all to Christ; and declaring Him worthy—not merely for any special mercies and kindnesses to themselves, not even for that crowning mercy of His incarnation, His death, His redemption; even that seems to have vanished from their minds at the sight of Him as He is. They glorify Him and worship Him simply for what He is in Himself, for what He would have been even if—which God forbid—He had never stooped from heaven to live and die on earth—for what He is and was and will be through eternity, the Creator and the Ruler, who has made all things, and for whose pleasure they are and were created. Consider that one text. The more I consider it, the more awful and yet most blessed depths of teaching do I find therein: and consider this text also, another glimpse of the worship which is in heaven.

"I heard a great voice of much people in heaven, singing Alleluia; salvation, and glory, and honour, and power, unto the Lord our God; for true and righteous are His judgments." What the special judgment was, for which these blessed souls worshipped God, I shall not argue here. It is enough for us that they worshipped God, as we should worship Him, because His judgments were righteous and true, were like Himself, proved Him to be what He was, worthy in Himself, because He is righteous and true. And consider then, again—the text. Before Him, the righteous and true Being who has created all things for His pleasure, and therefore has made them wisely and well; before Him who reigns, and will reign till He has put all His enemies under His foot; before Him, I say, bow down yourselves, and find true nobleness in confessing your own paltriness, true strength in confessing your own weakness, true wisdom in confessing your own ignorance, true holiness in confessing your own sins.

And not alone merely, each in your own chamber, or in your own heart. That is the place for private confessions of sin, for private prayers for help; for all the secrets which we dare not, and need not tell to any human being. They indeed are not out of place here in church. Those who composed our Prayer Book felt that, and have filled our services, the Litany especially, with prayers in which each of us can offer up his own troubles to God, if he but remember that he is offering up to God his neighbour's troubles also, and the troubles of all mankind. For this is the reason why we pray together in church; why all men, in all ages, heathen as well as Christian, have had the instinct of assembling together for public worship. They may have fancied often that their deity dwelt in one special spot, and that they must go thither to find him. They may have fancied that he or she dwelt in some particular image, and that they must visit, and pray to that particular image, if they wished their prayers to be heard. All this, however, have men done in their foolishness; but beneath that foolishness there have been always more rational ideas, sounder notions. They felt that it was God who had made them into families, and therefore whole families met together to worship in common Him of whom every family in heaven and earth is named. That God had formed them into societies whether into tribes, as of old, or into parishes, as here now; and therefore whole parishes came together to worship God, whose laws they were bound to obey in their parochial society. They felt that it was God who had made them into Nations (as the psalm says which we repeat every Sunday morning), and not they themselves; and therefore they conceived the grand idea of National churches, in which the whole nation should, if possible, worship Sunday after Sunday, at the same time, and in the same words, that God to whom they owed their order, their freedom, their strength, their safety, their National unity and life. And not in silence merely. These blessed souls in heaven are not silent. They in heaven follow out the human instinct which they had on earth, which all men (when they recollect themselves, will have), when they feel a thing deeply, when they believe a thing strongly, to speak it—to speak it aloud. They do not fancy in heaven, as the priests of Baal did on earth, that they must cry aloud, or God could not hear them. They do not fancy, as the heathen do, that they must make vain repetitions, and say the same words over and over again by rote, because they will be heard for their much speaking; neither need you and I. But yet they spoke aloud, because out of the fulness of the heart the mouth speaketh; and so should you and I.

And this brings me to the special object of my sermon. I have told you what (as it seems to me) Worship means; why we worship; why we worship together; and why we ought to worship aloud. Believe me, this last is your duty just as much as mine. The services of the Church of England are so constructed that the whole congregation may take part in them, that they may answer aloud in the responses, that they may say Amen at the end of each prayer, just as they read or chant aloud the alternate verses of the Psalms. The minister does not say prayers for them, but with them. He is only their leader, their guide. And if they are not to join in with their voices, there is really no reason why he should use his voice, why he should not say the prayers in silence and to himself, if the congregation are to say Amen in silence and to themselves. Each person in the congregation ought to join aloud, first for the sake of his neighbours, and then for his own sake.

For the sake of his neighbours: for to hear each other's voices stirs up earnestness, stirs up attention, keeps off laziness, inattention, and by a wholesome infection, makes all the congregation of one mind, as they are of one speech, in glorifying God. And for his own sake, too. For, believe me, when a man utters the responses aloud, he awakens his own thoughts and his own feelings, too. He speaks to himself, and he hears himself remind himself of God, and of his duty to God, and acknowledge himself openly (as in confirmation) bound to believe and do what he, by his own confession, has assented unto.

Believe me, my dear friends, this is no mere theory. It is to me a matter of fact and experience. I cannot, I have long found, keep my attention steady during a service, if I do not make the responses aloud;—if I do not join in with my voice, I find my thoughts wandering; and I am bound to suppose that the case is the same with you. Do not, therefore, think me impertinent or interfering, if I ask you all to take your due share in worshipping God in this church with your voices, as well as with your hearts. Let these services be more lively, more earnest, more useful to us all than they have been, by making them more a worship of the whole congregation, and not of the minister alone. I have read of a great church in the East, in days long, long ago, in which the responses of the vast congregation were so unanimous, so loud, that they sounded (says the old writer) like a clap of thunder. That is too much to expect in our little country church: but at least, I beg you, take such an open part in the responses, that you shall all feel that you are really worshipping together the same God and Christ, with the same heart and mind; and that if a stranger shall come in, he may say in his heart: Here are people who are in earnest, who know what they are about, and are not ashamed of trying to do it; people who evidently mean what they say, and therefore say what they mean.

SERMON XXV

THE PEACE OF GOD

Baltimore, U.S., 1874. Westminster Abbey. November 8, 1874.

Colossians. iii 15. "Let the peace of God rule in your hearts."

The peace of God. That is what the priest will invoke for you all, when you leave this abbey. Do you know what it is? Whether you do or not, let me tell you in a few words, what I seem to myself to have learned concerning that peace. What it is? how we can obtain it? and why so many do not obtain it, and are, therefore, not at peace?

It is worth while to do so. For these are not peaceful times. The peace of God is rare among us. Some say that it is rarer than it was. I know not how that may be; but I see all manner of causes at work around us which should make it rare. We live faster than our forefathers. We hurry, we bustle, we travel, we are eager for daily, almost for hourly news from every quarter, as if the world could not get on without us, or we without knowing a hundred facts which merely satisfy the curiosity of the moment; and as if the great God could not take excellent care of us all meanwhile. We are eager, too, to get money, and get more money still—piercing ourselves through too often, as the Apostle warned us—with many sorrows, and falling into foolish and hurtful lusts, which drown men in destruction and perdition. We are luxurious—more and more fond of show; more apt to live up to our incomes, and probably a little beyond; more and more craving for this or that gew-gaw, especially in dress and ornament, which if our neighbour has, we must have too, or we shall be mortified, envious. Nay, so strong is this temper of rivalry, of allowing no superiors, grown in us, that we have made now-a-days a god of what used to be considered the basest of all vices—the vice of envy—and dignify it with the names of equality and independence. Men in this temper of mind cannot be at peace. They are not content; they cannot be content.

But with what are they not content? That is a question worth asking. For there is a discontent (as I have told you ere now) which is noble, manful, heroic, and divine. Just as there is a discontent which is base, mean, unmanly, earthly—sometimes devilish. There is a discontent which is certain, sooner or later, to bring with it the peace of God. There is a discontent which drives the peace of God away, for ever and a day. And the noble and peace-bringing discontent is to be discontented with ourselves, as very few are. And the mean peace-destroying discontent is to be discontented with things around us, as too many are. Now, my friends, I cannot see into your hearts; and I ought not to see. For if I saw, I should be tempted to judge; and if I judged, I should most certainly judge rashly, shallowly, and altogether wrong. Therefore examine yourselves, and judge yourselves in this matter.

Ask yourselves each, Am I at peace? And if not, then apply to yourselves the rule of old Epictetus, the heroic slave, who, heathen though he was, sought God, and the peace of God, and found them, doubt it not, long, long ago. Ask yourselves with Epictetus, Am I discontented with things which are in my own power, or with things which are not in my own power?—that is, discontented with myself, or with things which are not myself? Am I discontented with myself, or with things about me, and outside of me? Consider this last question well, if you wish to be true Christians, true philosophers, and, indeed, true men and women.

But what is it that troubles you? What is it you want altered? On what have you set your heart and affections? Is it something outside you?—something which is not you yourself? If so, there is no use in tormenting your soul about it; for it is not in your own power, and you will never alter it to your liking; and more, you need not alter it, for you are not responsible for it. God sends it as it is, for better, for worse, and you must make up your mind to what God sends. Do I mean that we are to submit slavishly to circumstances, like dumb animals? Heaven forbid. We are not, like Epictetus, slaves, but free men. And we are made in God's image, and have each our spark, however dim, of that creative genius, that power of creating or of altering circumstances, by which God made all worlds; and to use that, is of our very birthright, or what would all education, progress, civilisation be, save rebellion against God? But when we have done our utmost, how little shall we have done! Canst thou,—asks our Lord, looking with loving sadness on the hurry and the struggle of the human anthill—canst thou by taking thought add one cubit to thy stature? Why, is there a wise man or woman in this abbey, past fifty years of age, who does not know that, in spite of all their toil and struggle, they have gone not whither they willed, but whither God willed? Have they not found out that for one circumstance of their lives which they could alter, there have been twenty which they could not, some born with them, some forced on them by an overruling Providence, irresistible indeed—but, as I hold, most loving and most fatherly, though often severe—even to agony—but irresistible still—till what they have really gained by fighting circumstance, however valiantly, has been the moral gain, the gain in character?—the power to live the heroic life, which

> "Is not as idle ore,
> But heated hot with burning fears,
> And bathed in baths of hissing tears,
> And batter'd, with the shocks of doom,
> To shape and use."

Ah! if a man be learning that lesson, which is the primer of eternal life, then I hardly pity him, though I see him from youth to age tearing with weak hands at the gates of brass, and beating his soul's wings to pieces against the bars of the iron cage. But, alas! the majority of mankind tear at the gates of brass, and beat against the iron cage, with no such good purpose, and therefore with no such good result. They fight with circumstances, not that they may become better themselves, not that they may right the wrongs or elevate the souls of their fellow-men, not even that they may fulfil the sacred duty of maintaining, and educating, and providing for the children whom they have brought into the world, and for whom they are responsible alike to God and to man; but simply because circumstances are disagreeable to them; because the things around them do not satisfy their covetousness, their luxury, their ambition, their vanity. And therefore the majority of mankind want to be, and to do, and to have a hundred things which are not in their own power, and of which they have no proof that God intends to give them; no proof either that if they had them, they would make right use of them, and certainly no proof at all that if they had them they would find peace. They war and fight, and have not, because they ask not. They ask, and have not, because they ask amiss, to consume it on their lusts; and so they spend their lives without peace, longing, struggling for things outside them, the greater part of which they do not get, because the getting them is not in their own power, and which if they got they could not keep, for they can carry nothing away with them when they die, neither can their pomp follow them. And therefore does man walk in a vain shadow, and disquiet himself in vain, looking for peace where it is not to be found—in everything and anything save in his own heart, in duty, and in God.

But happy are they who are discontented with the divine discontent, discontented with themselves. Happy are they who hunger and thirst after righteousness, that they may become righteous and good men. Happy are they who have set their hearts on the one thing which is in their own power—being better than they are, and doing better than they do. Happy are they who long and labour after the true riches, which neither mobs nor tyrants, man nor devil, prosperity nor adversity, or any chance or change of mortal life, can take from them—the true and eternal wealth, which is the Spirit of God. The man, I say, who has set his heart on being good, has set his heart on the one thing which is in his own power; the one thing which depends wholly and solely on his own will; the one thing which he can have if he chooses, for it is written, "If ye then being evil, know how to give good gifts unto your children, how much more shall your heavenly Father give the Holy Spirit to them that ask Him?" Moreover, he has set his heart on the one thing which cannot be taken from him. God will not take it from him; and man, and fortune, and misfortune, cannot take it from him. Poverty, misery, disease, death itself, cannot make him a worse man, cannot make him less just, less true, less pure, less charitable, less high-minded, less like Christ, and less like God.

Therefore he is at peace, for he is, as it were, intrenched in an impregnable fortress, against all men and all evil influences. And that castle is his own soul. And the keeper of that castle is none other than Almighty God, Jesus Christ our Lord, to whose keeping he has committed his soul, as unto a faithful and merciful Saviour, able to keep to the uttermost that which is committed to Him in faith and holiness.

Therefore that man is at peace with himself, for his conscience tells him that he is, if not doing his best, yet trying to do his best, better and better day by day. He is at peace with all the world; for most men are longing and quarrelling for pleasant things outside them, for which he does not greatly care, while he is longing and striving for good things inside him in his own heart and soul; and so the world goes one way, and he another, and their desires do not interfere with each other.

But, more, that man is at peace with God. He is at peace with God the Father; for he is behaving as the Father wishes His children to behave. He is at peace with God the Son; for he is trying to do that which God the Son did when He came not to do His own will, but His Father's; not to grasp at anything for himself, but simply to sacrifice himself for duty, for the good of man. And he is at peace with God the Holy Spirit; for he is obeying the gracious inspirations of that Spirit, and growing a better man day by day. And so the peace of God keeps that man's heart free from vain desires and angry passions, and his mind from those false and foolish judgments which make the world think things important which are quite unimportant; and, again, fancy things unimportant which are more important to them than the riches of the whole world.

My dear friends, take my words home with you, and if you wish for the only true and sound peace, which is the peace of God, do your duty. Try to be as good as you can, each in his station in life. So help you God.

Take an example from the soldier on the march; and if you do that, you will all understand what I mean. The bad soldier has no peace, just because he troubles himself about things outside himself, and not in his own power. "Will the officers lead us right?" That is not in his power. Let him go where the officers lead him, and do his own duty. "Will he get food enough, water enough, care enough, if he is wounded?" I hope and trust in God he will; but that is not in his own power. Let him take that, too, as it comes, and do his duty. "Will he be praised, rewarded, mentioned in the newspapers, if he fights well?" That, too, is not in his own power. Let him take that, too, as it comes, and do his duty; and so of everything else. If the soldier on the march torments himself with these matters which are not in his own power, he is the man who will be troublesome and mutinous in time of peace, and in time of war will be the first to run away. He will tell you, "A man must have justice done him; a man must see fair play for himself; a man must think of himself." Poor fool! He is not thinking of himself all the while, but of a number of things which are outside him, circumstances which stand round him, and outside him, and are not himself at all. Because he thinks of them—the things outside him—he is a coward or a mutineer, while he fancies he is taking care of himself—as it is written, "Whosoever shall seek to save his life shall lose it."

But if the man will really think of himself, of that which is inside him, of his own character, his own honour, his own duty—then he will say, Well fed or ill fed, well led or ill led, praised and covered with medals, or neglected and forgotten, and dying in a ditch, I, by myself I, am the same man, and I have the same work to do. I have to be—myself, and I have to do—my duty. So help me God. And therefore, so help me God, I will be discontented with no person or thing, save only with myself; and I will be discontented with myself, not when I have left undone something extraordinary, which I know I could not have done, but only when I have left undone something ordinary, some plain duty which I know I could have done, had I asked God to help me to do it. Then in that soldier would be fulfilled—has been fulfilled, thank God, a thousand times, by men who lie in this abbey, and by men, too, of whom we never heard, "whose graves are scattered far and wide, by mount, by stream, by sea,"—in him would be fulfilled, I say, the words, "He that will lose his life shall save it." Then would he have in his heart, and in his mind likewise, a peace which victory and safety cannot give, and which defeat, and wounds, ay, death itself, can never take away.

And are not you, too, soldiers—soldiers of Jesus Christ? Then even as that good soldier, you may be at peace, through all the battles, victories, defeats of mortal life, if you will be discontented with nothing save yourselves, and vow, in spirit and in truth, the one oath which is no blasphemy, but an act of faith, and an act of prayer, and a confession of the true theology—So help me God. For then God will help you. Neither you nor I know how; and I am sure neither you nor I know why—save that God is utterly good. God, I say, will help you, by His Holy Spirit the Comforter, to do your duty, and to be at peace. And then the peace of God will rule in your hearts and make you kings to God. For He will enable you each to rule, serene, though weary, over a kingdom—or, alas! rather a mob, the most unruly, the most unreasonable, the most unstable, and often the most fierce, which you are like to meet on earth. To rule, I say, over a mob, of which you each must needs be king or slave, according as you choose. And what is that mob? What but your own faculties, your own emotions, your own passions—in one word, your own selves? Yes, with the peace of God ruling in your hearts, you will be able to become what without it you will never be—and that is—masters of yourselves.

SERMON XXVI

SINS OF PARENTS VISITED

Eversley. 19th Sunday after Trinity, 1868.

Ezekiel xviii. 1-4. "The word of the Lord came unto me again, saying, What mean ye, that ye use this proverb concerning the land of Israel,
saying, The fathers have eaten sour grapes, and the children's teeth are
set on edge? As I live, saith the Lord God, ye shall not have occasion
any more to use this proverb in Israel. Behold, all souls are mine; as the
soul of the father, so also the soul of the son is mine: the soul that sinneth,
it shall die."

This is a precious chapter, and a comfortable chapter likewise, for it
helps us to clear up a puzzle which has tormented the minds of men in all
ages whenever they have thought of God, and of whether God meant them
well, or meant them ill.

For all men have been tempted. We are tempted at times to say,—The
fathers have eaten sour grapes, and the children's teeth are set on edge. That
is, we are punished not for what we have done wrong, but for what our fathers did wrong. One man says,—My forefathers squandered their money,
and I am punished by being poor. Or, my forefathers ruined their constitu-
tions, and, therefore, I am weakly and sickly. My forefathers were ignorant
and reckless, and, therefore, I was brought up ignorant, and in all sorts of
temptation. And so men complain of their ill-luck and bad chance, as they
call it, till they complain of God, and say, as the Jews said in Ezekiel's time,
God's ways are unequal—partial—unfair. He is a respecter of persons. He
has not the same rule for all men. He starts men unequally in the race of
life—some heavily weighted with their father's sins and misfortunes, some
helped in every way by their father's virtue and good fortune—and then He
expects them all to run alike. God is not just and equal. And then some go
on,—men who think themselves philosophers, but are none—to say things
concerning God of which I shall say nothing here, lest I put into your minds
foolish thoughts, which had best be kept out of them.

But, some of you may say, Is it not so after all? Is it not true? Is not
God harder on some than on others? Does not God punish men every day
for their father's sins? Does He not say in the Second Commandment that
He will do so, and visit the sins of the fathers upon the children to the third
and fourth generation; and how can you make that agree with what Ezekiel
says,—"The son shall not bear the iniquity of the father." My dear friends,
I know that this is a puzzle, and always has been one. Like the old puzzle
of God's foreknowledge and our free will, which seem to contradict each
other. Like the puzzle that we must help ourselves, and yet that God must
help us, which seem to contradict each other. So with this. I believe of it, as

of the two others I just mentioned, that there is no real contradiction between the two cases; and that some-when, somehow, somewhere, in the world to come, we shall see them clearly reconciled; and justify God in all His dealings, and glorify Him in all His ways. But surely already, here, now, we may see our way somewhat into the depths of this mystery. For Christ has come to give us light, and in His light we may see light, even into this dark matter.

For see: God visits the sins of the fathers upon the children unto the third and fourth generation—but of whom?—of them that hate Him. Now, by those who hate God is meant, those who break His commandments, and are bad men. If so, then, I say that God is not only just but merciful, in visiting the sins of the fathers on the children.

For, consider two cases. Suppose these bad men, from father to son, and from son to grandson, go on in the same evil ways, and are incorrigible. Then is not God merciful to the world in punishing them, even in destroying them out of the world, where they only do harm? The world does not want fools, it wants wise men. The world does not want bad men, it wants good men; and we ought to thank God, if, by His eternal laws, He gets rid of bad men for us; and, as the saying is, civilizes them off the face of the earth in the third or fourth generation. And God does so. If a family, or a class, or a whole nation becomes incorrigibly profligate, foolish, base, in three or four generations they will either die out or vanish. They will sink to the bottom of society, and become miserably poor, weak, and of no influence, and so unable to do harm to any but themselves. Whole families will sink thus, I have seen it; you may have seen it. Whole nations will sink thus; as the Jews sank in Ezekiel's time, and again in our Lord's time; and be conquered, trampled on, counted for nothing, because they were worth nothing.

But now suppose, again, that the children, when their father's sins are visited on them, are not incorrigible. Suppose they are like the wise son of whom Ezekiel speaks, in the 14th verse, who seeth all his father's sins, and considereth, and doeth not such like—then has not God been merciful and kind to him in visiting his father's sins on him? He has. God is justified therein. His eternal laws of natural retribution, severe as they are, have worked in love and in mercy, if they have taught the young man the ruinousness, the deadliness of sin. Have the father's sins made the son poor? Then he learns not to make his children poor by his sin. Have his father's sins made him unhealthy? Then he learns not to injure his children's health. Have his father's sins kept him ignorant, or in anywise hindered his rise in life? Then he learns the value of a good education, and, perhaps, stints himself to give his children advantages which he had not himself—and, as sure as he does so, the family begins to rise again after its fall. This is no fancy, it is fact. You may see it. I have seen it, thank God. How some of the purest and noblest women, some of the ablest and most right-minded men, will spring from families, will be reared in households, where everything was against them—where there was everything to make them profligate, false, reckless, in a word—bad—except the grace of God, which was trying to make them good, and succeeded in making them good; and how, though they have felt the punishment of their parents' sins upon them in many ways during their whole life, yet that has been to them not a mere punishment, but a chastisement, a purifying medicine, a cross to be borne, which only stirred them up to greater watchfulness against sin, to greater earnestness in educating their children, to greater activity and energy in doing right, and giving their children the advantages which they had not themselves. And so were fulfilled in them two laws of God. The one which Ezekiel lays down—that the bad man's son who executes God's judgments and walks in God's statutes shall not die for the iniquity of his father, but surely live; and the other law which Moses lays down—that God shews mercy unto thousands of generations, as I believe it means—that is, to son after father, and son after father again, without end—as long as they love Him and keep His commandments.

I do not, therefore, see that there is any real contradiction between what Moses says in the second commandment and what Ezekiel says in this chapter. They are but two different sides of the same truth; and Moses is shewing the Jews one side, because they needed most to be taught that in his time, and Ezekiel showing them the other, because that was the teaching which they needed most then. For they were fancying themselves, in their calamities, the victims of some blind and cruel fate, and had forgotten that, when God said that He visited the sins of the fathers on the children, He qualified it by saying, "of them that hate Me."

Therefore, be hopeful about yourselves, and hopeful about your children after you. If any one here feels—I am fallen very low in the world—here all has been so much against me—my parents were the ruin of me—Let him remember this one word of Ezekiel. "Have I any pleasure at all that the wicked should die? saith the Lord God: and not that he should return from his ways, and live?" Let him turn from his father's evil ways, and do that which is lawful and right, and then he can say with the Prophet, in answer to all the strokes of fortune and the miseries of circumstance, "Rejoice not against me, O mine enemy: when I fall I shall arise." Provided he will remember that God requires of all men something, which is, to be as good as they can be; then he may remember also that our Lord Himself says, "Unto whomsoever much is given, of him shall much be required;" implying that to whom little is given, of him will little be required. God's ways are not unequal. He has one equal, fair, and just rule for every human being; and that is perfect understanding, perfect sympathy, perfect good will, and therefore perfect justice and perfect love.

And if any one of you answers in his heart—these are good words, and all very well: but they come too late. I am too far gone. I ate the sour grapes in my youth, and my teeth must be on edge for ever and ever. I have been a bad man, or I have been a foolish woman too many years to mend now. I am down, and down I must be. I have made my bed, and I must lie on it, and die on it too. Oh my dear brother or sister in Christ, whoever you are who says that, unsay it again for it is not true. Ezekiel tells you that it is not true, and one greater than Ezekiel, Jesus Christ, your Saviour, your Lord, your God, tells you it is not true.

For what happens, by God's eternal and unchangeable laws of retribution, to a whole nation, or a whole family, may happen to you—to each individual man. They fall by sin; they rise again by repentance and amendment. They may rise punished by their sins, and punished for a long time, heavily weighted by the consequences of their own folly, and heavily weighted for a long time. But they rise—they enter into their new life weak and wounded, from their own fault. But they enter in. And from that day things begin to mend—the weather begins to clear, the soil begins to yield again—punishment gradually ceases when it has done its work, the weight lightens, the wounds heal, the weakness strengthens, and by God's grace within them, and by God's providence outside them, they are made men of again, and saved. So you will surely find it in the experience of life.

No doubt in general, in most cases,

The child is father of the man

for good and evil. A pious and virtuous youth helps, by sure laws of God, towards a pious and virtuous old age. And on the other hand, an ungodly and profligate youth leads, by the same laws, toward an ungodly and profligate old age. That is the law. But there is another law which may stop that law—just as the stone falls to the ground by the natural law of weight, and yet you may stop that law by using the law of bodily strength, and holding it up in your hand. And what is the gracious law which will save you from the terrible law which will make you go on from worse to worse?

It is this,—"when the wicked man turneth away from his wickedness that he hath committed, and doeth that which is lawful and right, he shall save his soul alive." It is not said that his soul shall come in a moment to perfect health and strength. No. There are old bad habits to be got rid of, old ties to be broken, old debts (often worse debts than any money debts) to be paid. But he shall save his soul alive. His soul shall not die of its disease. It shall be saved. It shall come to life, and gradually mend and be cured, and grow from strength to strength, as a sick man mends day by day after a deadly illness, slowly it may be, but surely:—for how can you fail of being cured if your physician is none other than Jesus Christ your Lord and your God?

Oh, recollect that last word. If you will but recollect that, you will never despair. How dare any man say—Bad I am, and bad I must remain—while the God who made heaven and earth offers to make you good? Who dare say,—I cannot amend—when God Himself offers to amend you? Who dare say,—I have no strength to amend—when God offers to give you strength, strength of His strength, and life of His life, even His Holy Spirit? Who dare say,—God has given me up; He has a grudge against me which He will not lay by, an anger against me which cannot be appeased, a score against me which will never be wiped out of His book? Oh foolish and faint-hearted soul. Look, look at Christ hanging on His cross, and see there what God's grudge, God's anger, God's score of your sins is like. Like love unspeakable, and nothing else. To wash out your sins, He spared not His only begotten Son, but freely gave Him for you, to shew you that God, so far from hating you, has loved you; that so far from being your enemy, He was your father; that so far from willing the death of a sinner, He willed that you and every sinner should turn from his wickedness and live. For that, Jesus the only begotten Son of God, came down and preached, and sorrowed, and suffered, and died upon the cross. He died that you may live; He suffered that you may be saved; He paid the debt, because you could never pay it; He bore your sins upon the cross, that you might not have to bear them for ever and for ever in eternal death. Now, even if you suffer somewhat in this life for your sins, that suffering is not punishment, but wholesome chastisement, as when a father chastens the son in whom he delighteth. All He asks of you is to long and try to give up your sins, for He will help you to give them up. All He asks of you is to long and try to lead a new life, for He will give you power to lead a new life. Oh, say not—I cannot—when Christ who died for you says you can. Say not—I dare not—when Christ bids you dare come boldly to His throne of grace. Say not—I must be as I am—when Christ died that you should not be as you are. Say not—there is no hope—when Christ died and rose again, and reigns for ever, to give hope to you and all mankind, that when the wicked man turns away from his wickedness that he has committed, and doeth that which is lawful and right, he shall save his soul alive, and all his transgressions shall not be mentioned unto him, but in his righteousness that he hath done shall he live.

SERMON XXVII

AGREE WITH THINE ADVERSARY

Eversley, 1861. Windsor Castle, 1867.

St. Matthew v. 25, 26. "Agree with thine adversary quickly, whiles thou art in the way with him; lest at any time the adversary deliver thee to the judge, and the judge deliver thee to the officer, and thou be cast into prison. Verily I say unto thee, Thou shalt by no means come out thence, till thou hast paid the uttermost farthing."

This parable our Lord seems to have spoken at least twice, as He did several others. For we find it also in the 12th chapter of St. Luke. But it is there part of quite a different discourse. I think that by seeing what it means there, we shall see more clearly what it means here.

Our Lord there is speaking of the sins of the whole Jewish nation. Here He is speaking rather of each man's private sins. But He applies the same parable to both. He gives the same warning to both. Not to go too far on the wrong road, lest they come to a point where they cannot turn back, but must go on to just punishment, if not to utter destruction.

That is what He warned the Jews all through the latter part of the 12th chapter of Luke. He will come again, He says, at an hour they do not think of, and then if their elders, the Scribes and Pharisees, are going on as they are now, beating the man-servants and maid-servants, and eating and drinking with the drunken, oppressing the people, and living in luxury and profligacy, He will cut them asunder, and appoint them their portion with the unbelievers.

In this, and in many other parables, He had been warning them that their ruin was near; and, at last, turning to the whole crowd, He appeals to them, to their common sense. "When ye see a cloud rise out of the west, straightway ye say, There cometh a shower; and so it is. And when ye see the south wind blow, ye say, There will be heat; and it cometh to pass. Ye hypocrites, ye can discern the face of the sky and of the earth; but how is it that ye do not discern this time?" If God can give you common sense about one thing, why not about another? Why can you not open your eyes and of yourselves judge what is right? "Agree with thine adversary quickly, whiles thou art in the way with him; lest at any time the adversary deliver thee to the judge, and the judge deliver thee to the officer, and thou be cast into prison. Verily I say unto thee, Thou shalt by no means come out thence, till thou hast paid the uttermost farthing."

So He spoke; and they did not fully understand what He meant. They thought that by their adversary He meant the Roman governor. For they immediately began to talk to Him about some Galileans whose blood Pilate, the Roman governor, had mingled with their sacrifices (I suppose in some of those wars which were continually breaking out in Judea). I think He meant more than that. "Suppose ye that these Galilæans were sinners above all the Galilæans? Except ye repent, ye shall all likewise perish." As much as to say, though ye did not rebel against the Romans like these Galilæans, you have your sins, which will ruin you. As long as you are hypocrites, with your mouths full of the cant of religion, and your hearts full of all mean and spiteful passions; as long as you cannot of yourselves discern what is right, and have lost conscience, and the everlasting distinction between right and wrong, so long are you walking blindfold to ruin. There is an adversary against you, who will surely deliver you to the judge some day, and then it will be too late to cry for mercy. And who was that adversary? Who but the everlasting law of God, which says, Thou shalt do justly?—and you Jews are utterly unjust, false, covetous, and unrighteous. Thou shalt love all men; and you are cruel and spiteful, hating each other, and making all mankind hate you. Thou shalt walk humbly with thy God; and you Jews are walking proudly with God; fancying that God belongs only to you; that because you are His chosen people, He will let you commit every sin you choose, as long as you keep His name on your lips, and keep up an empty worship of Him in the temple. That is your adversary, the everlasting moral law of God. And who is the Judge but God Himself, who is set on His throne judging right, while you are doing wrong? And who is the officer, to whom that judge will deliver you? There indeed the Jews were right. It was the Romans whom God appointed to punish them for their sins. All which our Lord had foretold, as all the world knows, came true forty years after in that horrible siege of Jerusalem, which the Jews brought on themselves entirely by their own folly, and pride, and wicked lawlessness. In that siege, by famine and pestilence, by the Romans' swords, by crucifixion, and by each other's hands (for the different factions were murdering each other wholesale up to the very day Jerusalem was taken), thousands of Jews perished horribly, and the rest were sold as slaves over the face of the whole earth, and led away into a captivity from which they could not escape till they had paid the uttermost farthing.

Now let us look at this same parable in the 5th chapter of St Matthew. Remember first that it is part of the sermon on the Mount, which is all about not doctrine, but morality, the law of right and wrong, the law of justice and mercy. You will see then that our Lord is preaching against the same sins as in the 12th chapter of St. Luke. Against a hypocritical religion, joined with a cruel and unjust heart. Those of old time, the Scribes and Pharisees, said merely, Thou shalt not kill. And as long as thou dost not kill thy brother, thou mayest hate him in thy heart and speak evil of him with thy lips. But our Lord says, Not so. Whosoever is angry with his brother without a cause is in danger of the judgment. Whosoever shall say to him Raca, or worthless fellow, shall speak insolently, brutally, cruelly, scornfully to him, is in danger of the council. But whosoever shall say unto him, Thou fool, is in danger of hell fire. For using that word to the Jews, so says the Talmudic tradition, Moses and Aaron were shut out of the land of promise, for it means an infidel, an atheist, a godless man, or rebel against God, as it is written, "The fool hath said in his heart there is no God." Whosoever shall curse his brother, who is trying to be a good Christian man to the best of his light and power, because he does not happen to agree with him in all things, and call him a heretic, and an infidel, and an atheist, and an enemy of God—he is in danger of hell fire. Let him agree with his adversary quickly, whiles he is in the way with him, lest he be delivered to God the judge, and to the just punishment of him who has not done justly, not loved mercy, not walked humbly with his God.

But who is the adversary of that man, and who is the judge, and who is the officer? Our adversary in every case, whenever we do wrong, knowingly or unknowingly, is the Law of God, the everlasting laws, by which God has ordered every thing in heaven and earth; and as often as we break one of these laws, let us agree with it again as quickly as we can, lest it hale us before God, the judge of all, and He deliver us over to His officer—to those powers of nature and powers of spirit, which He has appointed as ministers of His vengeance, and they cast us into some prison of necessary and unavoidable misery, from which we shall never escape till we have paid the uttermost farthing.

Do you not understand me? Then I will give you an example. Suppose the case of a man hurting his health by self-indulgence of any kind. Then his adversaries are the laws of health. Let him agree with them quickly, while he has the power of conquering his bad habits, by recovering his health, lest the time come when his own sins deliver him up to God his judge; and God to His terrible officers of punishment, the laws of Disease; and they cast him into a prison of shame and misery from which there is no escape—shame and misery, most common perhaps among the lower classes: but not altogether confined to them—the weakened body, the bleared eye, the stupified brain, the premature death, the children unhealthy from their parents' sins, despising their parents, and perhaps copying their vices at the same time. Many a man have I seen in that prison, fast bound with misery though not with iron, and how he was to pay his debt and escape out of it I know not, though I hope that God does know.

Are any of you, again, in the habit of cheating your neighbours, or dealing unfairly by them? Your adversary is the everlasting law of justice, which says, Do as you would be done by, for with what measure you mete to others, it shall be measured to you again.

This may show you how a bodily sin, like self-indulgence punishes itself by bringing a man into bondage of bodily misery, from which he cannot escape; and in the same way a spiritual sin, like want of charity, will bring a man into spiritual bondage from which he cannot escape. And this, as in bodily sins, it will do by virtue of that mysterious and terrible officer of God, which we call Habit. Habit, by which, we cannot tell how, our having done a thing once becomes a reason for our doing it again, and again after that, till, if the habit be once formed, we cannot help doing that thing, and become enslaved to it, and fast bound by it, in a prison from which there is no escape.

Look for instance at the case of the untruthful man. Let him beware in time. Who is his adversary? Facts are his adversary. He says one thing, and Fact says another, and a very stubborn and terrible adversary Fact is. The day will come, most probably in this life, when Facts will bring that untruthful man before God and before men likewise—and cry,—Judge between us which of us is right; and there will come to that false man exposure and shame, and a worse punishment still, perhaps, if he have let the habit grow too strong on him, and have not agreed with his adversary in time.

For have you not seen (alas, you have too surely seen) men who had contracted such a habit of falsehood that they could not shake it off—who had played with their sense of truth so long that they had almost forgotten what truth meant; men who could not speak without mystery, concealment, prevarication, half-statements; who were afraid of the plain truth, not because there was any present prospect of its hurting them, but simply because it was the plain truth—children of darkness, who, from long habit, hated the light—and who, though they had been found out and exposed, could not amend—could not become simple, honest, and truthful—could not escape from the prison of their own bad habits, and the net of lies which they had spread round their own path, till they had paid the uttermost penalty for their deceit?

Look, again, at the case of the uncharitable man, in the habit of forming harsh and cruel judgments of his neighbours. Then his adversary is the everlasting law of Love, which will surely at last punish him, by the most terrible of all punishments—loss of love to man, and therefore to God. Are we not (I am, I know, may God forgive me for it) apt to be angry with our brethren without a cause, out of mere peevishness? Let us beware in time. Are we not apt to say to them "Raca"—to speak cruelly, contemptuously, fiercely of them, if they thwart us? Let us beware in time still more. Are we not worst of all, tempted (as I too often am) to say to them "Thou fool;" to call better men, more useful men more pure men, more pious men than ourselves, hard and cruel names, names from which they would shrink with horror because they cannot see Christian truth in just exactly the same light that we do? Oh! let us beware then. Beware lest the everlasting laws of justice and fairness between man and man, of love and charity between man and man, which we have broken, should some day deliver us up, as they delivered those bigoted Jews of old to God our Judge, and He deliver our souls to His most terrible officers, who are called envy, hatred, malice, and all uncharitableness; and they thrust us into that blackest of all prisons, on the gate of which is written, Hardness of heart, and Contempt of God's Word and commandments, and within which is the outer darkness into which if a man falls, he cannot see the difference between right and wrong: but calls evil good, and good evil, like his companions in the outer darkness—namely, the devil and his angels. Oh! let us who are coming to lay our gift upon God's altar at this approaching Christmas tide, consider whether our brother hath aught against us in any of these matters, and, if so, let us leave our gift upon the altar, and be first reconciled to our brother, in heart at least, and with inward shame, and confession, and contrition, and resolution to amend. But we can only do that by recollecting what gift we are to leave on Christ's altar,—that it is the gift of self, the sacrifice of ourselves, with all our selfishness, pride, conceit, spite, cruelty. Ourselves, with all our sins, we are to lay upon Christ's altar, that our sins may be nailed to His cross, and washed clean in His blood, everlastingly consumed in the fire of His Spirit, the pure spirit of love, which is the Charity of God, that so, self being purged out of us, we may become holy and lively sacrifices to God, parts and parcels of that perfect sacrifice which Christ offered up for the sins of the whole world—even the sacrifice of Himself.

SERMON XXVIII

ST JOHN THE BAPTIST

Chester Cathedral. 1872.

St Luke iii. 2, 3, 7, 9-14. "The Word of God came unto John the son of Zacharias in the wilderness. And he came into all the country about Jordan, preaching the baptism of repentance for the remission of sins. . . . . Then said he to the multitude that came forth to be baptized of him, O generation of vipers, who hath warned you to flee from the wrath to come? Bring forth therefore fruits worthy of repentance. . . . And now also the axe is laid unto the root of the trees: every tree therefore that bringeth not forth good fruit is hewn down and cast into the fire. And the people asked him saying, What shall we do then? He answereth and saith unto them, He that hath two coats, let him impart to him that hath none; and he that hath meat, let him do likewise. Then came also publicans to be baptized unto them, and said unto him, Master, what shall we do? And he said, Exact no more than that which is appointed you. And the soldiers likewise demanded of him, saying, And what shall we do? And he said unto them, Do violence to no man, neither accuse any falsely, and be content with your wages."

This is St John Baptist's day. Let me say a very few words—where many might be said—about one of the noblest personages who ever has appeared on this earth.

Our blessed Lord said, "Among them that are born of women there hath not risen a greater than John the Baptist, notwithstanding, he that is least in the kingdom of heaven is greater than he." These are serious words; for which of us dare to say that we are greater than John the Baptist?

But let us at least think a while what John the Baptist was like. So we shall gain at least the sight of an ideal man. It is not the highest ideal. Our Lord tells us that plainly; and we, as Christians, should know that it is not. The ideal man is our Lord Christ Himself, and none other. Still, he that has not mounted the lower step of the heavenly stair, has certainly not mounted the higher; and therefore, if we have not attained to the likeness of John the Baptist, still more, we have not attained to the likeness of Christ. What, then, was John the Baptist like? What picture of him and his character can we form to ourselves in our own imaginations? for that is all we have to picture him by—helped—always remember that—by the Holy Spirit of God, who helps the imagination, the poetic and dramatic faculty of men; just as much as He helps the logical and argumentative faculty to see things and men as they really are, by the spirit of love, which also is the spirit of true understanding.

How, then, shall we picture John the Baptist to ourselves? Great painters, greater than the world seems likely to see again, have exercised their fancy upon his face, his figure, his actions. We must put out of our minds, I fear, at once, many of the loveliest of them all: those in which Raffaelle and others have depicted the child John, in his camel's hair raiment, with a child's cross in his hand, worshipping the infant Christ. There is also one exquisite picture, by Annibale Caracci, if I recollect rightly, in which the blessed babe is lying asleep, and the blessed Virgin signs to St John, pressing forward to adore him, not to awaken his sleeping Lord and God. But such imaginations, beautiful as they are, and true in a heavenly and spiritual sense, which therefore is true eternally for you, and me, and all mankind, are not historic fact. For St John the Baptist said himself, "and I knew him not."

He may have been, we must almost say, he must have been, brought up with or near our Lord. He may have seen in Him such a child (we must believe that), as he never saw before. He knew Him at least to be a princely child, of David's royal line. But he was not conscious of who and what He was, till the mysterious inner voice, of whom he gives only the darkest hints, said to him, "Upon whom thou shalt see the Spirit descending, and remaining on Him, the same is He which baptizeth with the Holy Ghost. And I saw and bare record that this is the Son of God." But what manner of man was St John the Baptist in the meantime? Painters have tried their hands at drawing him, and we thank them. Pictures, says St Augustine, are the books of the unlearned. And, my friends, when great painters paint, they are the books of the too-learned likewise. They bring us back, bring us home, by one glance at a human face, a human figure, a human scene of action, out of our philosophies, and criticisms, and doctrines, which narrow our hearts, without widening our heads, to the deeper facts of humanity, and therefore to the deeper facts of theology likewise. But what picture of St John the Baptist shall we choose whereby to represent him to ourselves, as the forerunner of the incarnate God?

The best which I can recollect is the great picture by Guido—ah, that he had painted always as wisely and as well—of the magnificent lad sitting on the rock, half clad in his camel's hair robe, his stalwart hand lifted up to denounce he hardly knows what, save that things are going all wrong, utterly wrong to him; his beautiful mouth open to preach, he hardly knows what, save that he has a message from God, of which he is half-conscious as yet—that he is a forerunner, a prophet, a foreteller of something and some one which is to come, and which yet is very near at hand. The wild rocks are round him, the clear sky is over him, and nothing more. He, the gentleman born, the clergyman born—for you must recollect who and what St John the Baptist was, and that he was neither democrat nor vulgar demagogue, nor flatterer of ignorant mobs, but a man of an ancestry as ancient and illustrious as it was civilised, and bound by long ties of duty, of patriotism, of religion, and of the temple worship of God:—he, the noble and the priest, has thrown off—not in discontent and desperation, but in hope and awe—all his family privileges, all that seems to make life worth having; and there aloft and in the mountains, alone with nature and with God, feeding on locusts and wild honey and whatsoever God shall send, and clothed in skins, he, like Elijah of old, renews not merely the habits, but the spirit and power of Elijah, and preaches to a generation sunk in covetousness and superstition, party spirit, and the rest of the seven devils which brought on the fall of his native land, and which will bring on the fall of every land on earth, preaches to them, I say—What?

The most common, let me say boldly, the most vulgar—in the good old sense of the word—the most vulgar morality. He tells them that an awful ruin was coming unless they repented and mended. How fearfully true his words were, the next fifty years proved. The axe, he said, was laid to the root of the tree; and the axe was the heathen Roman, even then master of the land. But God, not the Roman Cæsar merely, was laying the axe. And He was a good God, who only wanted goodness, which He would preserve; not badness, which He would destroy. Therefore men must not merely repent and do penance, they must bring forth fruits meet for penance; do right instead of doing wrong, lest they be found barren trees, and be cut down, and cast into that everlasting fire of God, which, thanks be to His Holy name, burns for ever—unquenchable by all men's politics, and systems, and political or other economies, to destroy out of God's Kingdom all that offendeth and whatsoever loveth and maketh a lie—oppressors, quacks, cheats, hypocrites, and the rest.

The people—the farming class—came to him with "What shall we do?" The young priest and nobleman, in his garment of camel's hair, has nothing but plain morality for them. "He that hath two coats, let him impart to him that hath none; and he that hath meat, let him do likewise." The publicans, the renegades, who were farming the taxes of the Roman conquerors, and making their base profit out of their countrymen's slavery, came to him,— "Master, what shall we do?" He does not tell them not to be publicans. He does not tell his countrymen to rebel, though he must have been sorely tempted to do it. All he says is, Make the bad and base arrangement as good as you can; exact no more than that which is appointed you. The soldiers, poor fellows, come to him. Whether they were Herod's mercenaries, or real gallant Roman soldiers, we are not told. Either had unlimited power under a military despotism, in an anarchic and half-enslaved country; but whichever they were, he has the same answer to them of common morality. You are what you are; you are where you are. Do it as well as you can. Do no violence to any man, neither accuse any man falsely, and be content with your wages.

Ah, wise politician, ah, clear and rational spirit, who knows and tells others to do the duty which lies nearest them; who sees (as old Greek Hesiod says), how much bigger the half is than the whole; who, in the hour of his country's deepest degradation, had divine courage to say, our deliverance lies, not in rebellion, but in doing right. But he has sterner words. Pharisees, the separatists, the religious men, who think themselves holier than any one else; and Sadducees, materialist men of the world, who sneer at the unseen, the unknown, the heroic, come to him. And for Pharisee and Sadducee—for the man who prides himself on believing more than his neighbours, and for the man who prides himself on believing less—he has the same answer. Both are exclusives, inhuman, while they are pretending to be more than human. He knew them well, for he was born and bred among them, and he forestalls our Lord's words to them, "O generation of vipers, who hath warned you to flee from the wrath to come?"

At last his preaching of common morality is put to the highest test. The king—the tyrant as we should call him—the Herod of the day, an usurper, neither a son of David, nor a king chosen by the people, tries to patronize him. The old spirit of his forefather Aaron, of his forefather Phineas, the spirit of Levi, which (rightly understood), is the Spirit of God, flashes up in the young priestly prophet, in the old form of common morality. "It is not lawful for thee to have thy brother's wife." We know the rest; how, at the request of Herodias' daughter, Herod sent and beheaded John in prison, and how she took his head in a charger and brought it to her mother. Great painters have shown us again and again the last act—outwardly hideous, but really beautiful—of St John's heroic drama, in a picture of the lovely dancing girl with the prophet's head in a charger—a dreadful picture; and yet one which needed to be painted, for it was a terrible fact, and is still, and will be till this wicked world's end, a matter for pity and tears rather than for indignation. The most perfect representations, certainly the most tragical I know of it, are those which are remarkable, not for their expression, but for their want of expression—the young girl in brocade and jewels, with the gory head in her hands, thinking of nothing out of those wide vacant foolish eyes, save the triumph of self-satisfied vanity; for the spite and re-venge is not in her, but in her wicked mother. She is just the very creature, who, if she had been better trained, and taught what John the Baptist really was, might have reverenced him, worshipped him, and ministered unto him. Alas! alas! how do the follies of poor humanity repeat themselves in every age. The butterfly has killed the lion, without after all meaning much harm. Ah, that such human butterflies would take warning by the fate of Herodias' daughter, and see how mere vanity will lead, if indulged too long and too freely, to awful crime.

One knows the old stories,—how Herod, and Herodias, and the vain foolish girl fell into disgrace with the Emperor, and were banished into Provence, and died in want and misery. One knows too the old legends, how Herodias' daughter reappears in South Europe—even in old German legends—as the witch-goddess, fair and ruinous, sweeping for ever through wood and wold at night with her troop of fiends, tempting the traveller to dance with them till he dies; a name for ever accursed through its own van-ity rather than its own deliberate sin, from which may God preserve us all, men as well as women. So two women, one wicked and one vain, did all they could to destroy one of the noblest human beings who ever walked this earth. And what did they do? They did not prevent his being the forerunner and prophet of the incarnate Son of God. They did not prevent his being the master and teacher of the blessed Apostle St John, who was his spiritual son and heir. They did not prevent his teaching all men and women, to whom God gives grace to understand him, that the true repentance, the true conversion, the true deliverance from the wrath to come, the true entrance into the kingdom of heaven, the true way to Christ and to God, is common morality.

And now let us bless God's holy name for all His servants departed in His faith and fear, and especially for His servant St John the Baptist, beseeching Him to give us grace, so to follow his doctrine and holy life, that we may truly repent after his preaching and after his example. May the Lord forgive our exceeding cowardice, and help us constantly to speak the truth, boldly rebuke vice, and patiently suffer for the truth's sake; through Jesus Christ our Lord. Amen.

SERMON XXIX

THE PRESENT RECOMPENSE

Chester Cathedral, Nave Service, Evening. May 1872.

Proverbs xi. 31. "Behold, the righteous shall be recompensed in the earth: much more the wicked and the sinner."

This is the key-note of the Book of Proverbs—that men are punished or rewarded according to their deeds in this life; nay, it is the key-note of the whole Old Testament. "The eyes of the Lord are over the righteous, and His ears are open unto their prayers; the countenance of the Lord is against them that do evil, to root out the remembrance of them from the earth."

But here, at the beginning of my sermon, I can fancy some one ready to cry—Stay! you have spoken too strongly. That is not the key-note of the whole Old Testament. There are words in it of quite a different note—words which complain to God that the good are not rewarded, and the wicked are not punished: as for instance, when the Psalmist says how the ungodly men of this evil world are filled with God's hid treasure, and how they have children at their desire, and leave the rest of their substance for their babes. And again, "I was envious at the foolish, when I saw the prosperity of the wicked. For there are no bands in their death; but their strength is firm. They are not in trouble as other men; neither are they plagued like other men. . . . They set their mouth against the heavens, and their tongue walketh through the earth. Therefore his people return hither; and waters of a full cup are wrung out to them. And they say, How doth God know? and is there knowledge in the most High?" And though the Psalmist says that such persons will come to a sudden and fearful end, yet he confesses that so long as they live they have prospered, while he had been punished all day long, and chastened every morning. And do we not know that so it is? Is it not obvious now, and has it not been notorious in every country, and in all times, that so it is? Do not good men often lead lives of poverty and affliction? Do not men make large fortunes, or rise to fame and power, by base and wicked means? and do not those same men often enough die in their beds, and leave children behind them, and found families, who prosper for generations after they are dead? How were they recompensed in the earth? Now this is one of the puzzles of life, which tries a man's faith in God, as it tried the psalmists and prophets in old time. But that the text speaks truth I do not doubt. I believe that the prosperous bad man is recompensed in the earth—is punished in this life—often with the most terrible of all punishments—Impunity; the not being punished at all; which is the worst thing in this life which can happen to a sinner. But I am not going to speak of that, but rather of the first part of the text, "The righteous shall be recompensed in the earth."

Now is not the answer to the puzzle this: That God is impartial; that He is no respecter of persons, but causing His sun to shine on the evil and on the good, and His rain to fall on the just and on the unjust; and so rewarding every man according to his work, paying him for all work done, of whatever kind it may be? Some work for this world, which we do see, and God gives them what they earn in this life; some work for the world above, which we cannot see, and God gives them what they earn in this life, for ever and ever likewise. If a man wishes for treasure on earth, he can have it if he will, and enjoy it as long as it lasts. If a man wishes for treasure in heaven, he can have it if he will, and enjoy it as long as it lasts. God deals fairly with both, and pays both what they have earned.

Some set their hearts on this world; some want money, some want power, some want fame and admiration from their fellow-men, some want merely to amuse themselves. Then they will have what they want if they will take the right way to get it. If a man wishes to make a large fortune, and die rich, he will very probably succeed, if he will only follow diligently the laws and rules by which God has appointed that money should be made. If a man longs for power and glory, and must needs be admired and obeyed by his fellow-men, he can have his wish, if he will go the right way to get what he longs for; especially in a free country like this, he will get most probably just as much of them as he deserves—that is, as much as he has talent and knowledge enough to earn. So did the Pharisees in our Lord's time. They wanted power, fame, and money as religious leaders, and they knew how to get them as well as any men who ever lived; and they got them. Our Lord did not deny that. They had their reward, He said. They succeeded—those old Pharisees—in being looked up to as the masters of the Jewish mob, and in crucifying our Lord Himself. They had their reward; and so may you and I. If we want any earthly thing, and have knowledge of the way to get it, and have ability and perseverance enough, then we shall very probably get it, and much good it will do us when we have got it after all. We shall have had our treasure upon earth and our hearts likewise; and when we come to die we shall leave both our treasure and our hearts behind us, and the Lord have mercy on our souls.

But again, there are those, thank God, who have, or are at least trying to get, treasure in heaven, which they may carry away with them when they die, and keep for ever. And who are they? Those who are longing and trying to be true and to be good; who have seen how beautiful it is to be true and to be good; to know God and the will of God; to love God and the will of God; and therefore to copy His likeness and to do His will. Those who long for sanctification, and who desire to be holy, even as their Father in heaven is holy, and perfect, even as their Father in heaven is perfect; and who therefore think, as St Paul bade them, of whatsoever things are just, true, pure, lovely, and of good report, if there be any true manhood, and if there be any just praise—in three words—who seek after whatsoever is true, beautiful, and good. These are they that have treasure in heaven. For what is really true, really beautiful, really good, is also really heavenly. God alone is perfect, good, beautiful, and true; and heaven is heaven because it is filled with the glory of His goodness, His beauty, and His truth. But wherever there is a soul on earth led by the Spirit of God, and filled by the Spirit of God with good and beautiful and true graces and inspirations, there is a soul which, as St Paul says, is sitting in heavenly places with Christ Jesus—a soul which is already in heaven though still on earth. We confess it by our own words. We speak of a heavenly character; we speak even of a heavenly countenance; and we speak right. We see that that character, though it be still imperfect, and marred by human weaknesses, is already good with the goodness which comes down from heaven; and that that countenance, though it may be mean and plain, is already beautiful with the beauty which comes down from heaven.

But how are such souls recompensed in the earth? Oh! my friends, is not a man recompensed in the earth whenever he can lift up his heart above the earth?—whenever he can lift up his heart unto the Lord, and behold His glory above all the earth? Does not this earth look brighter to him then? The world of man looks brighter to him, in spite of all its sins and sorrows, for he sees the Lord ruling it, the Lord forgiving it, the Lord saving it. He sees, by the eye of faith, the Lord fulfilling His own promise—"where two or three are gathered together in my name, there am I in the midst of them"; and he takes heart and hope for the poor earth, and says, The earth is not deserted; mankind is not without a Father, a Saviour, a Teacher, a King. Bad men and bad spirits are not the masters of the world; and men are not as creeping things, as the fishes of the sea, which have no ruler over them. For Christ has not left His church. He reigns, and will reign, till He has put all enemies under His feet, and cast out of His kingdom all that offend, and whatsoever loveth and maketh a lie; and then the heavenly treasure will be the only treasure; for whatsoever things are just, whatsoever things are true, pure, lovely, and of good report, if there be any valour, and if there be any praise, those things, and they alone, will be left in the kingdom of Christ and of God. Is not that man recompensed in the earth? Must he not rise each morning to go about his daily work with a more cheerful heart, saying, with Jeremiah, in like case, "Upon this I awaked, and beheld, and my sleep was sweet to me?"

Yes, I see in experience that the righteous man is recompensed in the earth, every day, and all day long. In proportion as a man's mind is heavenly, just so much will he enjoy this beautiful earth, and all that is therein. I believe that if a man walks with God, then he can walk nowhither without seeing and hearing what the ungodly and bad man will never see and hear, because his eyes are blinded, and his heart hardened from thinking of himself, his own selfish wants, his own selfish sins. Which, for instance, was the happier man—which the man who was the more recompensed in the earth this very day—the poor man who went for his Sunday walk into the country, thinking of little but the sins and the follies of the week past, and probably of the sins and the follies of the week to come; or the man who went with a clear conscience, and had the heart to thank God for the green grass, and the shining river, and the misty mountains sleeping far away, and notice the song of the birds, and the scent of the flowers, as a little child might do, and know that his Father in heaven had made all these?

Yes, my friends, Christ is very near us, though our eyes are holden by our own sins, and therefore we see Him not. But just in proportion as a man walks with God, just in proportion as the eyes of his soul are opened by the Spirit of God, he recovers, I believe, the privilege which Adam lost when he fell. He hears the Word of the Lord walking among the trees of the garden in the cool of the day; and instead of trying, like guilty Adam, to hide himself from his Maker, answers, with reverence and yet with joy, Speak, Lord, for thy servant heareth.

Nay, I would go further still, and say, Is not the righteous man recompensed on the earth every time he hears a strain of noble music? To him who has his treasure in heaven, music speaks about that treasure things far too deep for words. Music speaks to him of whatsoever is just, true, pure, lovely, and of good report, of whatsoever is manful and ennobling, of whatsoever is worthy of praise and honour. Music, to that man, speaks of a divine order and a divine proportion; of a divine harmony, through all the discords and confusions of men; of a divine melody, through all the cries and groans of sin and sorrow. What says a wiser and a better man than I shall ever be, and that not of noble music, but of such as we may hear any day in any street? "Even that vulgar music," he says, "which makes one man merry, another mad, strikes in me a deep fit of devotion, and a profound contemplation of God, the first composer. There is something more of divinity in it than the ear discovers. It is an hieroglyphical and shadowed lesson of the whole world, and of the creatures of God. Such a melody to the ear as the whole world, well understood, would afford to the understanding." That man, I insist, was indeed recompensed on the earth, when music, which is to the ungodly and unrighteous the most earthly of all arts, which to the heathens and the savages, to frivolous and profligate persons, only tempts to silly excitement or to brutal passion, was to him as the speech of angels, a remembrancer to him of that eternal and ever-present heaven, from which all beauty, truth, and goodness are shed forth over the universe, from the glory of the ever-blessed Trinity—Father, Son, and Holy Spirit.

Does any one say—These things are too high for me; I cannot understand them? My dear friends, are they not too high for me likewise? Do you fancy that I understand them, though my reason, as well as Holy Scripture, tells me that they are true? I understand them no more than I understand how I draw a single breath, or think a single thought. But it is good for you, and for me, and for every man, now and then, to hear things which we do not understand; that so we may learn our own ignorance, and be lifted up above ourselves, and renounce our fancied worldly wisdom, and think within ourselves:—Would it not be wiser to confess ourselves fools, and take our Lord's advice, and be converted, and become as little children? For otherwise, our Lord says, we shall in nowise enter into this very kingdom of heaven of which I have been telling you. For this is one of the things which God hides from the wise and prudent, and yet revealeth unto babes. Yes, that is the way to understand all things, however deep—to become as little children. A little child proves that all I say is true, and that it knows that all I say is true. Though it cannot put its feelings into words, it acts on them by a mere instinct, which is the gift of God. Why does a little child pick flowers? Why does a little child dance when it hears a strain of music? And deeper still, why does a little child know when it has done wrong? Why does it love to hear of things beautiful and noble, and shrink from things foul and mean, if what I say is not true? The child does so, because it is nearer heaven, not further off, than we grown folk.

Ah! that we would all lay to heart what one said of old, who walked with God:—

> "Dear soul, could'st thou become a child,
> Once more on earth, meek, undefiled,
> Then Paradise were round thee here,
> And God Himself for ever near."

SERMON XXX

THE KINGDOM OF HEAVEN

Chapel Royal, St James'. 1873.

St. Matt. xxii. 2-7. "The kingdom of heaven is like unto a certain king, which made a marriage for his son, and sent forth his servants to call them that were bidden to the wedding: and they would not come. Again, he sent forth other servants, saying, Tell them which are bidden, Behold, I have prepared my dinner: my oxen and fatlings are killed, and all things are ready: come unto the marriage. But they made light of it, and went their ways, one to his farm, another to his merchandise: And the remnant took his servants, and entreated them spitefully, and slew them. But when the king heard thereof, he was wroth: and he sent forth his armies, and destroyed those murderers, and burned up their city."

This parable, if we understand it aright, will help to teach us theology—that is, the knowledge of God, and of the character of God. For it is a parable concerning the kingdom of heaven, and the laws and customs of the kingdom of heaven—that is, the spiritual and eternal laws by which God governs men.

Now, what any kingdom or government is like must needs depend on what the king or governor of it is like; at least if that king is all-powerful, and can do what he likes. His laws will be like his character. If he be good, he will make good laws. If he be bad, he will make bad laws. If he be harsh and cruel—if he be careless and indulgent—so will his laws be. If he be loving and generous, delighting in seeing his subjects happy, then his laws will be so shaped that his subjects will be happy, if they obey those laws. But also—and this is a very serious matter, and one to which foolish people in all ages have tried to shut their eyes, and false preachers in all ages have tried to blind men's eyes—also, I say, if his laws be good, and bountiful, and sure to make men happy, then the good king will have those laws obeyed. He will not be an indulgent king, for in his case to be indulgent will be cruelty, and nothing less. The good king will not say,—I have given you laws by which you may live happy; but I do not care whether you obey them or not. I have, as it were, set you up, in life, and given you advantages by which you may prosper if you use them; but I do not care whether you use them or not. For to say that would be as much as to say that I do not care if you make yourselves miserable, and make others miserable likewise. The good king will say,—You shall obey my laws, for they are for your good. You shall use my gifts, for they are for your good. And if you do not, I will punish you. You shall respect my authority. And if you do not—if you go too far, if you become wanton and cruel, and destroy your fellow-subjects unjustly off the face of the earth; then I will destroy you off the face of he earth, and burn up your city. I will destroy any government or system of society which you set up in opposition to my good and just laws. And if you merely despise the gifts, and refuse to use them—then I will cast you out of my kingdom, inside which is freedom and happiness, and light and knowledge, into the darkness outside, bound hand and foot, into the ignorance and brutal slavery which you have chosen, where you may reconsider yourself, weeping and gnashing your teeth as you discover what a fool you have been.

Our Lord's parable has fulfilled itself again and again in history, and will fulfil itself as long as foolish and rebellious persons exist on earth. This is one of the laws of the kingdom of heaven. It must be so, for it arises by necessity out of the character of Christ, the king of heaven.—Infinite bounty and generosity; but if that bounty be despised and insulted, or still more, if it be outraged by wanton tyranny or cruelty, then—for the benefit of the rest of mankind—awful severity. So it is, and so it must be; simply because God is good.

At least, this is the kind of king which the parable shows to us. The king in it begins, not by asking his subjects to pay him taxes, or even to do him service, but to come to a great feast—a high court ceremonial—the marriage of his son. Whatsoever else that may mean, it certainly means this—that the king intended to treat these men, not as his slaves, but as his guests and friends. They will not come. They are too busy; one over his farm, another over his merchandise. They owe, remember, safe possession of their farm, and safe transit for their merchandise, to the king, who governs and guards the land. But they forget that, and refuse his invitation. Some of them, seemingly out of mere insolence, and the spirit of rebellion against authority, just because it is authority, go a step too far. To show that they are their own masters, and intend to do what they like, they take the king's messengers, and treat them spitefully, and kill them.

Then there arises in that king a noble indignation. We do not read that the king sentimentalised over these rebels, and said,—"After all, their evil, like all evil, is only a lower form of good. They had a fine instinct of freedom and independence latent in them, only it was in this case somewhat perverted. They are really only to be pitied for knowing no better; but I trust, by careful education, to bring them to a clearer sense of their own interests. I shall therefore send them to a reformatory, where, in consideration of the depressing circumstances of their imprisonment, they will be better looked after, and have lighter work, than the average of my honest and peaceable subjects." If the king had spoken thus, he would have won high applause in these days; at least till the farms and the merchandise, the property and the profits of the rest of his subjects, were endangered by these favoured objects of his philanthropy; who, having found that rebellion and even murder was pardonable in one case, would naturally try whether it was not pardonable in other cases likewise. But what we read of the king—and we must really remember, in fear and trembling, who spoke this parable, even our Lord Himself,—is this—He sent forth his armies, soldiers, men disciplined to do their duty at all risks, and sworn to carry out the law, and destroyed those murderers, and burned up their city.

Yes, the king was very angry, as he had a right to be. Yes, let us lay that to heart, and tremble, from the very worst of us all to the very best of us all. There is an anger in God. There is indignation in God. Our highest reason ought to tell us that there must be anger in God, as long as sin and wrong exist in any corner of the universe. For all that is good in man is of the likeness of God. And is it not a good feeling, a noble feeling, in man, to be indignant, or to cry for vengeance on the offender, whenever we hear of cruelty, injustice, or violence? Is that not noble? I say it is. I say that the man whose heart does not burn within him at the sight of tyranny and cruelty, of baseness and deceit, who is not ready to say, Take him, and do to him as he has done to others; that man's heart is not right with God, or with man either. His moral sense is stunted. He is on the way to become, first, if he can, a tyrant, and then a slave.

And shall there be no noble indignation in God when He beholds all the wrong which is done on earth? Shall the just and holy God look on carelessly and satisfied at injustice and unholiness which vexes even poor sinful man? God forbid! To think that, would, to my mind, be to fancy God less just, less merciful, than man. And if any one says, Anger is a passion, a suffering from something outside oneself, and God can have no passions; God cannot be moved by the sins and follies of such paltry atoms as we human beings are: the answer is, Man's anger—even just anger—is, too often, a passion; weak-minded persons, ill-educated persons, especially when they get together in mobs, and excite each other, are carried away when they hear even a false report of cruelty or injustice, by their really wholesome indignation, and say and do foolish, and cruel, and unjust things, the victims of their own passion. But even among men, the wiser a man is, the purer, the stronger-minded, so much the more can he control his indignation, and not let it rise into passion, but punish the offender calmly, though sternly, according to law. Even so, our reason bids us believe, does God, who does all things by law. His eternal laws punish of themselves, just as they reward of themselves. The same law of God may be the messenger of His anger to the bad, while it is the messenger of His love to the good. For God has not only no passions, but no parts; and therefore His anger and His love are not different, but the same. And His love is His anger, and His anger is His love.

An awful thought and yet a blessed thought. Think of it, my friends— think of it day and night. Under God's anger, or under God's love, we must be, whether we will or not. We cannot flee from His presence. We cannot go from His spirit. If we are loving, and so rise up to heaven, God is there—in love. If we are cruel, and wrathful, and so go down to hell, God is there also—in wrath: with the clean He will be clean, with the froward man He will be froward. In God we live and move, and have our being. On us, and on us alone, it depends, what sort of a life we shall live, and whether our being shall be happy or miserable. On us, and on us alone, it depends, whether we shall live under God's anger, or live under God's love. On us, and on us alone, it depends whether the eternal and unchangeable God shall be to us a consuming fire, or light, and life, and bliss for evermore.

We never had more need to think of this than now; for there has spread over the greater part of the civilised world a strong spirit of disbelief in the living God. Men do not believe that God punishes sin and wrong-doing, either in this world or in the world to come. And it is not confined to those who are called infidels, who disbelieve in the incarnation and kingdom of our Lord Jesus Christ. Would to God it were so! Everywhere we find Christians of all creeds and denominations alike, holding the very same ruinous notion, and saying to themselves, God does not govern this present world. God does not punish or reward in this present life. This world is all wrong, and the devil's world, and therefore I cannot prosper in the world unless I am a little wrong likewise, and do a little of the devil's work. So one lies, another cheats, another oppresses, another neglects his plainest social duties, another defiles himself with base political or religious intrigues, another breaks the seventh commandment, or, indeed, any and every one of the commandments which he finds troublesome. And when one asks in astonishment—You call yourselves Christians? You believe in God, and the Bible, and Christianity? Do you not think that God will punish you for all this? Do you not hear from the psalmists, and prophets, and apostles, of a God who judges and punishes such generations as this? Of a wrath of God which is revealed from heaven against all unrighteousness of men, who, like you, hold down the truth in unrighteousness, knowing what is right and yet doing what is wrong? Then they answer, at least in their hearts, Oh dear no! God does not govern men now, or judge men now. He only did so, our preachers tell us, under the old Jewish dispensation; and such words as you quote from our Lord, or St Paul, have only to do with the day of judgment, and the next life, and we have made it all right for the next life. I, says one, regularly perform my religious duties; and I, says another, build churches and chapels, and give large sums in charity; and I, says another, am converted, and a member of a church; and I, says another, am elect, and predestined to everlasting life— and so forth, and so forth. Each man turning the grace of God into a cloak for licentiousness, and deluding himself into the notion that he may break the eternal laws of God, and yet go to heaven, as he calls it, when he dies: not knowing, poor foolish man, that as the noble commination service well says, the dreadful judgments of God are not waiting for certain people at the last day, thousands of years hence, but hanging over all our heads already, and always ready to fall on us. Not knowing that it is as true now as it was two thousand years ago, that "God is a righteous judge, strong and patient." "If a man will not turn, He will whet His sword; He hath bent His bow, and made it ready," against those who travail with mischief, who conceive sorrow, and bring forth ungodliness. They dig up pits for their neighbours, and fall themselves into the destruction which they have made for others; not knowing that it is as true now as it was two thousand years ago, that God is for ever saying to the ungodly, "Why dost thou preach my laws, and takest my covenant in thy mouth; whereas thou hatest to be reformed, and hast cast my words behind thee? Thou hast let thy mouth speak wickedness, and with thy tongue thou hast set forth deceit. These things hast thou done, and I held my tongue, and thou thoughtest, wickedly, that I am even such a one as thyself. But I will reprove thee, and set before thee the things which thou hast done. O consider this, ye that forget God: lest I pluck you away, and there be none to deliver you."

Let us lay this to heart, and say, there can be no doubt—I at least have none—that there is growing up among us a serious divorce between faith and practice; a serious disbelief that the kingdom of heaven is about us, and that Christ is ruling us, as He told us plainly enough in His parables, by the laws of the kingdom of heaven; and that He does, and will punish and reward each man according to those laws, and according to nothing else.

We pride ourselves on our superior light, and our improved civilisation, and look down on the old Roman Catholic missionaries, who converted our forefathers from heathendom in the Middle Ages. Now, I am a Protestant, if ever there was one, and I know well that these men had their superstitions and false doctrines. They made mistakes, and often worse than mistakes, for they were but men. But this I tell you, that if they had not had a deep and sound belief that they were in the kingdom of God, the kingdom of heaven; and that they and all men must obey the laws of the kingdom of heaven; and that the first law of it was, that wrongdoing would be punished, and right-doing rewarded, in this life, every day, and all day long, as sure as Christ the living Lord reigned in righteousness over all the earth; if they had not believed that, I say, and acted on it, we should probably have been heathen at this day. As it is, unless we Protestants get back the old belief, that God is a living God, and that His judgments are abroad in the earth, and that only in keeping His commandments can we get life, and not perish, we shall be seriously in danger of sinking at last into that hopeless state of popular feeling, into which more than one nation in our own time has fallen,—that, as the prophet of old says, a wonderful and horrible thing is committed in the land; the prophets—that is, the preachers and teachers—prophesy falsely; and the priests—the ministers of religion—bear rule by their means; and my people love to have it so—love to have their consciences drugged by the news that they may live bad lives, and yet die good deaths.

"And what will ye do in the end thereof?" asks Jeremiah. What indeed! What the Jews did in the end thereof you may read in the book of the prophet Jeremiah. They did nothing, and could do nothing—with their morality their manhood was gone. Sin had borne its certain fruit of anarchy and decrepitude. The wrath of God revealed itself as usual, by no miracle, but through inscrutable social laws. They had to submit, cowardly and broken-hearted, to an invasion, a siege, and an utter ruin. I do not say, God forbid, that we shall ever sink so low, and have to endure so terrible a chastisement: but this I say, that the only way in which any nation of which I ever read in history, can escape, sooner or later, from such a fate, is to remember every day, and all day long, that the wrath of God is revealed from heaven against all ill-doing of men, who hold the truth in unrighteousness, knowing what is true and what is right, yet telling lies, and doing wrong.

Let us lay this to heart, with seriousness and godly fear. For so we shall look up with reverence, and yet with hope, to Christ the ascended king, to whom all power is given in heaven and earth; for ever asking Him for His Holy Spirit, to put into our minds good desires, and to enable us to bring these desires to good effect. And so we shall live for ever under our great taskmaster's eye, and find out that that eye is not merely the eye of a just judge, not merely the eye of a bountiful king, but more the eye of a loving and merciful Saviour, in whose presence is life even here on earth; and at whose right hand, even in this sinful world, are pleasures for evermore.

SERMON XXXI

THE UNCHANGEABLE CHRIST

Eversley. 1845.

Hebrews xiii. 8. "Jesus Christ the same yesterday, and to-day, and for ever."

Let me first briefly remind you, as the truth upon which my whole explanation of this text is built, that man is not meant either for solitude or independence. He is meant to live with his fellow-men, to live by them, and to live for them. He is healthy and godly, only when he knows all men for his brothers; and himself, in some way or other, as the servant of all, and bound in ties of love and duty to every one around him.

It is not, however, my intention to dwell upon this truth, deep and necessary as it is, but to turn your attention to one of its consequences; I mean to the disappointment and regret of which so many complain, who try, more or less healthily, to keep that truth before them, and shew it forth in their daily life.

It has been, and is now, a common complaint with many who interest themselves about their fellow-creatures, and the welfare of the human race, that nothing in this world is sure,—nothing is permanent; a continual ebb and flow seems to be the only law of human life. Men change, they say; their friendships are fickle; their minds, like their bodies, alter from day to day. The heart whom you trust to-day, to-morrow may deceive; the friend for whom you have sacrificed so much, will not in his turn endure the trial of his friendship. The child on whom you may have reposed your whole affection for years, grows up and goes forth into the world, and forms new ties, and you are left alone. Why then love man? Why care for any born of woman, if the happiness which depends on them is exposed to a thousand chances—a thousand changes? Again; we hear the complaint that not only men, but circumstances change. Why knit myself, people will ask, to one who to-morrow may be whirled away from me by some eddy of circumstances, and so go on his way, while I see him no more? Why relieve distress which fresh accidents may bring back again to-morrow, with all its miseries? Why attach ourselves to a home which we may leave to-morrow,—to pursuits which fortune may force us to relinquish,—to bright hopes which the rolling clouds may shut out from us,—to opinions which the next generation may find to have been utterly mistaken,—to a circle of acquaintances who must in a few years be lying silent and solitary, each in his grave? Why, in short, set our affections on anything in this earth, or struggle to improve or settle aught in a world where all seems so temporary, changeful, and uncertain, that "nought doth endure but mutability?"

Such is and has been the complaint, mixed up of truth and falsehood, poured out for ages by thousands who have loved (as the world would say) "too well"—who have tried to build up for themselves homes in this world; forgetting that they were strangers and pilgrims in it; and so, when the floods came, and swept away that small fool's paradise of theirs, repined, and were astonished, as though some strange thing had happened to them.

The time would fail me did I try fully to lay before you how this dread and terror of change, and this unsatisfied craving after an eternal home and an unchanging friendship embittered the minds of all the more thoughtful heathens before the coming of Christ, who, as the apostle says, all their lives were in bondage to the fear of death. How all their schemes and conceptions of the course of this world, resolved themselves into one dark picture of the terrible river of time, restless, pitiless, devouring all life and beauty as fast as it arose, ready to overwhelm the speakers themselves also with the coming wave, as it had done all they loved before them, and then roll onward for ever, none knew whither! The time would fail me, too, did I try to explain how after He had appeared, Who is the same yesterday, to-day, and for ever, men have still found the same disappointment in all the paths of life. Many, not seeing that the manifestation of an incarnate God was the answer to all such doubts, the healer of all such wounds, have sickened at this same change and uncertainty, and attempted self-deliverance by all kinds of uncouth and most useless methods. Some have shielded themselves, or tried to shield themselves, in an armour of stoical indifference—of utter selfishness, being sure that at all events there was one friendship in the world which could neither change nor fade—Self-love.

Others, again, have withdrawn themselves in disgust, not indeed from their God and Saviour, but from their fellow-men, and buried themselves in deserts, hoping thereby to escape what they despaired of conquering, the chances and changes of this mortal life. Thus they, alas, threw away the gold of human affections among the dross of this world's comfort and honour. Wiser they were, indeed, than those last mentioned; but yet shew I you a more excellent way.

It is strange, and mournful, too, that this complaint, of unsatisfied hopes and longings should still be often heard from Christian lips! Strange, indeed, when the object and founder of our religion, the king and head of all our race, the God whom we are bound to worship, the eldest brother whom we are bound to love, the Saviour who died upon the cross for us, is "the same yesterday, and to-day, and for ever!" Strange, indeed, when we remember that God was manifest in the flesh, that He might save humanity and its hopes from perpetual change and final destruction, and satisfy all those cravings after an immutable object of man's loyalty and man's love.

Yes, He has given us, in Himself, a king who can never misgovern, a teacher who can never mislead, a priest whose sacrifice can never be unaccepted, a protector who can never grow weary, a friend who can never betray. And all that this earth has in it really worth loving,—the ties of family, of country, of universal brotherhood—the beauties and wonders of

God's mysterious universe—all true love, all useful labour, all innocent enjoyment—the marriage bed, and the fireside circle—the bounties of harvest, and the smiles of spring, and all that makes life bright and this earth dear—all these things He has restored to man, spiritual and holy, deep with new meaning, bright with purer enjoyment, rich with usefulness, not merely for time, but for eternity, after they had become, through the accumulated sin and folly of ages, foul, dead, and well nigh forgotten. He has united these common duties and pleasures of man's life to Himself, by taking them on Himself on earth; by giving us His spirit to understand and fulfil those duties; by making it a duty to Him to cultivate them to the uttermost. He has sanctified them for ever, by shewing us that they are types and patterns of still higher relations to Himself, and to His Father and our Father, from whom they came.

Christ our Lord and Saviour is a witness to us of the enduring, the everlasting nature of all that human life contains of beauty and holiness, and real value. He is a witness to us that Wisdom is eternal; that that all-embracing sight, that all-guiding counsel, which the Lord "possessed in the beginning of His way, before His works of old," He who "was set up from everlasting," who was with Him when He made the world, still exists, and ever shall exist, unchanged. The word of the Lord standeth sure! That Word which was "in the beginning," and "was with God," and "was God!" Glorious truth! that, amid all the inventions which man has sought out, while every new philosopher has been starting some new method of happiness, some new theory of human life and its destinies, God has still been working onward, unchecked, unaltered, "the same yesterday, and to-day, and for ever." O, sons of men! perplexed by all the apparent contradictions and cross purposes and opposing powers and principles of this strange, dark, noisy time, remember to your comfort that your King, a man like you, yet very God, now sits above, seeing through all which you cannot see through; unravelling surely all this tangled web of time, while under His guiding eye all things are moving silently onward, like the stars in their courses above you, toward their appointed end, "when He shall have put down all rule and all authority, and power, for He must reign, till He hath put all enemies under His feet." And then, at last, this cloudy sky shall be all clear and bright, for He, the Lamb, shall be the light thereof.

Christ is the witness to us also of the eternity of Love,—Of God's love— the love of the Father who wills, of Himself who has purchased, of the Holy Ghost who works in us our salvation; and of the eternity of all love; that true love is not of the flesh, but of the spirit, and therefore hath its root in the spiritual world, above all change and accidents of time or circumstance. Think, think, my friends. For what is life that we should make such ado about it, and hug it so closely, and look to it to fill our hearts? What is all earthly life with all its bad and good luck, its riches and its poverty, but a vapour that passes away?—noise and smoke overclouding the enduring light of heaven. A man may be very happy and blest in this life; yet he may feel that, however pleasant it is, at root it is no reality, but only a shadow of realities which are eternal and infinite in the bosom of God, a piecemeal pattern, of the Light Kingdom—the city not made with hands—eternal in the heavens. For all this time-world, as a wise man says, is but like an image, beautifully and fearfully emblematic, but still only an emblem, like an air image, which plays and flickers in the grand, still mirror of eternity. Out of nothing, into time and space we all came into noisy day; and out of time and space into the silent night shall we all return into the spirit world—the everlasting twofold mystery—into the light-world of God's love, or the fire-world of His anger—every like unto its like, and every man to his own place.

> *"Choose well, your choice is*
> *Brief but yet endless;*
> *From Heaven, eyes behold you*
> *In eternity's stillness.*
> *There all is fullness,*
> *Ye brave to reward you,*
> *Work and despair not."*

SERMON XXXII

REFORMATION LESSONS

Eversley. 1861.

2 Kings xxiii. 3, 4, 25, 26. "And the king stood by a pillar, and made a covenant before the Lord, to "walk after the Lord, and to keep his commandments and his testimonies and his statutes with all their heart and all their soul, to perform the words of this covenant that were written in this book. And all the people stood to the covenant. And the king commanded Hilkiah the high priest, and the priests of the second order, and the keepers of the door, to bring forth out of the temple of the Lord all the vessels that were made for Baal, and for the grove, and for all the host of heaven: and he burned them without Jerusalem in the fields of Kidron, and carried the ashes of them unto Beth-el. . . . And like unto him was there no king before him, that turned to the Lord with all his heart, and with all his soul, and with all his might, according to all the law of Moses; neither after him arose there any like him. Notwithstanding the Lord turned not from the fierceness of his great wrath, wherewith his anger was kindled against Judah, because of all the provocations that Manasseh had provoked him withal."

You heard this chapter read as the first lesson for this afternoon's service; and a lesson it is indeed—a lesson for you and for me, as it was a lesson for our forefathers. If you had been worshipping in this church three hundred years ago, you would have understood, without my telling you, why the good and wise men who shaped our prayer-book chose this chapter to be read in church. You would have applied the words of it to the times in which you were living. You would have felt that the chapter spoke to you at once of joy and hope, and of sorrow and fear.

There is no doubt at all what our forefathers would have thought of, and did think of, when they read this chapter. The glorious reformation which young King Josiah made was to them the pattern of the equally glorious Reformation which was made in England somewhat more than three hundred years ago. Young King Josiah, swearing to govern according to the law of the Lord, was to them the pattern of young King Edward VI. determining to govern according to the laws of the Bible. The finding of the law of the Lord in Josiah's time, after it had been long lost, was to them the pattern of the sudden spread among them of the Bible, which had been practically hidden from them for hundreds of years, and was then translated into English and printed, and put freely into the hands of every man, rich and poor, who was able to read it. King Josiah's destruction of the idols, and the temples of the false gods, and driving out the wizards and workers with familiar spirits, were to them a pattern of the destruction of the monasteries and miraculous images and popish superstitions of every kind, the turning the monks out of their convents, and forcing them to set to honest work—which had just taken place throughout England. And the hearts of all true Englishmen were stirred up in those days to copy Josiah and the people of Jerusalem, and turn to the Lord with all their heart, and with all their soul, and with all their might, according to God's law and gospel, in the two Testaments, both Old and New.

One would have thought that at such a time the hearts of our forefathers would be full of nothing but hope and joy, content and thankfulness. And yet it was not so. One cannot help seeing that in the prayer-book, which was put together in those days, there is a great deal of fear and sadness. You see it especially in the Litany, which was to be said not only on Sundays, but on Wednesdays and Fridays also. Some people think the Litany painfully sad—too sad. It was not too sad for the time in which it was written. Our forefathers, three hundred years ago, meant what they said when they cried to God to have mercy upon them, miserable sinners, and not to remember their offences nor the offences of their forefathers, &c. They meant, and had good reason to mean, what they said, when they cried to God that those evils which the craft and subtilty of the devil and men were working against them might be brought to nought, and by the providence of His goodness be dispersed—to arise and help and deliver them for His name's sake and for His honour; and to turn from them, for the glory of His name, all those evils which they righteously had deserved. They were in danger and in terror, our forefathers, three hundred years ago. And when they heard this lesson read in church, it was not likely to make their terror less.

For what says the 26th verse of this chapter? "Notwithstanding," in spite of all this reformation, and putting away of idols and determining to walk according to the law of the Lord, "the Lord turned not from the fierceness of His great wrath, wherewith His anger was kindled against Judah." And what followed? Josiah was killed in battle—by his own fault too—by Pharaoh Nechoh, King of Egypt. And then followed nothing but disaster and misery. The Jews were conquered first by the King of Egypt, and taxed to pay to him an enormous tribute; and then, in the wars between Egypt and Babylon, conquered a second time by the King of Babylon, the famous Nebuchadnezzar, in that dreadful siege in which it is said mothers ate their own children through extremity of famine. And then after seventy years, after every one of that idolatrous and corrupt generation had died in captivity, the poor Jews were allowed to go back to their native land, chastened and purged in the fire of affliction, and having learnt a lesson which, to do them justice, they never forgot again, and have not forgotten to this day; that to worship a graven image, as well as to work unrighteousness, is abomination to the Lord—that God, and God alone, is to be worshipped, and worshipped in holiness and purity, in mercy and in justice.

And it was some such fate as this, some terrible ruin like that of the Jews of old, that our forefathers feared three hundred years ago. Their hearts were not yet altogether right with God. They had not shaken off the bad habits of mind, or the bad morals either, which they had learnt in the old Romish times—too many of them were using their liberty as a cloak of licentiousness; and, under pretence of religion, plundering not only God's Church, but God's poor. And many other evils were rife in England then, as there are sure to be great evils side by side with great good in any country in times of change and revolution. And so our forefathers needed chastisement, and they had it. King Edward, upon whom the Protestants had set their hopes, died young; and then came times which tried them literally as by fire. First came the terrible persecutions in Queen Mary's time, when hundreds of good men and women were burnt alive for their religion. And even after her death, for thirty years, came times, such as Hezekiah speaks of—times of trouble and rebuke and blasphemy, plots, rebellions, civil war, at home and abroad; dangers that grew ever more and more terrible, till it seemed at last certain that England would be conquered, in the Pope's name, by the King of Spain: and if that had come to pass (and it all but came to pass in the famous year 1588), the King of Spain would have become King of England; the best blood of England would have been shed upon the scaffold; the best estates parted among Spaniards and traitors; England enslaved to the most cruel nation of those times; and the Inquisition set up to persecute, torture, and burn all who believed in what they called, and what is, the gospel of Jesus Christ. That was to have happened, and it was only, as our forefathers confessed, by the infinite mercy of God that it did not happen. They were delivered strangely and suddenly, as the Jews were. For forty years they had been, chastised, and purged and humbled for their sins; and then, and not till then, came times of safety and prosperity, honour and glory, which have lasted, thanks be to God, ever since.

And now, my dear friends, what has this to do with us? If this chapter was a lesson to our forefathers, how is it to be a lesson to us likewise?

I have always told you (as those who have really understood their Bibles in all ages have told men) that the Bible sets forth the eternal laws of God's kingdom—the laws by which God, that is, our Lord Jesus Christ, governs nations and kingdoms—and not only nations and kingdoms, but you and me, and every individual Christian man; "all these things," says St Paul, are "written for our admonition." The history of the Jews is, or may be, your history or mine, for good or for evil; as God dealt with them, so is He dealing with you and me. By their experience we must learn. By their chastisements we must be warned. So says St Paul. So have all preachers said who have understood St Paul—and so say I to you. And the lesson that we may learn from this chapter is, that we may repent and yet be punished.

I know people do not like to believe that; I know that it is much more convenient to fancy that when a man repents, and, as he says, turns over a new leaf, he need trouble himself no more about his past sins. But it is a mistake; not only is the letter and spirit of Scripture against him, but facts are against him. He may not choose to trouble himself about his past sins; but he will find that his past sins trouble him, whether he chooses or not,—and that often in a very terrible way, as they troubled those poor Jews in their day, and our forefathers after the Reformation.

"What?" some will say, "is it not expressly written in Scripture that 'when the wicked man turneth away from his wickedness that he hath committed, and doeth that which is lawful and right, he shall save his soul alive?' and 'all his transgressions that he hath committed they shall not be mentioned unto him,' but that 'in his righteousness which he hath done he shall live?'"

No doubt it is so written, my friends. And no doubt it is perfectly and literally true: but answer me this, when does the wicked man do that which is lawful and right? The minute after he has repented? or the day after? or even seven years after?—the minute after he is forgiven, and received freely back again as God's child, as he will be, for the sake of that precious blood which Christ poured out upon the cross? Would to God it were so, my friends. Would to God it were so easy to do right, after having been accustomed to do wrong. Would to God it were so easy to get a clean heart and a right spirit. Would to God It were so easy to break through all the old bad habits—perhaps the habits of a whole life-time. But it is in vain to expect this sudden change of character. As well may we expect a man, who has been laid low with fever, to get up and go about to his work the moment his disease takes a favourable turn.

No. After the forgiveness of sin must come the cure of sin. And that cure, like most cures, is a long and a painful process. The sin may have been some animal sin, like drunkenness; and we all know how difficult it is to cure that. Or it may have been a spiritual sin—pride, vanity, covetousness. Can any man put off these bad habits in a moment, as he puts off his coat? Those who so fancy, can know very little of human nature, and have observed their own hearts and their fellow creatures very carelessly. If you will look at facts, what you will find is this:—that all sins and bad habits fill the soul with evil humours, just as a fever or any other severe disease fills the body; and that, as in the case of a fever, those evil humours remain after the acute disease is past, and are but too apt to break out again, to cause relapses, to torment the poor patient, perhaps to leave his character crippled and disfigured all his life—certainly to require long and often severe treatment by the heavenly physician, Christ, the purifier as well as the redeemer of our sin-sick souls. Heavy, therefore, and bitter and shameful is the burden which many a man has to bear after he has turned from self to God, from sin to holiness. He is haunted, as it were, by the ghosts of his old follies. He finds out the bitter truth of St Paul's words, that there is another law in his body warring against the law of his mind, of his conscience, and his reason; so that when he would do good, evil is present with him. The good that he would do he does not do; and the evil that he would not do he does. Till he cries with St Paul, "O wretched man that I am! who shall deliver me from the body of this death?" and feels that none can deliver him, save Jesus Christ our Lord.

Yes. But there is our comfort, there is our hope—Christ, the great healer, the great physician, can deliver us, and will deliver us from the remains of our old sins, the consequences of our own follies. Not, indeed, at once, or by miracle; but by slow education in new and nobler motives, in purer and more unselfish habits. And better for us, perhaps, that He should not cure us at once, lest we should fancy that sin was a light thing, which we could throw off whenever we chose; and not what it is, an inward disease, corroding and corrupting, the wages whereof are death. Therefore it is, that because Christ loves us He hates our sins, and cannot abide or endure them, will punish them, and is merciful and loving in punishing them, as long as a tincture or remnant of sin is left in us.

Let us then, if our consciences condemn us of living evil lives, turn and repent before it be too late; before our consciences are hardened; before the purer and nobler feelings which we learnt at our mothers' knees are stifled by the ways of the world; before we are hardened into bad habits, and grown frivolous, sensual, selfish and worldly. Let us repent. Let us put ourselves into the hands of Christ, the great physician, and ask Him to heal our wounded souls, and purge our corrupted souls; and leave to Him the choice of how He will do it. Let us be content to be punished and chastised. If we deserve punishment, let us bear it, and bear it like men; as we should bear the surgeon's knife, knowing that it is for our good, and that the hand which inflicts pain is the hand of one who so loves us, that He stooped to die for us on the cross. Let Him deal with us, if He see fit, as He dealt with David of old, when He forgave his sin, and yet punished it by the death of his child. Let Him do what He will by us, provided He does—what He will do—make us good men.

That is what we need to be—just, merciful, pure, faithful, loyal, useful, honourable with true honour, in the sight of God and man. That is what we need to be. That is what we shall be at last, if we put ourselves into Christ's hand, and ask Him for the clean heart and the right spirit, which is His own spirit, the spirit of all goodness. And provided we attain, at last, to that—provided we attain, at last, to the truly heroic and divine life, which is the life of virtue, it will matter little to us by what wild and weary ways, or through what painful and humiliating processes, we have arrived thither. If God has loved us, if God will receive us, then let us submit loyally and humbly to His law.

"Whom the Lord loveth He chasteneth, and scourgeth every son whom He receiveth."

SERMON XXXIII

HUMAN SOOT

Preached for the Kirkdale Ragged Schools, Liverpool, 1870.

St Matt, xviii. 14. "It is not the will of your Father which is in heaven, that one of these little ones should perish."

I am here to plead for the Kirkdale Industrial Ragged School, and Free School-room Church. The great majority of children who attend this school belong to the class of "street arabs," as they are now called; and either already belong to, or are likely to sink into, the dangerous classes—professional law-breakers, profligates, and barbarians. How these children have been fed, civilized, christianized, taught trades and domestic employments, and saved from ruin of body and soul, I leave to you to read in the report. Let us take hold of these little ones at once. They are now soft, plastic, mouldable; a tone will stir their young souls to the very depths, a look will affect them for ever. But a hardening process has commenced within them, and if they are not seized at once, they will become harder than adamant; and then scalding tears, and the most earnest trials, will be all but useless.

This report contains full and pleasant proof of the success of the schools; but it contains also full proof of a fact which is anything but pleasant—of the existence in Liverpool of a need for such an institution. How is it that when a ragged school like this is opened, it is filled at once: that it is enlarged year after year, and yet is filled and filled again? Whence comes this large population of children who are needy, if not destitute; and who are, or are in a fair way to become, dangerous? And whence comes the population of parents whom these children represent? How is it that in Liverpool, if I am rightly informed, more than four hundred and fifty children were committed by the magistrates last year for various offences; almost every one of whom, of course, represents several more, brothers, sisters, companions, corrupted by him, or corrupting him. You have your reformatories, your training ships, like your Akbar, which I visited with deep satisfaction yesterday—institutions which are an honour to the town of Liverpool, at least to many of its citizens. But how is it that they are ever needed? How is it—and this, if correct, or only half correct, is a fact altogether horrible—that there are now between ten and twelve thousand children in Liverpool who attend no school—twelve thousand children in ignorance of their duty to God and man, in training for that dangerous class, which you have, it seems, contrived to create in this once small and quiet port during a century of wonderful prosperity. And consider this, I beseech you—how is it that the experiment of giving these children a fair chance, when it is tried (as it has been in these schools) has succeeded? I do not wonder, of course, that it has succeeded, for I know Who made these children, and Who redeemed them, and Who cares for them more than you or I, or their best friends, can care for them. But do you not see that the very fact of their having improved, when they had a fair chance, is proof positive that they had not had a fair chance before? How is that, my friends?

And this leads me to ask you plainly—what do you consider to be your duty toward those children; what is your duty toward those dangerous and degraded classes, from which too many of them spring? You all know the parable of the Good Samaritan. You all know how he found the poor wounded Jew by the wayside; and for the mere sake of their common humanity, simply because he was a man, though he would have scornfully disclaimed the name of brother, bound up his wounds, set him on his own beast, led him to an inn, and took care of him.

Is yours the duty which the good Samaritan felt?—the duty of mere humanity? How is it your duty to deal, then, with these poor children? That, and I think a little more. Let me say boldly, I think these children have a deeper and a nearer claim on you; and that you must not pride yourselves, here in Liverpool, on acting the good Samaritan, when you help a ragged school. We do not read that the good Samaritan was a merchant, on his march, at the head of his own caravan. We do not read that the wounded man was one of his own servants, or a child of one of his servants, who had been left behind, unable from weakness or weariness to keep pace with the rest, and had dropped by the wayside, till the vultures and the jackals should pick his bones. Neither do we read that he was a general, at the head of an advancing army, and that the poor sufferer was one of his own rank and file, crippled by wounds or by disease, watching, as many a poor soldier does, his comrades march past to victory, while he is left alone to die. Still less do we hear that the sufferer was the child of some poor soldier's wife, or even of some drunken camp-follower, who had lost her place on the baggage-waggon, and trudged on with the child at her back, through dust and mire, till, in despair, she dropped her little one, and left it to the mercies of the God who gave it her.

In either case, that good Samaritan would have known what his duty was. I trust that you will know, in like case, what your duty is. For is not this, and none other, your relation to these children in your streets, ragged, dirty, profligate, sinking and perishing, of whom our Lord has said—"It is not the will of your Father which is in heaven that one of these little ones should perish?" It is not His will. I am sure that it is not your will either. I believe that, with all my heart. I do not blame you, or the people of Liverpool, nor the people of any city on earth, in our present imperfect state of civilisation, for the existence among them of brutal, ignorant, degraded, helpless people. It is no one's fault, just because it is every one's fault—the fault of the system. But it is not the will of God; and therefore the existence of such an evil is proof patent and sufficient that we have not yet discovered the whole will of God about this matter; that we have not yet mastered the laws of true political economy, which (like all other natural laws) are that will of God revealed in facts. Our processes are hasty, imperfect, barbaric—and their result is vast and rapid production: but also waste, refuse, in the shape of a dangerous class. We know well how, in some manufactures, a certain amount of waste is profitable—that it pays better to let certain substances run to refuse, than to use every product of the manufacture; as in a steam mill, where it pays better not to consume the whole fuel, to let the soot escape, though every atom of soot is so much wasted fuel. So it is in our present social system. It pays better, capital is accumulated more rapidly, by wasting a certain amount of human life, human health, human intellect, human morals, by producing and throwing away a regular percentage of human soot—of that thinking, acting dirt, which lies about, and, alas! breeds and perpetuates itself in foul alleys and low public houses, and all dens and dark places of the earth.

But, as in the case of the manufactures, the Nemesis comes, swift and sure. As the foul vapours of the mine and the manufactory destroy vegetation and injure health, so does the Nemesis fall on the world of man; so does that human soot, these human poison gases, infect the whole society which has allowed them to fester under its feet.

Sad, but not hopeless! Dark, but not without a gleam of light on the horizon! For I can conceive a time when, by improved chemical science, every foul vapour which now escapes from the chimney of a manufactory, polluting the air, destroying the vegetation, shall be seized, utilised, converted into some profitable substance; till the black country shall be black no longer, the streams once more crystal clear, the trees once more luxuriant, and the desert which man has created in his haste and greed shall, in literal fact, once more blossom as the rose. And just so can I conceive a time when, by a higher civilisation, formed on a political economy more truly scientific, because more truly according to the will of God, our human refuse shall be utilised, like our material refuse, when man, as man, even down to the weakest and most ignorant, shall be found to be (as he really is) so valuable, that it will be worth while to preserve his health, to develop his capabilities, to save him alive, body, intellect, and character, at any cost; because men will see that a man is, after all, the most precious and useful thing on the earth, and that no cost spent on the development of human beings can possibly be thrown away.

I appeal, then, to you, the commercial men of Liverpool, if there are any such in this congregation. If not, I appeal to their wives and daughters, who are kept in wealth, luxury, refinement, by the honourable labours of their husbands, fathers, brothers, on behalf of this human soot. Merchants are (and I believe that they deserve to be) the leaders of the great caravan, which goes forth to replenish the earth and subdue it. They are among the generals of the great army which wages war against the brute powers of nature all over the world, to ward off poverty and starvation from the ever-teeming millions of mankind. Have they no time—I take for granted that they have the heart—to pick up the footsore and weary, who have fallen out of the march, that they may rejoin the caravan, and be of use once more? Have they no time—I am sure they have the heart—to tend the wounded and the fever-stricken, that they may rise and fight once more? If not, then must not the pace of their march be somewhat too rapid, the plan of their campaign somewhat precipitate and ill-directed, their ambulance train and their medical arrangements somewhat defective? We are all ready enough to complain of waste of human bodies, brought about by such defects in the British army. Shall we pass over the waste, the hereditary waste of human souls, brought about by similar defects in every great city in the world?

Waste of human souls, human intellects, human characters—waste, saddest of all, of the image of God in little children. That cannot be necessary. There must be a fault somewhere. It cannot be the will of God that one little one should perish by commerce, or by manufacture, any more than by slavery, or by war.

As surely as I believe that there is a God, so surely do I believe that commerce is the ordinance of God; that the great army of producers and distributors is God's army. But for that very reason I must believe that the production of human refuse, the waste of human character, is not part of God's plan; not according to His ideal of what our social state should be; and therefore what our social state can be. For God asks no impossibilities of any human being.

But as things are, one has only to go into the streets of this, or any great city, to see how we, with all our boasted civilisation, are, as yet, but one step removed from barbarism. Is that a hard word? Why, there are the barbarians around us at every street corner! Grown barbarians—it may be now all but past saving—but bringing into the world young barbarians, whom we may yet save, for God wishes us to save them. It is not the will of their Father which is in heaven that one of them should perish. And for that very reason He has given them capabilities, powers, instincts, by virtue of which they need not perish. Do not deceive yourselves about the little dirty, offensive children in the street. If they be offensive to you, they are not to Him who made them. "Take heed that ye despise not one of these little ones; for I say unto you, That in heaven their angels do always behold the face of my Father which is in heaven." Is there not in every one of them, as in you, the Light which lighteth every man that cometh into the world? And know you not Who that Light is, and what He said of little children? Then, take heed, I say, lest you despise one of these little ones. Listen not to the Pharisee when he says, Except the little child be converted, and become as I am, he shall in nowise enter into the kingdom of heaven. But listen to the voice of Him who knew what was in man, when He said, "Except ye be converted, and become as little children, ye shall not enter into the kingdom of heaven." Their souls are like their bodies, not perfect, but beautiful enough, and fresh enough, to shame any one who shall dare to look down on them. Their souls are like their bodies, hidden by the rags, foul with the dirt of what we miscall civilisation. But take them to the pure stream, strip off the ugly, shapeless rags, wash the young limbs again, and you shall find them, body and soul, fresh and lithe, graceful and capable—capable of how much, God alone who made them knows. Well said of such, the great Christian poet of your northern hills—

> *"Not in entire forgetfulness,*
> *And not in utter nakedness,*
> *But trailing clouds of glory do we come*
> *From God, who is our home."*
> *Truly, and too truly, alas! he goes on to say—*
> *"Shades of the prison-house begin to close*
> *Upon the growing boy."*

Will you let the shades of that prison-house of mortality be peopled with little save obscene phantoms? Truly, and too truly, he goes on—

> *"The youth, who daily further from the east*
> *Must travel, still is Nature's priest,*
> *And by the vision splendid,*
> *Is on his way attended."*

Will you leave the youth to know nature only in the sense in which an ape or a swine knows it; and to conceive of no more splendid vision than that which he may behold at a penny theatre? Truly again, and too truly, he goes on—

> *"At length the man perceives it die away,*
> *And fade into the light of common day."*

Yes, to weak, mortal man the prosaic age of manhood must needs come, for good as well as for evil. But will you let that age be—to any of your fellow citizens—not even an age of rational prose, but an age of brutal recklessness; while the light of common day, for him, has sunk into the darkness of a common sewer?

And all the while it was not the will of their Father in heaven that one of these little ones should perish. Is it your will, my friends; or is it not? If it be not, the means of saving them, or at least the great majority of them, is easier than you think. Circumstances drag downward from childhood, poor, weak, fallen, human nature. Circumstances must help it upward again once more. Do your best to surround the wild children of Liverpool with such circumstances as you put round your own children. Deal with them as you wish God to deal with your beloved. Remember that, as the wise man says, the human plant, like the vegetable, thrives best in light; and you will discover, by the irresistible logic of facts, by the success of your own endeavours, by seeing these young souls grow, and not wither, live, and not die—that it is not the will of your Father which is in heaven that one of these little ones should perish.

SERMON XXXIV

NATIONAL SORROWS AND NATIONAL LESSONS

On the illness or the Prince of Wales.
Chapel Royal, St James's, December 17th, 1871.

2 Sam. xix. 14. "He bowed the heart of all the men of Judah, even as the heart of one man."

No circumstances can be more different, thank God, than those under which the heart of the men of Judah was bowed when their king commander appealed to them, and those which have, in the last few days, bowed the heart of this nation as the heart of one man. But the feeling called out in each case was the same—Loyalty, spontaneous, contagious, some would say unreasoning: but it may be all the deeper and nobler, because for once it did not wait to reason, but was content to be human, and to feel.

If those men who have been so heartily loyal of late—respectable, business-like, manful persons, of a race in nowise given to sentimental excitement—had been asked the cause of the intense feeling which they have shown during the last few days, they would probably, most of them, find some difficulty in giving it. Many would talk frankly of their dread lest business should be interfered with; and no shame to them, if they live by business. Others would speak of possible political complications; and certainly no blame to them for dreading such. But they would most of them speak, as frankly, of a deeper and less selfish emotion. They would speak, not eloquently it may be, but earnestly, of sympathy with a mother and a wife; of sympathy with youth and health fighting untimely with disease and death—they would plead their common humanity, and not be ashamed to have yielded to that touch of nature, which makes the whole world kin. And that would be altogether to their honour. Honourably and gracefully has that sympathy showed itself in these realms of late. It has proved that in spite of all our covetousness, all our luxury, all our frivolity, we are not cynics yet, nor likely, thanks be to Almighty God, to become cynics; that however encrusted and cankered with the cares and riches of this world, and bringing, alas, very little fruit to perfection, the old British oak is sound at the root—still human, still humane.

But there is, I believe, another and an almost deeper reason for the strong emotion which has possessed these men; one most intimately bound up with our national life, national unity, national history; one which they can hardly express to themselves; one which some of them are half ashamed to express, because they cannot render a reason for it; but which is still there, deeply rooted in their souls; one of those old hereditary instincts by which the histories of whole nations, whole races, are guided, often half-unconsciously, and almost in spite of themselves; and that is Loyalty, pure and simple Loyalty—the attachment to some royal race, whom they conceived to be set over them by God. An attachment, mark it well, founded not on their own will, but on grounds very complex, and quite independent of them; an attachment which they did not make, but found; an attachment which their forefathers had transmitted to them, and which they must transmit to their children as a national inheritance,—at once a symbol of and a support to the national unity of the whole people, running back to the time when, in dim and mythic ages, it emerged into the light of history as a wandering tribe. This instinct, as a historic fact, has been strong in all the progressive European nations; especially strong in the Teutonic; in none more than in the English and the Scotch. It has helped to put them in the forefront of the nations. It has been a rallying point for all their highest national instincts. Their Sovereign was to them the divinely appointed symbol of the unity of their country. In defending him, they defended it. It did not interfere, that instinct of loyalty, with their mature manhood, freedom, independence. They knew that if royalty were indeed God's ordinance, it had its duties as well as its rights. And when their kings broke the law, they changed their kings. But a king they must have, for their own sakes; not merely for the sake of the nation's security and peace, but for the sake of their own self-respect. They felt, those old forefathers of ours, that loyalty was not a degrading, but an ennobling influence; that a free man can give up his independence without losing it; that—as the example of that mighty German army has just shown an astounded world—independence is never more called out than by subordination; and that a free man never feels himself so free as when obeying those whom the laws of his country have set over him; an able man never feels himself so able as when he is following the lead of an abler man than himself. And what if, as needs must happen at whiles, the sovereign were not a man, but a woman or a child? Then was added to loyalty in the hearts of our forefathers, and of many another nation in Europe, an instinct even deeper, and tenderer, and more unselfish—the instinct of chivalry; and the widowed queen, or the prince, became to them a precious jewel committed to their charge by the will of their forefathers and the providence of God; an heirloom for which they were responsible to God, and to their forefathers, and to their children after them, lest their names should be stained to all future generations by the crime of baseness toward the weak.

This was the instinct of the old Teutonic races. They were often unfaithful to it—as all men are to their higher instincts; and fulfilled it very imperfectly—as all men fulfil their duties. But it was there—in their heart of hearts. It helped to make them; and, therefore, it helped to make us. It ennobled them; it called out in them the sense of unity, order, discipline, and a lofty and unselfish affection. And I thank God, as an Englishman, for any event, however exquisitely painful, which may call out those true graces in us, their descendants. And, therefore, my good friends, if any cynic shall sneer, as he may, after the present danger is past, at this sudden outburst of loyalty, and speak of it as unreasoning and childish, answer not him.

"Give not that which is holy unto the dogs, neither cast ye your pearls before swine, lest they trample them under their feet, and turn again and rend you." But answer yourselves, and answer too your children, when they ask you what has moved you thus—answer, I say, not childishly, but childlike: "We have gone back, for a moment at least, to England's childhood—to the mood of England when she was still young. And we are showing thereby that we are not yet decayed into old age. That if we be men, and not still children, yet the child is father to the man; and the child's heart still beats underneath all the sins and all the cares and all the greeds of our manhood."

More than one foreign nation is looking on in wonder and in envy at that sight. God grant that they may understand all that it means. God grant that they may understand of how wide and deep an application is the great law, "Except ye be converted," changed, and turned round utterly, "and become as little children, ye shall not enter into the kingdom of heaven." God grant that they may recover the childlike heart, and replace with it that childish heart which pulls to pieces at its own irreverent fancy the most ancient and sacred institutions, to build up ever fresh baby-houses out of the fragments, as a child does with its broken toys.

Therefore, my friends, be not ashamed to have felt acutely. Be not ashamed to feel acutely still, till all danger is past, or even long after all danger is past; when you look back on what might have been, and what it might have brought, ay, must have brought, if not to you, still to your children after you. For so you will show yourselves worthy descendants of your forefathers: so you will show yourselves worthy citizens of this British empire. So you will show yourselves, as I believe, worthy Christian men and women. For Christ, the King of kings and subjects, sends all sorrow, to make us feel acutely. We do not, the great majority of us, feel enough. Our hearts are dull and hard and light, God forgive us; and we forget continually what an earnest, awful world we live in—a whole eternity waiting for us to be born, and a whole eternity waiting to see what we shall do now we are born. Yes; our hearts are dull and hard and light; and, therefore, Christ sends suffering on us to teach us what we always gladly forget in comfort and prosperity—what an awful capacity of suffering we have; and more, what an awful capacity of suffering our fellow-creatures have likewise. We sit at ease too often in a fool's paradise, till God awakens us and tortures us into pity for the torture of others. And so, if we will not acknowledge our brotherhood by any other teaching, He knits us together by the brotherhood of common suffering.

But if God thus sends sorrow to ennoble us, to call out in us pity, sympathy, unselfishness, most surely does He send for that end such a sorrow as this, which touches in all alike every source of pity, of sympathy, of unselfishness at once. Surely He meant to bow our hearts as the heart of one man; and He has, I trust and hope, done that which He meant to do. God grant that the effect may be permanent. God grant that it may call out in us all an abiding loyalty. God grant that it may fill us with some of that charity which bears all things, hopes all things, believes all things, which rejoices not in iniquity, but rejoices in the truth; and make us thrust aside henceforth, in dignified disgust, the cynic and the slanderer, the ribald and the rebel.

But more. God grant that the very sight of the calamity with which we have stood face to face, may call out in us some valiant practical resolve, which may benefit this whole nation, and bow all hearts as the heart of one man, to do some one right thing. And what right thing? What but the thing which is pointed to by plain and terrible fact, as the lesson which God must mean us to learn, if He means us to learn any, from what has so nearly befallen? Let our hearts be bowed as the heart of one man, to say—that so far as we have power, so help us God, no man, woman, or child in Britain, be he prince or be he beggar, shall die henceforth of preventable disease. Let us repent of and amend that scandalous neglect of the now well-known laws of health and cleanliness which destroys thousands of lives yearly in this kingdom, without need and reason; in defiance alike of science, of humanity, and of our Christian profession. Two hundred thousand persons, I am told, have died of preventable fever since the Prince Consort's death ten years ago. Is that not a sin to bow our hearts as the heart of one man? Ah, if this foul and needless disease, by striking once at the very highest, shall bring home to us the often told, seldom heeded fact that it is striking perpetually at hundreds among the very lowest, whom we leave to sicken and die in dens unfit for men—unfit for dogs; if this tragedy shall awaken all loyal citizens to demand and to enforce, as a duty to their sovereign, their country, and their God, a sanatory reform in town and country, immediate, wholesale, imperative; if it shall awaken the ministers of religion to preach about that, and hardly aught but that—till there is not a fever ally or a malarious ditch left in any British city;—then indeed this fair and precious life will not have been imperilled in vain, and generations yet unborn will bless the memory of a prince who sickened as poor men sicken, and all but died, as poor men die, that his example—and, it may be hereafter, his exertions—might deliver the poor from dirt, disease, and death.

For him himself I have no fear. We have committed him to God. It may be that he has committed himself to God. It may be that he has already learned lessons which God alone can teach. It may be that those lessons will bring forth hereafter royal fruit right worthy of a royal root. At least we can trust him in God's hands, and believe that if this great woe was meant to ennoble us it was meant to ennoble him; that if it was meant to educate us it was meant to educate him; that God is teaching him; and that in God's school-house he is safe. For think, my friends, if we, who know him partly, love him much; then God, who knows him wholly, loves him more. And so God be with him, and with you, and with your prayers for him. Amen.

SERMON XXXV

GRACE AND GLORY

Chapel Royal, Whitehall. 1865. For the consumptive hospital.

St John ii. 11. "This beginning of miracles did Jesus in Cana of Galilee, and manifested forth his glory."

This word glory, whether in its Greek or its Roman shape, had a very
definite meaning in the days of the Apostles. It meant the admiration of
men. The Greek word, as every scholar knows, is derived from a root sig-
nifying to seem, and expresses that which a man seems, and appears to his
fellow men. The Latin word glory is expressly defined by Cicero to mean
the love, trust, and admiration of the multitude; and a consequent opinion
that the man is worthy of honour. Glory, in fact, is a relative word, and
can be only used of any being in relation to other rational beings, and their
opinion of him.

The glory of God, therefore, in Scripture, must needs mean that admiration which men feel, or ought to feel for God. There is a deeper, an altogether abysmal meaning for that word: "And now, O Father, glorify thou
me with thy own self, with the glory which I had with thee before the world
was." But on that text, speaking of the majesty of the ever-blessed Trinity, I
dare not attempt to comment; though, could I explain it, I should. When St.
John says that Christ manifested forth His glory, and His disciples believed
on Him, it is plain that He means by His glory that which produced admiration and satisfaction, not alone in the mind of God the Father, but in the
minds of men.

Now, what the Romans thought glorious in their days is notorious
enough. No one can look upon the picture of a Roman triumph without
seeing that their idea of glory was force, power, brute force, self-willed do-
minion, selfish aggrandizement. But this was not the glory which St. John
saw in Christ, for His glory was full of grace, which is incompatible with
self-will and selfishness.

The Greek's meaning of glory is equally notorious. He called it wisdom. We call it craft—the glory of the sophist, who could prove or disprove
anything for gain or display; the glory of the successful adventurer, whose
shrewdness made its market out of the stupidity and vice of the barbarian.
But this is not the glory of Christ, for St. John saw that it was full of truth.

Therefore, neither strength nor craft are the glory of Christ; and, there-
fore, they are not the glory of God. For the glory of Christ is the glory of
God, and none other, because He is very God, of very God begotten. In
Christ, man sees the unseen, and absolute, and eternal God as He is, was,
and ever will be. "No man hath seen God at any time; the only begotten
Son, which is in the bosom of the Father, He hath declared Him:"—and

that perfectly and utterly; for in Him dwells all the fulness of the Godhead bodily, so that He Himself could say, "He that hath seen me hath seen the Father." This is the Catholic Faith. God grant that I may believe it with my whole heart. God grant that you may believe it with your whole hearts likewise, and not merely with your intellects and brains.

But, it may be said, though God be not glorious and admirable for selfish force, which it were blasphemous to attribute to Him, He is still admirable for His power. Though He be not glorious for craft, He is still glorious for His wisdom. I deny both. I deny that power is any object of admiration, unless it be used well for good ends. To admire power for its own sake is one of those errors, which has been well called Titanolatry, the worship of giants. Neither is wisdom an object of admiration, unless it be used for good ends. To worship it for its own sake is a common error enough—the idolatry of Intellect. But it is none the less an error, and a grievous one. God's power and wisdom are glorious only in as far as they are used (as they are utterly) for good ends; only, in plain words, as far as God is (as He is perfectly) good. And the true glory of God is that God is good. So says the Scripture; and so I bid you all remember, for it is a truth which you and I and all mankind are perpetually ready to forget.

Let me but ask you one question as a test whether or not I am right. If the Supreme Being used His power, as the Roman Cæsar used his; if He used His wisdom as the Greek sophist used his, would He be glorious then and worthy of admiration? The old heathen Æschylus answered that question for mankind long ago on the Athenian stage. I should be ashamed to answer it again in a Christian pulpit. And when I say good, I mean good, even as man can be, and ought to be, and is, more or less, good. The theory that because God's morality is absolute, it may, therefore, be different from man's morality, in kind as well as in degree, is equally contrary to the letter and to the spirit of Scripture. Man, according to Scripture, is made in God's moral image and likeness, and however fallen and degraded that image may be, still the ultimate standard of right and wrong is the same in God and in man. How else dare Abraham ask of God, "Shall not the Judge of all the earth do right?" How else has God's command to the old Jews any meaning, "Be ye holy, for I am holy?" How else have all the passages in the Psalms, Prophets, Evangelists, Apostles, which speak of God's justice, mercy, faithfulness, any honest or practical meaning to human beings? How else can they be aught but a mockery, a delusion, and a snare to the tens of thousands who have found in them hope and trust, that God would deliver them and the world from evil? What means the command to be perfect as our Father in heaven is perfect? What mean the words that we partake of a divine nature? How else is the command to love God anything but an arbitrary and impossible demand,—demanding love, which every writer of fiction tells you, and tells you truly, cannot be compelled—can only go forth toward a being who shows himself worthy of our love, by possessing those qualities which we admire in our fellow men? No. Against such a theory I must quote, as embodying all that I would say, and corroborating, on entirely independent ground, the Scriptural account of human morality—against such a theory, I say I must quote the words of our greatest living logician. "Language has no meaning for the words Just, Merciful, Benevolent" (he might have added truthful likewise) "save that in which we predicate them of our fellow creatures; and unless that is what we intend to express by them, we have no business to employ the words. If in affirming them of God we do not mean to affirm these very qualities, differing only as greater in degree, we are neither philosophically nor morally entitled to affirm them at all ... What belongs to" God's goodness "as Infinite (or more properly Absolute) I do not pretend to know; but I know that infinite goodness must be goodness, and that what is not consistent with goodness is not consistent with infinite goodness. ... Besides," he says—and to this sound reductio ad absurdum I call the attention of all who believe their Bibles—"unless I believe God to possess the same moral attributes which I find, in however inferior a degree, in a good man, what ground of assurance have I of God's veracity? All trust in a Revelation presupposes a conviction that God's attributes are the same, in all but degree, with the best human attributes. If, instead of the 'glad tidings' that there exists a Being in whom all the excellences which the highest human mind can conceive, exist in a degree inconceivable to us, I am informed that the world is ruled by a being whose attributes are infinite, but what they are we cannot learn, nor what are the principles of his government, except that 'the highest human morality which we are capable of conceiving' does not sanction them; convince me of it and I will bear my fate as I may. But when I am told that I must believe this, and at the same time call this being by the names which express and affirm the highest human morality, I say in plain terms that I will not. Whatever power such a being may have over me, there is one thing which he shall not do: he shall not compel me to worship him. I will call no being good, who is not what I mean when I apply that epithet to my fellow creatures."

That St. John would have assented to these bold and honest words, that such is St. John's conception of human and divine morality, the story in the text shows, to my mind, especially. It is, so to speak, a crucial experiment, by which the truth of the Scripture theory is verified. The difficulty in all ages about a standard of morality has been—How can we fix it? Even if we agree that man's goodness ought to be the counterpart of God's goodness, we know that in practice it is not, as mankind has differed in all ages and countries about what is right and wrong. The Hindoo thinks it right to burn widows, wrong to eat animal food; and between such extremes there are numberless minor differences. Hardly any act is conceivable which has not been thought by some man, somewhere, somehow, morally right or morally wrong. If all that we can do is, to choose out those instances of morality which seem to us most right, and impute them to God, shall we not have an ever-shifting, probably a merely conventional standard of right and wrong? And worse—shall we not be always in danger of deifying our own superstitions—perhaps our own vices: of making a God in our own image, because we cannot know that God in whose image we are made? Most true, unless "we believe rightly the incarnation of our Lord Jesus Christ," "perfect God and perfect man." In Him, says the Bible, the perfect human morality is manifested, and shown by His life and conduct to be identical with the divine. He bids us be perfect even as our Father in heaven is perfect; and He only has a right—in the sense of a sound and fair reason—for so doing; because He can say, and has said, "He that hath seen me hath seen the Father."

At least, such is the doctrine of St. John. He tells us that the Word, who was God, was made flesh, and dwelt in his land and neighbourhood; and that he and his fellows beheld His glory; and saw that it was the glory of the only-begotten of the Father, full of grace and truth. And then, in the next chapter, he goes on to tell us how that glory was first manifested forth—by turning water into wine at a marriage feast. On the truth of the story, I say simply, in passing, that I believe it fully and literally; as I do also St. John's assertions about our Lord's Divinity. But I only wish to point out to you why I called this miracle the crucial experiment, which proved God's goodness to be identical with that which we call (and rightly) goodness in man. It is by the seeming insignificance thereof, by the seeming non-necessity, by the seeming humbleness of its circumstances, by the seeming smallness of its results, issuing merely (as far as Scripture tells us, and therefore as far as we need know, or have a right to imagine) in the giving of a transitory and unnecessary physical pleasure. In short, by the very absence of that Dignus deo vindice nodus, that knot which only a God could untie, which heathens demanded ere a god was allowed to interfere in the plot of a tragedy; which too many who call themselves Christians demand before the living God is allowed to interfere in that world in which without Him not a sparrow falls to the ground. In a moral case of this kind, if you will consider, that which seems least is often the greatest. That which seems the lowest, because the simplest and meanest manifestation of a moral law, may be—probably is—the deepest, the highest, the most universal.

Life is made up of little things, say the practically wise, and they say true, for our Lord says so likewise. "He that is faithful in that which is least is faithful also in much." If you look on morality, virtue, goodness, holiness, sanctification—call it what you will—as merely the obligation of an external law, you will be tempted to say, "Let me be faithful to it in its greater and more important cases, and that is enough. The pettier ones must take care of themselves, I have not time enough to attend to them, and God will not, it may be, require them of me." But if the morality, goodness, holiness be in you what it was in Christ, without measure—a spirit, even the spirit of God—a spirit within you, possessing you, and working on you, and in you—then that which seems most petty and unimportant will often be most important, the test of the soundness of your heart, of the reality of your feelings.

We all know—every writer of fiction, at least, should know—how true this is in the case of love between man and woman, between parent and child: how the little kindnesses, the half-unconscious gestures, the petty labours of love, of which their object will never be aware, the scrupulousness which is able "to greatly find quarrel in a straw, when honour is at stake,"—how these are the very things which show that the affection is neither the offspring of dry and legal duty, nor of selfish enjoyment, but lies far down in the unconscious abysses of the heart and being itself:—as Christ—to compare (for He Himself permits, nay commands, us to do so in His parables) our littleness with His immensity—as Christ, I say, showed, when He chose first to manifest His glory—the glory of His grace and truth—by increasing for a short hour the pleasures of a village feast.

I might say much more on the point; how He showed these by His truth; how He proved that He, and therefore His Father and your Father, was not that Deus quidam deceptor, whom some suppose Him, mocking the intellect of His creatures by the facts of nature which He has created, tempting the souls of His creatures by the very faculties and desires which He Himself has given them.

But I wish now to draw your minds rather to that one word Grace—Grace, what it means, and how it is a manifestation of glory. Few Scriptural expressions have suffered more that this word Grace from the storms of theological controversy. Springing flesh in the minds of Apostles, as did many other noble words in that heaven-enriched soil, the only adequate expressions of an idea which till then had never fully possessed the mind of man, it meant more than we can now imagine; perhaps more that we shall ever imagine again. We, alas! only know the word with its fragrance battered out, its hues rubbed off, its very life anatomized out of it by the battles of rival divines, till its mere skeleton is left, and all that grace means to most of us is simply and dryly a certain spiritual gift of God. Doubtless it means that; but if it meant nothing more at first, why was not the plain word Gift enough for the Apostles? Why did they use Grace? Why did they use, too, in the sense of giving and gifts, nouns and verbs derived from that root-word, charis, grace, which plainly signified so much to them? A word, the root-meaning of which was neither more nor less than a certain heathen goddess, or goddesses—the inspirer of beauty in art, the impersonation of all that is pure, charming, winning, bountiful—in one word, of all that is graceful and gracious in the human character. The fact is strange, but the fact is there; and being there, we must face it and explain it. Of course, the Apostles use the word grace in a far deeper and loftier meaning; raise it, mathematically speaking, to a far higher power. There is no need to remind you of that. But why did they choose and use the word at all—a word whose old meaning every heathen knew—unless for some innate fitness in it to express something in the character of God? To tell men that there was in God a graciousness, as of the most gracious of all human beings, which gave to His character a moral beauty, a charm, a winningness, which, as even the old Jewish prophet, before the Incarnation, could perceive and boldly declare, drew them with the cords of a man and with the bands of love, attracting them by the very human character of its graciousness.

"The glory as of the only-begotten of the Father, full of grace." Meditate on those words. "Full of grace,"—of that spirit which we, like the old heathens, consider rather a feminine than a masculine excellence; the spirit, which, as St. James says of God the Father, gives simply and upbraideth not; gives gracefully, as we ourselves say—in the right and happy use of the adverb; does not spoil its gifts by throwing them in the teeth of the giver, but gives for mere giving's sake; pleases where it can be done, without sin or harm, for mere pleasing's sake; most human and humane when it is most divine; the spirit by which Christ turned the water into wine at the marriage feast, and so manifested forth His absolute and eternal glory. And how? How?

Thus, if you will receive it; if you will believe a truth which is too often hidden from the wise and prudent, and yet revealed unto babes; which will never be understood by the proud Pharisee, the sour fanatic, the ascetic who dreads and distrusts his Father in heaven; but which is clear and simple enough to many a clear and simple heart, honest and single-eyed, sunny itself, and bringing sunshine wherever it comes, because it is inspired by the gracious spirit of God, and delights to show kindness for kindness' sake, and to make happy for happiness' sake, taking no merit to itself for doing that, which is as instinctive as its very breath.

This,—that the graciousness which Christ showed at that marriage feast is neither more nor less than the boundless love of God, who could not live alone in the abyss, but must needs, out of His own Divine Charity, create the universe, that He might have somewhat beside Himself whereon to pour out the ocean of His love, which finds its own happiness in giving happiness to all created things, from the loftiest of rational beings down to the gnat which dances in the sun, and for aught we know, to the very lichen which nestles in the Alpine rock.

This is the character of God, unless Scripture be a dream of man's imagination. Thus far you may know God; thus far you may see God as He is; and know and see that He is just with the justice of a man, only more just; merciful with the mercy of a man, only more merciful; truthful with the truthfulness of a man, only more truthful; gracious with the graciousness of a man, only more gracious; and loving? That we dare not say: for if we say so much, the Scripture commands us to say more. The Scripture tells us that the whole absolute morality of God is summed up—as our own human morality ought to be—in His Love. That love is the fulfilment of the Moral Law in Him as in us; that it is the root and cause and spirit of His justice, mercy, truth, and graciousness; that it belongs not to His attributes, as they may be said to be, but to His essence and His spirit; that we must not, if we be careful of our words, say, God is loving, because we are bidden to say, "God is Love."

Thus, the commands, Thou shalt love the Lord thy God—and thy neighbour as thyself, are shown to be not arbitrary and impossible demands, miscalled moral obligations, while they are merely legal and external ones; but true moral obligations, in the moral sense, to which heart and spirit can answer, "I rejoice to do thy will, O God; Thy law is within my heart." You ought to love God, because He is supremely loveable and worthy of your love. You can love God, because you can appreciate and know God; for you are His child, made in His moral likeness, and capable of seeing Him as He is morally, and of seeing in Him the full perfection of all that attracts your moral sense, when it is manifested in any human being. And you can love your neighbour as yourselves, because, and in as far as you have in you the Spirit of God, the spirit of universal love, which proceedeth out for ever both from the Father and the Son to all beings and things which They have made.

And of one thing I am sure, that in proportion as you are led and inspired by that Spirit of God which showed in our Lord, in the very deepest and truest sense, as the spirit of humanity, just so you will feel a genial and hearty pleasure in lessening all human suffering, however slight; in increasing all harmless human pleasure, however transitory; and in copying Him who, at the marriage feast, gracefully and graciously turned the water into wine. I do not, of course, mean that you are to do no more than that; to prefer sentiment to duty, to amuse and glorify yourselves by paying tithe of mint, anise, and cummin, and neglect the weightier matters of the law, judgment, mercy, and faith. But I do mean that you are not to distrust your own sentiments, not to crush your own instinctive sympathies. The very lowest of them—that which makes you shrink at the sight of pain, and rejoice in the sight of pleasure, is not natural, and common to you with the animals; it is supernatural and divine. It is a schoolmaster to bring you to Christ, to that higher inspiration of His, which tells your heart to alleviate the unseen woes which will never come into painful contact with your sensibilities, to bestow pleasures in which you yourself have no immediate share. It will tell your hearts especially in the case of this very Hospital for Consumption not to be slack in giving, because so much of what you will give—it is painful to recollect how much—will be spent, not in prevention, not even in cure, but in mere alleviation, mere increased bodily ease, mere savoury food, even mere passing amusements for wearied minds. Be it so. If (which God forbid) we could do nothing save alleviate; if (which God forbid) permanent cure, even lengthening of life, were impossible, I should say just as much, Give. Give money to alleviate; give, even though what you give were, in the strictly economic sense, wasted. We are ready enough, most of us, to waste upon ourselves. It is well for us to taste once in a way the luxury of wasting on others; though I have yet to learn that anything can be called wasted which lessens, even for a moment, the amount of human suffering. A plan, for instance, is on foot for sending twenty of the patients to Madeira for the winter. The British Consul, to his honour, guarantees their maintenance, if the Hospital will pay their passage out and home. Some may say—An unnecessary expense—a problematical benefit. Be it so. I believe that it will not be such; that it may save many lives—they may revive: but were it not so, I would still say Give. Let them go, even if every soul in that ship were doomed. Let them go. Let them drink the fresh sea breeze before they die; let them see the green tropic world; let them forget their sorrow for a while; let them feel springing up afresh in them the celestial fount of hope.

We let the guilty criminal eat and drink well the morn ere he is led forth to die—shall we not do as much by those who are innocent?

But especially would I say, try to lessen such suffering as that for which I plead to-day, because it is undeserved in the true sense of that word—not earned by any act of their own. These poor souls suffer for no sins of their own; they have done nothing to bring on themselves a disease which attacks too often the fairest, the seemingly strongest and healthiest, the most temperate and most pure. They suffer, some it may be for the sins of their forefathers, some from causes of disease which science cannot as yet control, cannot even discover. They are objects of unmixed pity and sympathy: they should be so to us; for they are so to Him who made them. On this disease God does bestow a special alleviation—a special mark of His pity, of His tenderness, in a word of His grace. That unclouded intellect, that unruffled temper, that cheerful resignation, that brave and yet calm facing of the inevitable future, that ever-fresh hope, which is no delusion but a token that God Himself has taken away the sting of death and the victory of the grave, till the very thought of death has vanished, or is looked on merely as the gate to a life of health, and strength, and peace, and joy:—all these symptoms, so common, so normal, all but universal—this Euthanasia which God has provided for those who, humanly speaking, are innocent, yet must, for the general good of humanity, leave this world for another;—what are they but the voice of God to us, telling that He loves, that He pities, that He alleviates; and bidding us go and do likewise? God has alleviated where we cannot. He has bidden us thereby, if His likeness and spirit be indeed in us, to alleviate where we can; and believe that by every additional comfort, however petty, which we provide, we are copying the Ideal Man, who, because He was very God of very God, could condescend, at the marriage feast, to turn the water into wine.

SERMON XXXVI

USELESS SACRIFICE

Preached at Southsea for the Mission of the
Good Shepherd. October 1871.

Isaiah i. 11-17. "To what purpose is the multitude of your sacrifices unto me? saith the Lord: . . . When ye come to appear before me, who hath required this at your hand, to tread my courts? Bring no more vain oblations; incense is an abomination to me; the new moons and sabbaths, the calling of assemblies, I cannot away with; it is iniquity, even the solemn meeting. Your new moons and your appointed feasts my soul hateth: they are a trouble to me; I am weary to bear them. And when ye spread forth your hands, I will hide mine eyes from you: yea, when ye make many prayers, I will not hear: your hands are full of blood. Wash you, make you clean; put away the evil of your doings from before mine eyes; cease to do evil; learn to do well; seek judgement, relieve the oppressed, judge the fatherless, plead for the widow."

I have been asked to plead to-day for the mission of the Good Shepherd in Portsea.

I am informed that Portsea contains some thirteen thousand souls, divided between two parishes. That they, as I feared, include some of the most ignorant and vicious of both sexes which can be found in the kingdom; that there are few or no rich people in the place; that the rich who have an interest in the labour of these masses live away from the place, and from the dwellings of those whom they employ—a social evil new to England; but growing, alas! fearfully common in it; and that vice, and unthrift, uncertain wages, and unhealthy dwellings produce there, as elsewhere, misery and savagery most deplorable. I am told, too, that this mission has been working, nobly and self-denyingly, among these unhappy people for some years past. That it can, and ought to largely extend its operations; that it is in want of fresh funds; that it is proposed to build a new church, which, it is hoped, will be a centre of civilization and organization, as well as of religion and morality, for the district; and I am bidden to invite you, as close neighbours of Portsea, to help in the good work. I, of course, know too little of local facts, or of the temper of the people of Southsea. But I am bound to believe it to be the same as I have found it elsewhere. And I therefore shall confine myself to general questions, and shall treat this case of Portsea, as what it is, alas! one among a hundred similar ones, and say to you simply what I have said for twenty-five years, wherever and whenever I can get a hearing. And therefore if I seem here and there to speak sharply and sternly, recollect that I pay you a compliment in so doing—first, that I speak not to you, but to all English men and women; and next, that I speak as to those who have noble instincts, if they will be only true to them:—as to English people, who are not afraid of being told the truth; to English people who do wrong rather from forgetfulness and luxury, than from meanness and cruelty aforethought; who, as far as I have seen, need, for the most part, only to be reminded that they are doing wrong, to reawaken them to their better selves, and set them trying honestly and bravely to do right.

Let me then begin this sermon with a parable. Alas! that the parable should represent a common and notorious fact. Suppose yourselves in some stately palace, amid marbles and bronzes, statues and pictures, and all that cunning brain and cunning hand, when wedded to the high instinct of beauty, can produce. The furniture is of the very richest, and kept with the most fastidious cleanliness. The floors of precious wood are polished like mirrors. The rooms have every appliance for the ease of the luxurious inmates. Everywhere you see, not mere brute wealth, but taste, purity, and comfort. There is no lack of intellect either.—wise and learned books fill the library shelves; maps and scientific instruments crowd the tables. Nor of religion either;—for the house contains a private chapel, fitted up in the richest style of mediæval ecclesiastical art. And as you walk along from polished floor to polished floor, you seem to pass in review every object which the body, or the mind, or the spirit, of the most civilized human being can need for its satisfaction.

But, next to the chapel itself, a scent of carrion makes you start. You look, against the will of your smart and ostentatious guide, through a half-open door, and see another sight—a room, dark and foul, mildewed and ruinous; and, swept carelessly into a corner, a heap of dirt, rags, bones, waifs and strays of every kind, decaying all together.

You ask, with astonishment and disgust, how comes that there? and are told, to your fresh astonishment and disgust, that that is only where the servants sweep the litter. But crouching behind the litter, in the darkest corner, something moves. You go up to it, in spite of the entreaties of your guide, and find an aged idiot gibbering in her rags.

Who is she? Oh, an old servant—or a child, or possibly a grand-child, of some old servant—your guide does not remember which. She is better out of the way there in the corner. At all events she can find plenty to eat among the dirt-heap; and as for her soul, if she has one, the clergyman is said to come and see her now and then, so probably it will be saved.

Would you not turn away from that palace with the contemptuous thought—Civilized? Refined? These people's civilization is but skin-deep. Their refinement is but an outside show. Look into the first back room, and you find that they are foul barbarians still.

And yet such, literally such and no better, is the refinement of modern England; such, and no better, is the civilization of our great towns. Such I fear from what I am told, is the civilization of Southsea, beside the barbarism to be found in Portsea close at hand. Dirt and squalor, brutality and ignorance close beside such luxury as the world has not seen, it may be, since the bad days of Heathen Rome.

But more, if you turned away, you would say to yourselves, if you were thoughtful persons—not only what barbarism, but what folly. The owner and his household are in daily danger. The idiot in discontent, or even in mere folly, may seize a lighted candle, burn petroleum, as she did in Paris of late, and set the whole palace on fire. And more, the very dirt is in itself inflammable, and capable, as it festers, of spontaneous combustion. How many a stately house has been burnt down ere now, simply by the heating of greasy rags, thrust away in some neglected closet. Let the owner of the house beware. He is living, voluntarily, over a volcano of his own making.

But more—what if you were told that the fault lay not so much in the negligence of servants as in that of the owner himself, that the master of that palace had over him a King, to whom all that was foul, neglectful, cruel, was inexpressibly hateful, so hateful that He once had actually stepped off the throne of the universe to die for such creatures as that poor idiot and her forgotten parents? Would you not question whether the prayers offered up in that chapel would have any answer from Him, save that awful answer He once gave? "When ye spread forth your hands, I will hide mine eyes: yea, when ye make many prayers, I will not hear; your hands are full of blood."

Oh, my friends, you who understand my parable, has the awful thought never struck you that such may be God's answer to the prayers of a nation which leaves in its midst such barbarism, such heathenism, as exists in every great town of this realm? And what if you were told next that the laws of His kingdom were eternal and inexorable, and that one of His cardinal laws is—that as a man sows, so shall he reap; that every sin punishes itself, even though the sinner does not know that he has sinned; that he who knew not his master's will, and did it not, shall be beaten with few stripes; that the innocent babe does not escape unburnt, because it knew not that fire burns; that the good man who lives in a malarious alley does not escape fever and cholera, because he does not know that dirt breeds pestilence; that, in a word, he who knew not his master's will, and did it not, shall be beaten with few stripes; but that he who knew his master's will, and did it not, shall be beaten with many stripes? Then of how many and how heavy stripes, think you, will the inhabitant of that palace be counted worthy, who has been taught by Christianity for the last fifteen hundred years, and by physical science and political economy for the last fifty years, and yet persists, in defiance of his own knowledge, in leaving his used-up servants, and their children and grand-children after them, to rot, body, mind, and soul, in the very precincts of the palace, having no other excuse to offer for this than that it is too much trouble to treat them better, and that, on the whole, he can make money more rapidly by thus throwing away that human dirt, and leaving it to decay where it can, regardless what it pollutes and poisons; just as the manufacturer can make money more rapidly by not consuming his own smoke, but letting it stream out of the chimney to poison with blackness and desolation the green fields where God meant little children to gather flowers?

Ladies, to you I appeal, not merely as women, but as Ladies, if (as I am assured by those who know you), ladies you are, in the grand old meaning of that grand old word.

If so—you know then, what it is to be a lady and what not. You know that it is not to go, like the daughters of Zion in Isaiah's time, with mincing gait, and borrowed head-gear, and tasteless finery, the head well-nigh empty, the heart full of little save vanity and vexation of spirit, busy all the week over cheap novels and expensive dresses, and on Sunday over a little dilettante devotion. You know, I take for granted, that whatever the world may think or say, that to be that, is not to be a lady.

For you know, I take for granted, what that word lady meant at first. That it meant she who gave out the loaves, the housewife who provided food and clothes; the stewardess of her household and dependants; the spinner among her maidens; the almsgiver to the poor; the worshipper in the chapel, praying for wild men away in battle. The being from whom flowed forth all gracious influences of thought and order, of bounty and compassion, of purity and piety, civilizing and Christianizing a whole family, a whole domain. This it was to be a lady, in the old days when too many men had little care save to make war. And this it is to be a lady still, in the new days in which too many men have little care save to make money. Show then that you can be ladies still. That the spirit is the spirit of your ancestresses, though the form in which it must show itself is changed with the change of society.

To you I appeal; to as many in this church as are ladies, not in name only, but in spirit and in truth. Say to your fathers, husbands, brothers, sons, and say too, and that boldly, to the tradesmen with whom you deal—Do you hear this? Do you hear that there are savages and heathens, generations of them, within a rifle-shot of the house? And you cannot exterminate them; cannot drive them out, much less kill them. You must convert them, improve them, make them civilized and Christian, if not for their own sakes, at least for our sakes, and for our children.

And if they should answer: My dears, it is too true. But we did not make them or put them there, and they are not in our parish. They are no concern of ours, and besides they will not hurt us.

Answer them: Not made by our fault! True, our hands are more or less clean: but what of that? There they are. If you had a tribe of Red Indians on the frontier of your settlement, would you take the less guard against them, because you did not put them there? Not in our parish, and what of that? They are in our county; they are in England. Has man the right, has man the power in the sight of God to draw any imaginary line of demarcation between Englishman and Englishman, especially when that line is drawn between rich and poor? England knows no line of demarcation, save the shore of the great sea; and even that her generosity is overleaping at this moment at the call of mere humanity, in bounty to sufferers by the West Indian hurricane, and by the Chicago fire. Will you send your help across the Atlantic; and deny it to the sufferers at your own doors? At least, if the rich be confined by an imaginary line across, the poor on the other side will not—they will cross it freely enough; and what they will bring with them will be concern enough of ours. Would it not be our concern if there was small-pox, scarlet fever, cholera among them? Should we not fear lest that might hurt us? Would you not bestir yourselves then? And do you not know that it is among such people as these that pestilence is always bred? And if not, is not the pestilence of the soul more subtle and more contagious than any pestilence of the body? What is the spreading power of fever to the spreading power of vice, which springs from tongue to tongue, from eye to eye, from heart to heart? What matter whether they be one mile off or five? Will not they corrupt our servants; and those servants again our children?

And say to them, if you be prudent and thrifty housewives, Do not tell us that their condition costs you nothing. Even in pocket you are suffering now—as all England is suffering—from the existence of heathens and savages, reckless, profligate, pauperized. For if you pay no poor-rates for their support, the shop-keepers with whom you deal pay poor-rates; and must and do repay themselves, out of your pockets, in the form of increased prices for their goods.

And when you have said all this, ladies, and more,—for more will suggest itself to your woman's wit,—say to them with St Paul—"And yet show we unto you a more excellent way,"—a nobler argument—and that is Charity.

Not almsgiving. I had almost said, anything but that; making bad worse, the improvident more improvident, the liar more ready to lie, the idler more ready to idle. But the Charity which is Humanity, which is the spirit of pure pity, the Spirit of Christ and of God.

Say then, Even if these poor creatures did us no harm, as they must and will do—civilize and christianize them for their own sakes, simply because they must be so very miserable—miserable too often with acute and conscious misery; too often with a worse misery, dull and unconscious, which knows not, stupified by ignorance and vice, that it is miserable, and ought to be more miserable still. For who is so worthy of our pity, as he who knows not that he is pitiable?—who takes ignorance, dirt, vice, passion, and the wretchedness which vice and passion bring, as all in the day's work, as he takes the rain and hail, the frost and snow,—as unavoidable necessities of mortal life, for which the only temporary alleviation is—drink?

If the refined and pure-minded lady does not pity such beings as that, I know not of what her refinement is made. If the religious lady will not bestir herself, and make sacrifices to teach such people that that is not what God meant them to be—to stir up in them a noble self-discontent, a noble self-abhorrence, which may be the beginning of repentance and amendment of life—I know not of what her religion is made.

One word more—I know that such thoughts as I have put before you to-day are painful. I know that we all—I as much as anyone in this church—are tempted to put them by, and say, I will think of things beautiful, not of things ugly; of art, poetry, science—all that is orderly, graceful, ennobling; and not of dirt, ignorance, vice, misery, all that is disorderly, degrading.

Nay, even the most pious at times are tempted to say, I will think of heaven and not of earth. I will lift up my heart, and try to behold the glory and the goodness of God, and not the disgrace and sin of man.

But only for a time may they thus think and speak. Happy if they can, at moments, lift up their hearts unto the Lord, and catch one glimpse of Him enthroned in perfect serenity and perfect order, governing the worlds with that all-embracing justice, which is at the same time all-embracing love, and so, giving Him thanks for His great glory, gain heart and hope to—what? To descend again, even were it from the beatific vision itself, to this disordered earth, to work a little—and, alas how little—at lessening the sum of human ignorance, human vice, human misery—even as their Lord and Saviour stooped from the throne of the universe, and from the bosom of the Father, to toil and die for such as curse about the streets outside.

SERMON XXXVII

THE SURPRISE OF THE RIGHTEOUS

Preached at Southsea for the Mission of the
Good Shepherd. October 1871.

St Matt. xxv. 34-37. "Then shall the King say unto them on his right hand, Come, ye blessed of my Father, inherit the kingdom prepared for you from the foundation of the world: For I was an hungred, and ye gave me meat: I was thirsty, and ye gave me drink: I was a stranger, and ye took me in: naked, and ye clothed me: I was sick, and ye visited me: I was in prison, and ye came unto me. Then shall the righteous answer him, saying, Lord, when saw we Thee an hungred, and fed Thee? or thirsty, and gave Thee drink?"

Let us consider awhile this magnificent parable, and consider it carefully, lest we mistake its meaning. And let us specially consider one point about it, which is at first sight puzzling, and which has caused, ere now, many to miss (as I believe, with some of the best commentators,) the meaning of the whole—which is this: that the righteous in the parable did not know that when they did good to their fellow-creatures, they did it to Christ the Lord.

Now there are two kinds of people who do know that, because they have been taught it by Holy Scripture, who would make two very different answers to the Lord, when He spoke in such words to them. At least so we may suppose, for they are ready to make such answers here on earth; and therefore, we may suppose that if they dared, they would answer so at the day of judgment. One party would—or at least might say, "Yes, Lord, I knew that whatever I did to the poor, I did to Thee; and therefore I did all I could for the poor. I started charitable institutions, I spoke at missionary meetings, I put my name down for large sums in every subscription list, I built churches and chapels, schools and hospitals; I gained the reputation among men of being a leading philanthropist, foremost in every good work."

What answer the man who said that would receive from the Lord, I know not; for who am I that I should put words into the mouth of my Creator and my God? But I think that the awful majesty of the Lord's very countenance might strike such a man dumb, ere he had time to say those vain proud words, and strike his conscience through with the thought, Yes, I have been charitable: but have I been humane? I have been a philanthropist: but have I really loved my fellow-men? Have I not made my interest in the heathen whom I have not seen, an excuse for despising and hating my countrymen whom I have seen, if they dared to differ from me in religion or in politics? I have given large sums in charity: but have I ever sacrificed anything for my fellow-men? I have given Christ back a pound in every hundred—perhaps even out of every ten which He has given me: but what did I do with the other nine pounds save spend them on myself? Is there a luxury in which a respectable man could safely indulge, which I have denied myself? What have I been after all, with all my philanthropy and charity, but a selfish, luxurious, pompous personage? an actor doing my alms to be seen of men? I did my good works as unto Christ?—No; I did them as unto myself—to get honour from men while I lived, and to save my selfish soul when I died. God be merciful to me a sinner! That such thoughts ought to pass through too many persons' hearts in this generation, I fear is too certain. God grant that they may do so before it is too late. But it is plain, at least, that these are not the sheep of whom Christ speaks.

Again, there are another, and a very different kind of persons, who we have a right to fancy, would answer the Lord somewhat thus: "Oh Lord, speak not of it. It may be I have tried to do a little good to a poor suffering creature here and there; to feed a few hungry, clothe a few naked, visit a few sick and prisoners. But Lord, how could I do less? after all that Thou hast done and suffered for me; and after Thy own gracious saying, that inasmuch as I did anything to the least of Thy brethren, I did it to Thee. What less could I do, Lord?—and after all, what a pitifully small amount I have done! Thou did'st hunger for me—for whom have I ever hungered? Thou did'st suffer for me—for whom have I ever suffered? Thou did'st die for me—for whom have I ever died? And I did not—I fear in the depth of my heart—do what I did really for Thee; but for the very pleasure of doing it. I began to do good from a sense of duty to Thee; but after a while I did good, I fear, only because it was so pleasant—so pleasant to see human faces looking up into mine with gratitude; so pleasant to have little children, even though they were none of my own, clinging to me in trust; so pleasant when I went home at night to feel that I had made one human being a little happier, a little better, even only a little more comfortable; so pleasant to give up my own pleasure, in order to give pleasure to others, that I fear I forgot Thee in my own enjoyment. If I sinned in that, Lord forgive. But at least, I have had my reward. My work among Thy poor was its own reward, a reward of inward happiness beyond all that earth can give—and now Thou speakest of rewarding me over and above, with I know not what of undeserved bliss. Thou art too good, O Lord, as is Thy wont from all eternity. Let me go and hide myself—a more than unprofitable servant, who has not done the hundredth part of that which it was my duty to do."

What answer the Lord would make to the modest misgivings of that sweet soul, I cannot say; for again, who am I, that I should put words into the mouth of my Creator and my God? But this I know, that I had rather be—what I am not, and never shall be—such a soul as that in the last day, than own all the kingdoms of the world and the glory thereof. Still, it is plain that such persons, however holy, however loving, are not those of whom our Lord speaks in this parable. For they, too, know, and must know, that inasmuch as they showed mercy unto one of the least of the Lord's brethren, they showed it unto Him. But the special peculiarity of the persons of whom our Lord speaks, is that they did not know, that they had no suspicion, that in showing kindness to men, they were showing kindness to Christ. "Lord," they answer, "when saw we Thee?"

It is a revelation to them, in the strictest and deepest sense of the word. A revelation, that is an unveiling, a drawing away of a veil which was before their eyes and hiding from them a divine and most blessed fact, of which they had been unaware. But who are they? I think we must agree with some of the best commentators, among others with that excellent divine and excellent man, now lost to the Church on earth, the late Dean of Canterbury, that they are persons who, till the day of judgment, have never heard of Christ; but who then, for the first time, as Dean Alford says, "are overwhelmed with the sight of the grace which has been working in and for them, and the glory which is now their blessed portion." Such persons, perhaps, as those two poor negresses—to remind you of a story which was famous in our fathers' time—those two poor negresses, I say, who found the African traveller, Mungo Park, dying of fever and starvation, and saved his life, simply from human love—as they sung to themselves by his bedside—

> *"Let us pity the poor white man;*
> *He has no mother to make his bed,*
> *No wife to grind his corn."*

Perhaps it is such as those, who have succoured human beings they knew not why, simply from a divine instinct, from the voice of Christ within their hearts, which they felt they must obey, though they knew not whose voice it was. Perhaps, I say, it is such as those, that Christ will astonish at the last day by the words, "Come ye blessed of my Father, inherit the kingdom prepared for you from the foundation of the world."

If this be the true meaning of our Lord's words, what comfort and hope they may give us, when we think, as we are bound to think, if we have a true humanity in us, of the hundreds of millions of heathen now alive, and of the thousands of millions of heathen who have lived and died. Sinful they are as a whole. Sinning, it may be, without law, but perishing without law. For the wages of sin are death, and can be nothing else. But may not Christ have His elect among them? May not His Spirit be working in some of them? May He not have His sheep among them, who hear His voice though they know not that it is His voice? They hear a voice within their hearts whispering to them, "Be loving, be merciful, be humane, in one word be just, and do to others as you would they should do to you." And whose voice can that be but the voice of Christ, and the Spirit of God? Those loving instincts come not from the fleshly fallen nature, or natural man. That says to us, "Be selfish; do not be loving. Do to others not what you would they should do to you, but do to others whatever is pleasant and profitable to yourselves." And alas! the heathen, and too many who call themselves Christians, listen to that carnal voice, and live the life of selfishness and pleasure, of anger and revenge, of tyranny and cruelty—the end of which is death.

But if any among those heathen—hearing within their hearts the other voice, the gracious voice which says, "Do unto others as you would they should do unto you,"—feel that that voice is a good voice and a right command, which must be obeyed, and which it is beautiful and delightful to obey, and so obey it; may we not hope then, that Christ, who has called them, will perfect His own work; and in His own good way, and His own good time, deliver them from their sin and ignorance, and vouchsafe to them at last that knowledge of the true and holy God, Father, Son, and Holy Spirit, whom truly to know is everlasting life? They are Christ's lost sheep: but they are still His sheep who hear His voice. May He not fulfil His own words to them, and go forth and seek such souls, and lay them on His shoulder, and bring them home; saying to His Church on earth, and to His Church in heaven, "Rejoice with Me: for I have found my sheep which was lost?"

Now if we can thus have hope for some among the heathen abroad, shall we not have hope, too, for some among the heathen at home? for some among that mass of human corruption which welters around the walls of so many of our cities? I am not going to make vain excuses for them; and say they are but the victims of circumstance. The great majority of them are the victims of their own low instincts. They have chosen the broad and easy road of animalism, which leads to destruction. They have sown to the flesh, and they will of the flesh reap corruption. For the laws of God are inexorable; and the curse of the law is sure, namely, "The wages of sin are death." Neither dare I encourage too vast hopes and say, If we had money enough, if we had machinery enough, if we had zeal enough, we might convert them all, and save them all. I dare not believe it. The many, I fear, will always go the broad road; the few the narrow one. And all we dare say is, if we have faith enough, we can convert some. We can at least fulfil our ordination vow. We can seek out Christ's sheep scattered abroad about this naughty world, and tell them of His fold, and try to bring them home.

But how shall we know Christ's sheep when we see them? How, but by the very test which Christ has laid down, it seems to me, in this very parable? Is there in one of them the high instincts—even the desire to do a merciful act? Let us watch for that: and when in the most brutal man, and—alas that I should have to use the words—in the most brutal woman, we see any touch of nobleness, justice, benevolence, pity, tenderness—in one word, any touch, however momentary, of unselfishness,—let us spring at that, knowing that there is the soul we seek; there is a lost sheep of Christ; there is Christ Himself, working unknown upon a human soul; there is a soul ready for the gospel, and not far from the kingdom of God. But what shall we say to that lost sheep? Shall we terrify it by threats of hell? Shall we even allure it by promises of heaven? Not so—not so at least at first—for that would be to appeal to bodily fear and bodily pleasure, to the very selfishness from which Christ is trying to deliver it; and to neglect the very prevenient grace, the very hold on the soul which Christ Himself offers us. Let us determine with St. Paul to know nothing among our fellow-men but Christ crucified. Let us appeal just to that in the soul which is unselfish; not to the instincts of loss and gain, but to those nobler instincts of justice and mercy; just because they are not the man's or the woman's instincts; but Christ's within them, the light of Christ and the Spirit of Christ, the spirit of love and justice saying, "Do unto others as you would they should do unto you." Do you doubt that? I trust not. For to doubt that is to doubt whether God be truly the Giver of all good things. To doubt that is to begin to disbelieve St. Paul's great saying, "In me, that is, in my flesh, dwelleth no good thing." To doubt that is to lay our hearts and minds open to the insidious poison of that Pelagian heresy which, received under new shapes and names, is becoming the cardinal heresy of modern disbelief. No; we will have faith in Christ, faith in our creeds, faith in catholic doctrine; and will say to that man or that woman, even as they wallow still in the darkness and the mire, "Behold your God! That cup of cold water which you gave, you knew not why,—Christ told you to give it, and to Him you gave. That night watch beside the bed of a woman as fallen as yourself,—Christ bade you watch, and you watched by Him. For that drunken ruffian, whom you, a drunken ruffian yourself, leaped into the sea to save, Christ bade you leap, and like St. Christopher of old, you bore, though you knew it not, your Saviour and your God to land." And if they shall make answer, "And who is He that I did not know Him? who is He that I should know Him now?" Let us point them—and whither else should we point them in heaven or earth?—to Christ upon the cross, and say, "Behold your God! This He did, this He condescended, this He dared, this He suffered for you, and such as you. This is what He, the Maker of the universe, is like. This is what He has been trying to make you like, in your small degree, every time a noble, a generous, a pitiful, a merciful emotion crossed your heart; every time you forgot yourself, even for a moment, and thought of the welfare of a fellow-man."

If that tale, if that sight, if that revelation and unveiling of Christ to the poor sinful soul does not work in it an abhorrence of past sin, a craving after future holiness, an admiration and a reverence for Christ Himself, which is, ipso facto, saving faith; if that soul does not reply—it may not be in words, but in feelings too deep for words,—"Yes; this is indeed noble, indeed Godlike, worthy of a God, and worthy therefore to be at once imitated and adored:" then, indeed, the Cross of Christ must have lost that miraculous power which it has possessed, for more than eighteen hundred years, as the highest "moral ideal" which ever was seen, or ever can be seen, by the reason and the heart of man.

SERMON XXXVIII

THE LORD'S PRAYER

Windsor Castle, 1867. Chester Cathedral, 1870.

Matthew vi. 9, 10. "After this manner, therefore, pray ye, Our Father which art in heaven, hallowed be thy name, thy kingdom come, thy will be done, on earth as it is in heaven."

Let us think for a while on these great words. Let us remember that some day or other they will certainly be fulfilled. Let us remember that Christ would not have bidden us use them, unless He intended that they should be fulfilled. And let us remember, likewise, that we must help to fulfil them We need to be reminded of this from time to time, for we are all inclined to forget it. We are inclined to forget that mankind has a Father in heaven, who is ruling, and guiding, and educating us, His human children, to

> *"One far off divine event,*
> *Toward which the whole creation moves."*

We are apt to fancy that the world will always go on very much as it goes on now; that it will be guided, not by the will of God, but by the will of man; by man's craft; by man's ambition; by man's self-interest; by man's cravings after the luxuries, and even after the mere necessities of this life. In a word, we are apt to fancy that man, not God, is the master of this earth on which we live, and that men have no king over them in heaven.

The Lord's Prayer tells us that men have a king over them in heaven, and that that king is a Father likewise—a Father whose name will one day be hallowed above all names. That the world will not always go on as it goes on now, but that the Father's kingdom will come. That above the will of man, there is a will of God, which must be done, and therefore will be done some day. In a word, the Lord's Prayer tells us that this world is under a Divine government; that the Lord, even Jesus Christ our Saviour, is King, be the people never so impatient. That He sitteth between the cherubim, master of all the powers of nature, be the earth never so unquiet. That His power loves justice. That He has prepared equity. That He has executed, and therefore will execute to the end, judgment and righteousness in the earth. That Christ reigns in justice and in love. That He has for those who disobey His laws the most terrible penalties; for those who obey them blessings such as eye hath not seen nor ear heard, nor hath it entered into the heart of man to conceive. That He must reign till He has put all enemies under His feet and delivered up the kingdom to God, even the Father. That on that great day He will prove His royalty, and His Father's royalty, in the sight of all heaven and earth, and make every soul of man aware, in a fashion which none shall mistake, that He is Lord and King. This is the message which the Lord's Prayer brings—a message of mingled fear and joy.

But a message of more joy than fear. Else why does our Lord bid us pray for it that it may come to pass?—pray daily, before we even pray for our daily bread, or the forgiveness of our sins—that His Father's name may be hallowed, His Father's kingdom come, His Father's will be done?

He bids us pray for that because it will bring blessings. Blessings to every soul of man who desires to be good and true. Because it will satisfy every aspiration which has ever risen up from the heart of man after what is noble, what is generous, what is just, what is useful, what is pure. Surely it is so. Consider but these short words of my text, and think what the world would be like if they were fulfilled; what the next world will actually be like when they are fulfilled.

"Hallowed be thy name." But what name? The name of Father. If that name were hallowed by men, there would be an end of all superstitions. The root of all superstitions, fanaticisms, and false religions is this—that they do not hallow the name of Father. They do not see that it is a Holy name, a beautiful and tender as well as an awful and venerable name. They think of fathers, like too many among themselves, proud, and arbitrary, selfish and cruel. They say in their hearts, even such fathers as we are, such is God. Therefore, they shrink from God, and turn from Him to idols, to the Virgin Mary, or Saints, or any other beings who can deliver them (as they fancy) out of the hands of their Father in heaven. If men once learnt to hallow the name of Father, to think of a father as one who not only possessed power but felt love, who not only had rights which he would enforce, and issued commands which must be obeyed, but who felt yearning sympathy for his children's weakness, an active interest in their education, and was ready to labour for, to sacrifice himself for, his family—That would be truly to hallow the name of Father, and look on it as a holy thing, whether in heaven above or in earth beneath.

To hallow the Father's name would abolish all the superstition of the world. And so the coming of the Father's kingdom would abolish all the misrule and anarchy of the world. For the kingdom of God the Father is a kingdom of perfect order, perfect justice, perfect usefulness. Surely the first consequences of that kingdom's coming would be, that every one would be exactly in his right place, and that every one would get his exact deserts. That would indeed be the kingdom of God on earth. The prospect of such a kingdom would be painful enough to those who were in their wrong place, to those who were undeserving. All who were useless, taking wages either from man or from God, without doing any work in return, all these would have but too good reason to dread the coming of the kingdom of God.

But those who were trying earnestly to do their work, though amid many mistakes and failures, why should they dread the coming of the kingdom of God? Why should they shrink from remembering that, though God's kingdom is not come in perfection and fulness, it is here already, and they are in it? Why should they shrink from that thought? They will find it full of comfort, of strength, and hope, if they will but hallow their Father's name, and remember the fact of all facts—that they have a Father in heaven. There are thousands on earth, from the highest to the lowest, who can say honestly—to take the commonest instance—every parent can say it—"I have a heavy work to do, a heavy responsibility to fulfil. God knows I did not seek it, thrust myself into it; it was thrust upon me. It came to me in the course of nature or of society, and circumstances over which I had no control. In one word it was my Duty. But now that I have my duty to do, behold I cannot do it. I try my best, but I fail. I come short daily of my own low standard of duty. How much more of God's perfect standard of it! And the burden of responsibility, the regret for failure, is more than I can bear.

To such we may answer, hallow your Father's name, and be of good cheer. Your Father has given you your work. Because He is a Father, He is surely educating you for your work. Because He is a Father, He will surely set you no task which you are unable to fulfil. Because He is a Father, He will help you to fulfil your task. Your station and calling is His will; and because it is a Father's will it is a good will.

And the Judge of your work—He is no stern taskmaster, no unfeeling tyrant, but Jesus Christ, your Lord, who died for you on the Cross. He knows what is in man. He remembereth that we are but dust. Else the spirit would fail before Him and the souls which He has made. He can be touched with the feeling of our infirmities, seeing that He was tempted in all things like as we are, yet without sin. He can sympathise utterly; He can make all just allowances; He will judge not by outward results, but by the inward will and desire. He will judge not by the hearing of the ear, nor the seeing of the eye, as the shallow cruel world judges, but He will judge righteous judgment. Trust your cause to Him, and trust yourself to Him. Believe that if He can sympathise, He can also help; for from Him, as well as from His Father, proceeds the Holy Spirit, the Lord and giver of life, the spirit of wisdom and understanding, the spirit of power and might, the spirit of knowledge and the fear of the Lord, and He will inspire you to see your duty, and do your duty, and rejoice in your duty, in spite of weariness and failure, and all the burdens of the flesh and of the spirit.

"Thy will be done on earth as it is in heaven." If that were done, it would abolish all the vice of the world, and therefore the misery which springs from vice. Ah, that God's will were but done on earth as it is in the material heaven overhead, in perfect order and obedience, as the stars roll in their courses, without rest, yet without haste; as all created things, even the most awful, fire and hail, snow and vapour, wind and storm, fulfil God's word, who hath made them sure for ever and ever, and given them a law which shall not be broken. But above them; above the divine and wonderful order of the material universe, and the winds which are God's angels, and the flames of fire which are His messengers; above all, the prophets and apostles have caught sight of another divine and wonderful order of rational beings, of races, loftier and purer than man—angels and archangels, thrones and dominions, principalities and powers, fulfilling God's will in heaven as it is not alas! fulfilled on earth.

And beside them, beside the innumerable company of angels, are there not the spirits of just men made perfect, freed from the fetters of the gross animal body, and now somewhere in that boundless universe in which this earth is but a tiny speck, doing God's will, as they longed to do it on earth, with clearer light, fuller faith, deeper love, mightier powers of usefulness? Ah, that we were like to them! Ah, that we could perform the least part of our day's work on earth as it is performed by saints and angels for ever in heaven! When we think of what this poor confused world is, and then what it might be, were God's will done therein as it is done in heaven; what it might be if even the little of God's will which we already know, the little of God's laws which are proved already to be certain, were carried out with any earnestness by the majority of mankind, or even of one civilized nation—when we think—to take the very lowest ground—of the health and wealth, the peace and happiness, which would cover this earth did men only do the will of God; then, if we have human hearts within us—if we care at all for the welfare of our fellow-men—ought not this to be the prayer of all our prayers, and ought we not to welcome any event, however awful, which would bring mankind to reason and to virtue, and to God, and abolish the sin and misery of this unhappy world?

To abolish the superstition, the misrule, the vice, the misery of this world. That is what Christ will do in the day when He has put all enemies under His feet. That is what Christ has been doing, step by step, ever since that day when first He came to do His Father's will on earth in great humility. Therefore, that is what we must do, each in our place and station, if we be indeed His subjects, fellow-workers with Him in the improvement of the human race, fellow-soldiers with Him in the battle against evil.

But what we wish to do for our fellow-creatures, we must do first for ourselves. We can give them nothing save what God has already given us. We must become good before we can make them good, and wise before we can make them wise. Let us pray, then, the Lord's Prayer in spirit and in truth. Let us pray that we may hallow the name of God, our Father. Let us pray that His kingdom may come in our own hearts. Let us pray that we may do His will on earth as those whom we love and honour do it in heaven. Let us keep that before us, day and night, as the aim and purpose of our lives. Let us pray for forgiveness of our failures in that; for help to do that better as our years run on. So we shall be ready for the day in which Christ shall have accomplished the number of His elect, and hastened His kingdom. So we shall be found in that dread day, not on the side of evil, but of God; not on the side of darkness, anarchy, and vice, but on the side of light, of justice, and of virtue, which is the side of Christ and of God. And so we, with all those that are departed in the faith of His holy name, shall have our perfect consummation and bliss in His eternal and everlasting glory, to which may He, of His great mercy, bring us all. Amen.

SERMON XXXIX

THE DISTRACTED MIND

Eversley. 1871.

Matthew vi. 34. "Take no thought for the morrow, for the morrow shall take thought for the things of itself. Sufficient unto the day is the evil thereof."

Scholars will tell you that the words "take no thought" do not exactly express our Lord's meaning in this text. That they should rather stand, "Be not anxious about to-morrow." And doubtless they are right on the whole. But the truth is, that we have no word in English which exactly expresses the Greek word which St Matthew uses in his gospel, and which we are bound to believe exactly expresses our Lord's meaning, in whatever language He spoke. The nearest English word, I believe, is—distracted. Be ye not distracted about to-morrow. I do not mean the vulgar sense of the word—which is losing one's senses. But the old and true sense, which is still used by those who speak good English.

To distract, means literally to pull a thing two different ways—even to pull it asunder. We speak of distracting a man's attention, when we call him off from looking at one thing to make him look at something else, and we call anything which interrupts us in our business, or puts a thought suddenly out of our heads, a distraction. Now the Greek word which St Matthew uses, means very nearly this—Be not divided in your thoughts—do not think of two things at once—do not distract your attention from to-day's work, by fearing and hoping about to-morrow. Sufficient for the day is the evil thereof; and you will have quite trouble enough to get through to-day honestly and well, without troubling yourself with to-morrow—which may turn out very unlike anything which you can dream. This, I think, is the true meaning of the text; and with it, I think, agrees another word of our Lord's which St Luke gives—And be ye not of doubtful mind. Literally, Do not be up in the air—blown helpless hither and thither, by every gust of wind, instead of keeping on the firm ground, and walking straight on about your business, stoutly and patiently, step after step. Have no vain fears or vain hopes about the future; but do your duty here and now. That is our Lord's command, and in it lies the secret of success in life.

For do we not find, do we not find, my friends, in practice, that our Lord's words are true? Who are the people who get through most work in their lives, with the least wear and tear, not merely to their bodily health, but to their tempers and their characters? Are they the anxious people? Those who imagine to themselves possible misfortunes, and ask continually—What if this happened—or that? What would become of me then? How should I be able to pull through such a trouble? Where shall I find friends? How shall I make myself safe against the chances and changes of life? Do we not know that those people are the very ones who do little work, and often less than none, by thus distracting their attention and their strength from their daily duty, daily business? That while they are looking anxiously for future opportunities, they are neglecting the opportunities which they have already. While they are making interest with others to help them, they forget to help themselves. That in proportion as they lose faith in God and His goodness, they lose courage and lose cheerfulness; and have too often to find a false courage and a false cheerfulness, by drowning their cares in drink, or in mean cunning and plotting and planning, which usually ends in failure and in shame?

Are those who do most work, either the plotting or intriguing people? I do not mean base false people. Of them I do not speak here. But really good and kind people, honest at heart, who yet are full of distractions of another sort; who are of double mind—look two ways at once, and are afraid to be quite open, quite straightforward—who like to compass their ends, as the old saying is, that is to go round about, towards what they want, instead of going boldly up to it; who like to try two or more ways of getting the same thing done; and, as the proverb has it, have many irons in the fire; who love little schemes, and plots, and mysteries, even when there is no need for them. Do such people get most work done? Far, far from it. They take more trouble about getting a little matter done, than simpler and braver men take about getting great matters done. They fret themselves, they weary themselves, they waste their brains and hearts—and sometimes their honesty besides—and if they fail, as in the chances and changes of this mortal life they must too often fail, have nothing for all their schemings save vanity and vexation of spirit.

But the man who will get most work done, and done with the least trouble, whether for himself, for his family, or in the calling and duty to which God has called him, will be the man who takes our Lord's advice. Who takes no thought for the morrow, and leaves the morrow to take thought for itself. That man will believe that this world is a well-ordered world, as it needs must be, seeing that God made it, God redeemed it, God governs it; and that God is merciful in this—that He rewardeth every man according to his works. That man will take thought for to-day, earnestly and diligently, even at times anxiously and in fear and trembling; but he will not distract, and divide, and weaken his mind by taking thought for to-morrow also. Each day he will set about the duty which lies nearest him, with a whole heart and with a single eye, giving himself to it for the time, as if there was nothing else to be done in the world. As for what he is to do next, he will think little of that. Little, even, will he think of whether his work will succeed or not. That must be as God shall will. All that he is bound to do is to do his best; and his best he can only do by throwing his whole soul into his work. As his day, he trusts his strength will be; and he must not waste the strength which God has given him for to-day on vain fears or vain dreams about to-morrow. To-day is quite full enough of anxiety, of care, of toil, of ignorance. Sufficient for the day is the evil thereof. Yes; and sufficient for the day is the good thereof likewise. To-day, and to-morrow, too, may end very differently from what he hoped. Yes; but they may end, too, very differently from what he feared. Let him throw his whole soul into the thing which he is about, and leave the rest to God.

For so only will he come to the day's end in that wholesome and manful temper, contented if not cheerful, satisfied with the work he has had to do, if not satisfied with the way in which he has done it, which will leave his mind free to remember all his comforts, all his blessings, even to those commonest of all blessings, which we are all too apt to forget, just because they are as necessary as the air we breathe; which will show him how much light there is, even on the darkest day.

He has not got this or that fine thing, it may be, for which he longed: but he has at least his life, at least his reason, at least his conscience, at least his God. Are not they enough to possess? Are not they enough wherewith to lie down at night in peace, and rise to-morrow to take what comes to-morrow, even as he took what came to-day? And will he not be most fit to take what comes to-morrow like a Christian man, whether it be good or evil, with his spirit braced and yet chastened, by honest and patient labour, instead of being weakened and irritated by idling over to-day, while he dreamed and fretted about to-morrow?

Ah! I fancy that I hear some one say—perhaps a woman—"So easy to preach, but so difficult to practise. So difficult to think of one thing at a time. So difficult not to plot, not to fret, with a whole family of children dependent on you! What does the preacher know of a woman's troubles? How many things she has to think of, day by day, not one of which she dares forget—and yet can seldom or never, for all her recollecting, contrive to get them all done? How can she help being distracted by the thought of to-morrow? Can he feel for frail me? Does he know what I go through?" Yes. I do know; and I wonder, and admire. To me the sight of any poor woman managing her family respectably and thriftily, is one of the most surprising sights on earth, as it is one of the most beautiful sights on earth. How she finds time for it, wit for it, patience for it, courage for it, I cannot conceive. I have wondered often why many a woman does not lie down and die, for sheer weariness of body and soul. I have fancied often that God must give some special grace to all good mothers, to enable them to do all that they do, and bear all they bear. But still, the women who do most, who bring up their families best, are surely those who obey their Lord's command, who give their whole souls to each day's work, and think as little as they can of to-morrow. With them, surely, the true wisdom is, not to fret, not to plot, to do the duty which lies nearest them, and leave the rest to God; to get each week's bill paid, trusting to God to send money for the week to come; to get their children every day to school; to correct in them each fault as it shews itself, without looking forward too much to how the child will turn out at last. For them, and for parents of all ranks, the wisest plan, I believe, is to make no far-fetched plans for their children's future, certainly no ambitious intrigues for their marriage: but simply to educate them—that is, to bring out in them, day by day, all that is purest and best, wisest and ablest, and leave the rest to God; sure that if they are worth anything, their Father in heaven will find them work to do, and a place at His table, in this life and in the life to come.

Yes, my dear friends, this is the true philosophy, the philosophy which Christ preaches to us all—to old and young, rich and poor, ploughman and scholar, maid, wife, and widow, all alike.

Fret not. Plot not. Look not too far ahead.

Fret not—lest you lose temper, and be moved to do evil. Plot not—lest you lose faith in God, and be moved to be dishonest. Look not too far ahead—So far only, as to keep yourselves out of open and certain danger—lest you see what is coming before you are ready for the sight. If we foresaw the troubles which may be coming, perhaps it would break our hearts; and if we foresaw the happiness which is coming, perhaps it would turn our heads. Let us not meddle with the future, and matters which are too high for us, but refrain our souls, and keep them low, like little children, content with the day's food, and the day's schooling, and the day's play-hours, sure that the Divine Master knows that all is right, and how to train us, and whither to lead us, though we know not, and need not know, save this—that the path by which He is leading each of us—if we will but obey and follow, step by step—leads up to Everlasting Life.

SERMON XL

THE LESSON OF LIFE

Fifth Sunday in Lent.
Chester Training College, 1870. Windsor Castle, 1871.

Hebrews v. 7, 8. "Who in the days of His flesh, when He had offered up prayers and supplications with strong crying and tears, unto Him that was able to save Him from death, and was heard in that He feared; though He were a Son, yet learned He obedience by the things which He suffered."

This is the lesson of life. This is God's way of educating us, of making us men and women worthy of the name of men and women, worthy of the name of children of God. As Christ learnt, so must we. If it was necessary for Him who knew no sin, how much more for us who have sins enough and to spare. Though He was the eternal Son of God, yet He learnt obedience by the things which He suffered. Though we are God's adopted children, we must learn obedience by what we suffer. He had to offer up prayer with strong crying. So shall we have to do again and again before we die. He was heard in that He feared God, and said, "Father not my will, but Thine be done." And so shall we. He was perfected by sufferings. God grant that we may be so likewise. He had to do like us. God grant that we may do like Him.

God grant it. That is all I can say. I cannot be sure of it, for myself or for any of you. I can only hope, and trust in God. Life is hard work—any life at least which is worth being called life, which is not the life of a swine, who thinks of nothing but feeding himself, or of a butterfly which thinks of nothing but enjoying itself. Those are easy lives enough: but the end thereof is death. The swine goes to the slaughter. The butterfly dies of the frost—and there is an end of them. But the manly life, the life of good deeds and noble thoughts, and usefulness, and purity, the life which is discontented with itself, and which the better it is, longs the more to be better still; the life which will endure through this world into the world to come, and on and upward for ever and for ever.—That life is not an easy life to live; it is very often not a pleasant life; very often a sad life—so sad that that is true of it which the great poet says—

"Who ne'er his bread in sorrow ate,
Who never in the midnight hours
Sat weeping on his lonely bed,
He knows you not, you Heavenly Powers."

You may say this is bad news. I do not believe it is. I believe it is good news, and the very best of news: but if it is bad news, I cannot help it. I did not make it so. God made it so. And God must know best. God is love. And we are His children, and He loves us. And therefore His ways with us must be good and loving ways, and any news about them must be good news, and a gospel, though we cannot see it so at first.

In any case, if it is so, it is better to remember that it is so. And Lent, and Passion Week, and Good Friday are meant to put us in mind of it year by year, because we are all of us only too ready to forget it, and shut our eyes to it. Lent and Passion Week, I say, are meant to put us in mind. And the preacher is bound to put you in mind of it now and then. He is bound, not too often perhaps, lest he should discourage young hearts, but now and then, to put you in mind of the old Greek proverb, the very words of which St. Paul uses in the text, that τα παθηματα μαθηματα—sorrows are lessons; and that the most truly pitiable people often are those who have no sorrows, and ask for no man's pity.

For so it is. The very worst calamity, I should say, which could befall any human being would be this—To have his own way from his cradle to his grave; to have everything he liked for the asking, or even for the buying; never to be forced to say, "I should like that: but I cannot afford it. I should like this: but I must not do it"—Never to deny himself, never to exert himself, never to work, and never to want. That man's soul would be in as great danger as if he were committing great crimes. Indeed, he would very probably before he died commit great crimes—like certain negroes whom I have seen abroad, who live a life of such lazy comfort and safety, and superabundance of food, that they are beginning more and more to live the life of animals rather than men. They are like those of whom the Psalmist says, "Their eyes swell out with fatness, and they do even what they lust." So do they, and indulge in gross vices, which, if not checked in some way, will end in destroying them off the face of the earth in a few generations more. I had rather, for the sake of my character, my manhood, my immortal soul, I had rather, I say, a hundred times over, be an English labourer, struggling on on twelve shillings a week, and learning obedience, self-denial, self-respect, and trust in God, by the things suffered in that hard life here at home, than be a Negro in Tropic islands, fattening himself in sloth under that perpetual sunshine, and thinking nought of God, because, poor fool, he can get all he wants without God's help.

No, my dear young friends, this is good for a man. It is necessary for a man, if he is to be a man and a child of God, and not a mere animal, to have to work hard whether he likes or not. It is good for a man to bear the yoke in his youth, as Jeremiah told the Jews, when, because they would not bear God's light yoke in their youth, but ran riot into luxury and wantonness, and superstition and idolatry which come thereof, they had to bear the heavy yoke of the Babylonish captivity in their old age. It is good for a man to be checked, crossed, disappointed, made to feel his own ignorance, weakness, folly; made to feel his need of God; to feel that, in spite of all his cunning and self-confidence, he is no better off in this world than a lost child in a dark forest, unless he has a Father in Heaven, who loves him with an eternal love, and a Holy Spirit in Heaven, who will give him a right judgment in all things; who will put into his mind good desires, and enable him to bring those desires to good effect; and a Saviour in Heaven who can be touched with the feeling of his infirmities, because He too was made perfect by sufferings; He too was tempted in all points like as we are, yet without sin.

And, therefore, my dear friends, those words which we read in the Visitation of the Sick about this matter are not mere kind words, meant to give comfort for the moment. They are truth and fact and sound philosophy. They are as true for the young lad in health and spirits as for the old folk crawling towards their graves. It is true, and you will find it true, that sickness and all sorts of troubles, are sent to correct and amend in us whatever doth offend the eyes of our Heavenly Father. It is true, and you will find it true, that whom the Lord loveth He chasteneth, and scourgeth every son whom He receiveth. It is true, and you will find it true (though God knows it is a difficult lesson enough to learn), that there should be no greater comfort to Christian persons, than to be made like Christ, by suffering patiently not only the hard work of every-day life, but adversities, troubles, and sicknesses, and our Heavenly Father's correction, whensoever, by any manner of adversity, it shall please His gracious goodness to visit them. For Christ Himself went not up to joy, but first He suffered pain; He entered not into His glory, before He was crucified.

So truly our way to eternal joy is to labour and to suffer here with Christ. It is true, and you will find it true, when years hence you look back, as I trust you all will, calmly and intelligently, on the events of your own lives—you will find, I say, that the very events in your lives which seemed at the time most trying, most vexing, most disastrous, have been those which wore most necessary for you, to call out what was good in you, and to purge out what was bad; that by those very troubles your Lord, who knows the value of suffering, because He has suffered Himself, was making true men, true women of you; hardening your heads, while He softened your hearts; teaching you to obey Him, while He taught you not to obey your own fancies and your own passions; refining and tempering your characters in the furnace of trial, as the smith refines soft iron into trusty steel; teaching you, as the great poet says—

> "That life is not as idle ore,
> But heated hot with burning fears,
> And bathed in baths of hissing tears,
>   And battered with the strokes of doom,
> To shape and use."

Yes, you will learn that, and more than that, and say in peace—"Before I was troubled I went wrong, but now have I kept thy commandments." And to such an old age may our Lord Jesus Christ bring you and me and all we love. Amen.

SERMON XLI

SACRIFICE TO CÆSAR OR TO GOD

Eversley, 1869. Chester Cathedral, 1872.

Matthew xxii. 21. "Render therefore unto Cæsar the things which are Cæsar's; and unto God the things that are God's."

Many a sermon has been preached, and many a pamphlet written, on this text, and (as too often has happened to Holy Scripture), it has been made to mean the most opposite doctrines, and twisted in every direction, to suit men's opinions and superstitions. Some have found in it a command to obey tyrants, invaders, any and every government, just or unjust. Others have found in it rules for drawing a line between the authority of the State and of the Church, i.e., between what the Government have a right to command, and what the Clergy have a right to demand; and many more matters have they fancied that they discovered in the text which I do not believe are in it at all.

For to understand the original question—Is it lawful to pay tribute to Cæsar or no? we must imagine to ourselves a state of things in Judea utterly different, thank God, from anything which has been in these realms for now eight hundred years. The Cæsar, or Emperor of Rome, had obtained by conquest an authority over the Jews very like that which we have over the Hindoos in India. And what was working in the mind of the Jews was very like that which was working in the minds of the Hindoos in the Sepoy Rebellion—whether it was not a sacred and religious duty to rise against their conquerors and drive them out. We know from the New Testament that both our Lord and His apostles again and again warned them not to rebel, warned them that they would not succeed: but ruin themselves thereby; for that those who took the sword would perish by the sword. And we know, too, that the Jews would not take our Lord's advice, nor the apostles', but did rise again and again, both in Judea and elsewhere, gallantly and desperately enough, poor creatures, in mad useless rebellion, till the Romans all but destroyed them off the face of the earth. But what has that to do with us, free self-governed Englishmen, in this peaceful and prosperous land? In the early middle age, when the clergy represented and defended Roman pure Christianity and civilization against the half-heathen and half-barbaric Teutons who had conquered the Roman Empire, then doubtless the text became once more full of meaning, and the clergy had again and again to defend the things which belonged to God against the rapacity or the wilfulness of many a barbaric Cæsar. But what has that, again, to do with us? Those who apply the text to any questions which can at present arise between the Church and the State, mistake alike, it seems to me, the nature and functions of an Established Church, and the nature and functions of a free Government.

Do I mean, then, that the text has nothing to do with us? God forbid! I believe that every word of our Lord's has to do with us, and with every human being, for their meaning is infinite, eternal, and inexhaustible. And what the latter half of the text has to do with us, I will try to show you, while I tell you openly, that the first half of it, about rendering to Cæsar the things which are Cæsar's, has nothing to do with us, and never need, save through our own cowardice and effeminacy, or folly.

We have no Cæsar over us in free England, and shall not have, while Queen Victoria, and her children after her reign; but if ever one, or many (which God forbid!), should arise and try to set themselves up as despots over us, I trust we shall know how to render them their due, be they native or foreigner, in the same coin in which our forefathers have always paid tyrants and invaders. No. The only Cæsar which we have to fear—and he is a tyrant who seems ready, nowadays, to oppose and exalt himself above all that is called God, or is worshipped,—patronizing, of course, Religion, as a harmless sanction for order and respectability, but dictating morality, while telling us all day long, with a thousand voices and a thousand pens— "Right is not the eternal law of God. Whatever profits me, whatever I like, whatever I vote—that and that alone is right, and you must do it at your peril." Do you know who that Cæsar is, my friends? He is called Public Opinion—the huge anonymous idol which we ourselves help to make, and then tremble before the creation of our own cowardice; whereas, if we will but face him, in the fear of God and the faith of Christ, determined to say the thing which is true, and do the thing which is right, we shall find the modern Cæsar but a phantom of our own imagination; a tyrant, indeed, as long as he is feared, but a coward as soon as he is defied.

To that Cæsar let us never bow the knee. Render to him all that he deserves—the homage of common courtesy, common respectability, common charity—not in reverence for his wisdom and strength, but in pity for his ignorance and weakness. But render always to God the things which are God's. That duty, my good friends, lies on us, as on all mankind still, from our cradle to our grave, and after that through all eternity. Let us go back, or rather, let us go home to the eternal laws of God, which were, ages before we were born, and will be, ages after we are dead—to the everlasting Rock on which we all stand, which is the will and mind of our Lord Jesus Christ the Son of God, to whom all power is given (as He said Himself) in heaven and on earth. And we have need to do so, for in such times of change as these are, there will always be too many who fancy that changes in society and government change their duty about religion, and are, some of them, sorely puzzled as to their duty to God: and others ready to take advantage of the change to throw off their duty to God, and run into licence and schism and fanaticism.

Now let all people clearly understand, and settle it in their hearts, that no change in Church or in State can change in the least their duty to God and to man. If the world were turned upside down, God would still be where He is, and we where we are—in His presence. Right would still be right, my friends, and wrong wrong, though all the loud voices in the world shouted that wrong is right and right wrong. No change of time, place, society, government, circumstance of any kind, can alter our duty to God, and our power of doing that duty. Whatever the Cæsar of the hour may require us to render to him, what we are bound to render to God remains the same. The two things are different in kind, so different, that they never need interfere with each other.

Even if, which God forbid, the connection between Church and State were dissolved; even if, which God forbid, the Church of England were destroyed for a while—if all Churches were destroyed—yea, if not a place of worship were left for a while in this or any other land; yet even then, I say, we could still render to God the things which are God's, and offer to Him spiritual sacrifices, more pleasing to Him than the most gorgeous ceremonies which the devotion, and art, and wealth of man ever devised— sacrifices, by virtue of which the Church would arise out of her ruins, like the Jewish Church after the captivity, more pure, more glorious, and more triumphant than ever.

What do I mean? I mean this—that there are three sacrifices which every man, woman, and child can offer, and should offer, however lowly, however uneducated in what the world calls education nowadays. Those they can offer to God, and with them they can worship God, and render to God the things which are God's, wherever they are, whatever they are doing, what- ever be the laws of their country, or the state of society round them. For of these sacrifices our Lord Himself said, The true worshippers shall worship the Father in spirit and in truth: for the Father seeketh such to worship Him.

Now what are these spiritual sacrifices?

First and foremost, surely, the sacrifice of repentance, of which it is writ- ten, "The sacrifice of God is a broken spirit. A broken and a contrite heart, oh God, Thou wilt not despise." Surely when we—even the best of us— look back on our past lives; when we recollect, if not great and positive sins and crimes, yet the opportunities which we have neglected; the time, and often the money which we have wasted; the meannesses, the tempers, the spite, the vanity, the selfishness, which we have too often indulged—When we think of what we have been, and what we might have been, what we are, and what we might be; when we measure ourselves, not by the paltry, low, and often impure standard of the world around us, but by the pure, lofty, truly heroical standard of our Lord Jesus Christ—what can we say, but that we are miserable—that is, pitiful and pitiable sinners, who have left undone what we ought to have done, and done that which we ought not to have done, till there is no health in us?

And if you ask me, How is it a sacrifice to God to confess to Him that we are sinners? the answer is simple. It is a sacrifice to God, and a sacrifice well-pleasing to Him, simply because it is The Truth. God wants nothing from us; we can give Him nothing. The wild beasts of the forest are His, and so are the cattle on a thousand hills. If He be hungry He will not tell us for the whole world is His and all that is therein. But what He asks is, that for our own sakes we should see the truth about ourselves, see what we really are, and sacrifice that self-conceit which prevents our seeing ourselves as God our Father sees us. And why does that please God? Simply because it puts us in our right state, and in our right place, where we can begin to become better men, let us be as bad as we may. If a man be a fool, the best possible thing for him is that he should find out that he is a fool, and confess that he is a fool, as the first, and the absolutely necessary first step to becoming wise. Therefore repentance, contrition, humility, is the very foundation-stone of all goodness, virtue, holiness, usefulness; and God desires to see us contrite, simply because He desires to see us good men and good women.

Next, the sacrifice of thankfulness, of which it is written, "I will offer to thee the sacrifice of thanksgiving, and will call upon the name of the Lord." And again—By Christ let us offer the sacrifice of praise continually, that is, the fruit of our lips, giving thanks unto His name. Ah! my friends, if we offered that sacrifice oftener, we should have more seldom need to offer the first sacrifice of repentance. I am astonished when I look at my own heart, by which alone I can judge the hearts of others, to see how unthankful one is. How one takes as a matter of course, without one aspiration of gratitude to our Father in heaven—how one takes, as a matter of course, I say, life, health, reason, freedom, education, comfort, safety, and all the blessings of humanity, and of this favoured land. How we never really feel that these are all God's undeserved and unearned mercies; and then, how, if we set our hearts on anything which we have not got, forget all that we have already, and begin entreating God to give us something which, if we had, we know not whether it would be good for us; like children crying peevishly for sweets, after their parents have given them all the wholesome food they need. Ah! that we would offer to God more frankly the sacrifice of thanksgiving! So we should do God justice, by confessing all we owe to Him; and so, we must believe, we should please God; for if God be indeed our Father in heaven, as surely as a parent is pleased with the affection and gratitude of his child, so will our Father in heaven be pleased when He sees us love Him, who first loved us.

Next—the sacrifice of righteousness, of which it is written, "Present your bodies a living sacrifice, holy, acceptable to God, which is your reasonable service." To be good and to do good, even to long to be good and to long to do good, to hunger and thirst after righteousness, is the best and highest sacrifice which any human being can offer to his Father in heaven. For so he honours his father most truly; for he longs and strives to be like that Father; to be good as God is good, holy as God is holy, beneficent and useful even as God is infinitely beneficent and useful; being, in one word, perfect, as his Father in heaven is perfect. This is the best and highest act of worship, the truest devotion. For pure worship (says St James), and undefiled before God and the Father, is this, to visit the fatherless and widows in their affliction, and to keep ourselves unspotted from the world.

Yes—every time we perform an act of kindness to any human being, aye, even to a dumb animal; every time we conquer our own worldliness, love of pleasure, ease, praise, ambition, money, for the sake of doing what our conscience tells us to be our duty, we are indeed worshipping God the Father in spirit and in truth, and offering him a sacrifice which He will surely accept, for the sake of His beloved Son, by whose spirit all good deeds and thoughts are inspired.

Think of these things, my friends, always, but, above all, think of them as often as you come—as would to God all would come—to the altar of the Lord, and the Holy Communion of His body and blood. For there, indeed, you render to God that which is God's—namely, yourselves; there you offer to God the true sacrifice, which is the sacrifice of yourselves—the sacrifice of repentance, the sacrifice of thanksgiving, the sacrifice of righteousness, or at least of hunger and thirst after righteousness; and there you receive in return your share of God's sacrifice, the sacrifice which you did not make for Him, but which He made for you, when He spared not His only-begotten Son but freely gave Him for us.

That is the sacrifice of all sacrifices, the wonder of all wonders, the mystery of all mysteries; and it is also the righteousness of all righteousness, the generosity of all generosity, the nobleness of all nobleness, the beauty of all beauty, the love of all love. Thinking of that, beholding in that bread and wine the tokens of the boundless love of God, then surely, surely, our repentance for past follies, our thankfulness for present blessings, our longing to be good, pure, useful, humane, generous, high-minded—in one word, to be holy—ought to rise up in us, into a passion, as it were, of noble shame at our own selfishness, and admiration of God's unselfishness, a longing to follow His divine example, and to live, not for ourselves, but for our fellow-men. If we could but once understand the full meaning of those awful yet glorious words, "He that spared not His own Son, but delivered Him up for us all, how shall He not with Him also freely give us all things?" then, indeed, we should understand that the one overpowering reason for being unselfish and doing good is this—that we are God's children, and that God our Father is utterly unselfish, and utterly does good, even at the sacrifice of Himself; and that therefore when we are unselfish, and do good, even at the sacrifice of ourselves, we do indeed, in spirit and in truth, "render unto God the things that are God's."

SERMON XLII

THE UNJUST STEWARD

Eversley, 1866. Ninth Sunday After Trinity.

Luke xvi. 8. "And the Lord commended the unjust steward, because he had done wisely."

None of our Lord's parables has been as difficult to explain as this one. Learned and pious men have confessed freely, in all ages, that there is much in the parable which they cannot understand; and I am bound to confess the same. The puzzle is, plainly, why our Lord should seem to bid us to copy the conduct of a bad man and a cheat. For this is the usual interpretation. The steward has been cheating his master already. When he is found out and about to be dismissed, he cheats his master still further, by telling his debtors to cheat, and so wins favour with them.

But does our Lord bid us copy a cheat? I cannot believe that; and the text I should have said ought to give us a very different notion. We read that the lord—that is, the steward's master—commended the unjust steward. What? Commended him for cheating him a second time, and teaching his debtors to cheat him? He must have been a man of a strange character—very unlike any man whom we know, or, at all events, any man whom we should wish to know—to have done that. But it is said—he commended him for having acted wisely. Now that word "wisely" may merely mean prudently, sensibly, and with common sense. But if the master thought that to cheat, or to teach others to cheat, was acting either wisely or prudently, then he was a very foolish and short-sighted man, and altogether mistaken. For be sure and certain, and settle it in your minds, that neither falsehood or dishonesty is ever either wise or prudent, but short-sighted, foolish, certain to punish itself. Such teaching is totally contrary to our Lord's own teaching. Agree with thine adversary quickly, He says, while thou art in the way with him, lest he deliver thee to the Judge. If thou hast done wrong, right it again as soon as possible; for your sin will surely find you out, and avenge itself. Give the devil his due, says the good old proverb. Pay him at once and be done with him: but never think to escape out of his clutches, as too many wretched and foolish sinners do, by running up a fresh score with him, and trying to hide old sins by new ones. Be sure that if the steward cheated his master a second time, the master was foolish and mistaken, and as it were a partner in the steward's sin by commending him. But if so; why does our Lord mention it? What had our Lord to do, what have we to do, with the opinion of so foolish a man?

It seems to me that the only reason for our Lord's using the words of the text, must be, that the master was right, not wrong, in commending the steward. But it seems to me, also, that the master could be right only, if the steward was right also—if the steward had done the right and just thing at last, and, instead of cheating his master a second time, had done his best to make restitution for his own sins.

But how could that be? We know nothing of what these debtors were. All we know is that one believed that he owed the Lord a hundred measures of oil; and another believed that he owed him a hundred measures of wheat; and that the steward told one to put down in his bill eighty, and the other fifty. Now suppose that the steward had been cheating and oppressing these men, as was common enough in those days with stewards, and has been common enough since; suppose that he had been charging them more than they really owed, and, it may be, putting the surplus into his own pocket, and so wasting his master's goods—that the one really owed only eighty measures of oil, and the other really owed only fifty of wheat; what could be more simple, or more truly wise either, when he was found out, than to do this—to go round to the debtors and confess: I have been overcharging you; you do not owe what I have demanded of you; take your bill and write four-score, for that is what you really owe?

This is but a guess on my part. But all other explanations are only guesses likewise, because we do not know how business was transacted in those days and in that country. We do not know whether these debtors were tenants, paying rent in kind, or traders to whom goods had been advanced, or what they were. We do not know whether the steward was agent of the estate, or house steward, or what he was. But this we do know—that to mend one act of villainy by committing a fresh one, is not wisdom, but foolishness; and we may be sure that our Lord would never have held up the unjust steward as an example to us, or quoted his master's opinion of him, if all he did was to commit fraud on fraud, and make bad worse, thereby risking his own more utter ruin. And this view of the parable surely agrees with our Lord's own lesson, which He draws from it. "And I say unto you, Make to yourselves friends of the mammon of righteousness." But what does that mean? Wise men have been puzzled by that text as much as by the parable; but surely our Lord Himself explains it in the verses which follow: "He that is faithful in that which is least, is faithful also in much; and he that is unjust in that which is least, is unjust also in much." He that is faithful. The unjust steward was commended for acting wisely. Now, it seems the way to act wisely is to act faithfully—that is honestly. Our Lord bids us copy the unjust steward, and make ourselves friends of the mammon of unrighteousness. Now, it seems, He tells us that the way to make friends of men by money transactions is to deal faithfully and honestly by them. This then was perhaps why the Lord commended the unjust steward, because he had been converted in time, and seen his true interest; and for once at least in his life become just. He had found out that after all, honesty is the best policy; as God grant all of us may find out if any of us have not found it out already. Honesty is the best policy. Faithfulness, as our Lord calls it, is the true wisdom. And in that, as our Lord says, the children of this world are wiser in their generation than the children of light. The children of this world, the plain worldly men of business, find that to conduct their business they must be faithful, diligent, punctual, accurate, cautious, business-like. They must have practical common sense, which is itself a kind of honesty. They must be men of their word, just and true in their dealings, or sooner or later, they will fail. Their schemes, their money, their credit, their character, will fail them, and they will be overwhelmed by ruin.

And that is just what too often the children of light forget. The children of light have a higher light, a deeper teaching from God, than the children of the world. They have a great insight into what ought to be; they see that mankind might be far wiser, happier, better, holier than they are; they have noble and lofty hopes for the future; they desire the welfare and the holiness of mankind. But they are too apt to want practical common sense. And so they are laughed at (and deservedly) as dreamers, as fanatics, as foolish unpractical people, who are wasting their talents on impossible fancies. Often while their minds are full of really useful and noble schemes, they neglect their business, their families, their common duties, till they cause misery to those around them, and shame to themselves. Often, too, they are tempted to be actually dishonest, to fancy that the means sanctify the end; that it is lawful to do evil that good may come; and so, in order to carry out some fine scheme of theirs, to say false things, or do mean or cruel things, not for their own interest, but, as they fancy, for the cause of God: as if God, and God's cause, could ever be helped by the devil and his works. And so they cast a scandal on religion, and give the enemies of the Lord reason to blaspheme. So it was, it seems, in our Lord's time—so it has been too often since. The children of light—those who ought to be of most use to their own generation—are sometimes of least use to it, through their own weaknesses and follies. They will not remember that he that is not faithful in that which is least, in the every-day concerns of life, is not likely to be faithful in that which is greatest; that if they will not be faithful in the unrighteous mammon—that is, if they cannot resist the temptations to meanness and unfairness which come with all money transactions, God will not commit to them the true riches—the power of making their fellow creatures wiser, happier, better. If they will not be faithful in that which is another man's—in plain English, if they will not pay their debts honestly, who will give them that which is their own—the inspiration of God's indwelling Spirit? Would to God all high religious professors would recollect that, and be just and honest, before they pretend to higher graces and counsels of perfection.

This lesson, then, I think our Lord means to teach us. I do not say it is the only lesson in the parable; God forbid. But I think that our Lord's own words show us that this is one lesson. That, however pious we are, however enlightened we are, however useful we wish to be; in one word, however much we are, or fancy ourselves to be, children of light, our first duty as Christian men is the duty which lies nearest us—that of which it is written: "If a man know not how to rule his own house, how shall he take care of the Church of God?" And again, "If any provide not for his own and specially for those of his own house, he hath denied the faith, and is worse than an infidel." Our first duty, I say, as Christian men, is to be just and honest in money matters and every-day business; and over and above that, to be generous and liberal therein. Not merely to pay—which the very publicans in our Lord's time did—but to give, generously, liberally; lending, if we can afford it, as our Lord bids us, hoping for nothing again; and remembering that he who giveth to the poor lendeth to the Lord, and whatsoever he layeth out, it shall be repaid him again.

Yes, my friends, we must all needs take our Lord's advice—make to yourselves friends of the mammon of unrighteousness, that when ye fail, they may receive you into everlasting habitations. When ye fail—literally, when you are eclipsed, as the sun is eclipsed. That must happen to all of us, to the best, the wisest, the most famous. Each must be eclipsed, and passed in the race of life, and forgotten for some younger man. Each in turn must fail. One may fail in money—the mammon for which he toiled may take to itself wings and fly away; or he may fail in his plans, noble plans, and useful though they seemed; and he may find, as he grows old, that the world has not gone his way, but quite another one; or he may fail in health, and be cut down and crippled, and laid by in the midst of his work. And even if he escapes all these disasters, he must needs fail at last, by mere old age, when the days come "when thou shalt say, I have no pleasure in them;" when the sun and the light are darkened, and the clouds return after the rain, when the strong men bow themselves, and those who look out of the windows are dark; and he shall rise up at the voice of a bird, and fears shall be in the way, and the grasshopper shall be a burden, and desire shall fail: because man goeth to his long home, and the mourners go about the streets. Think for yourselves. What would you wish your end to be—lonely, unhappy, without the love, the respect, the care of your fellow-men; or surrounded by friends who comfort your failing body and soul on earth, and receive you at last into everlasting habitations?

Make friends, make friends against that day, whether or not you make them out of the mammon of unrighteousness. If you have been unrighteous, bring friends back to you, as the steward did, by being just and fair, by confessing your faults freely, by doing your best to atone for them. And if you have no share in the mammon of unrighteousness, still make friends. Make them by truth and justice, make them by generosity and usefulness. To ease every burden, and let the oppressed go free, to feed the hungry, clothe the naked, and what the very poorest can do—comfort the mourner; to nurse the sick, to visit the fatherless and widows in their affliction, and so keep ourselves unspotted from the selfishness of the world—This is that true Religion, acceptable in the sight of God the Father—and happy he who has so served God. Happy for him, when he begins to fail, to see round him attached hearts, and grateful faces, hands ready to tend him, as he has tended others. And happier still to remember that on the other side of the dark river of death are other grateful faces, other loving hearts, ready to welcome him into everlasting habitations—and among them, and above them all, one whose form is as the Son of Man, full of all humanity Himself, and loving and rewarding all humanity in His creatures, saying, "Inasmuch as ye did it to one of the least of these my brethren, ye have done it unto Me."

SERMON XLIII

THE RICH AND THE POOR

Chapel Royal, Whitehall, 1871.

Proverbs xxii. 2. "The rich and poor meet together: the Lord is the maker of them all."

I have been asked to preach here this afternoon on behalf of the Parochial Mission Women's Fund. I may best describe the object for which I plead, as an attempt to civilise and Christianise the women of the lower classes in the poorer districts of London and other great towns, by means of women of their own class—women, who have gone through the same struggles as they have, and who will be trusted by them to understand and to sympathize with their needs and difficulties. These mission women are in communication with lady-superintendents in each ecclesiastical district. These are, I understand, usually the wives of small tradesmen, or of clerks. They, again, are in communication with ladies at the West End of London, who are willing to give personal help and money for certain objects, but not indiscriminate alms. And thus a series of links is established between the most prosperous and the least prosperous classes, by means of which the rich and the poor may meet together, and learn—to the infinite benefit of both—that the Lord is the maker of them all. Considering this excellent scheme, I could not help seeing as a background to it, a very different and a far darker scene. I could not help remembering that during these very days, the poorer classes of another great city had taken up an attitude full of awful lessons to us, and to every civilized country upon earth. We have been reading of a hundred thousand armed men encamped in the suburbs of Belleville and Montmartre, with cannon and mitrailleuses, uttering through their organs, threats which leave no doubt that the meaning of this movement is—as some of them boldly phrase it,—a war of the poor against the rich. There is no mistaking what that means. This madness has been stopped for the time, we are told, principally (as was to be expected), by the superior common sense of their wives. But only, I fear, for a time. Such men will go far, if not this time, then some other time. For they believe what they say, and know what they want. They have done with phrases, done with illusions. They are no longer deceived and hampered by party cries against this and that grievance, real or imaginary, the abolition of which the working classes demand so eagerly from time to time, in the vain belief that if it were only got rid of the millennium would be at hand. They have done long ago with remedial half-measures. Landed aristocracy, Established Church, military classes, privileged classes, restricted suffrage, and all the rest, have been abolished in their country for two generations and more: but behold, the poor man finds himself (or fancies himself, which is just as dangerous) no richer, safer, happier after all, and begins to see a far simpler remedy for all his ills. He has too little of this world's goods, while others have too much. What more fair, more simple, than that he should take some of the rich man's goods, and if he resists, kill him, crying, "Thou sayest, let me eat and drink, for to-morrow I die. Then I too will eat and drink, for to-morrow I die?" And so will the rich and poor meet together with a vengeance, simply because neither of them has learnt that the Lord is the maker of them all.

This is a hideous conclusion. But it is one towards which the poor will tend in every country in which the rich are merely rich, spending their wealth in self-enjoyment, atoned for by a modicum of alms.

I said a modicum of alms. I ought to have said, any amount of alms, any amount of charity. Throughout the great cities of Europe—in London as much as anywhere—hundreds of thousands are saying, "We want no alms. We intend to reconstitute society, even at the expense of blood, so that no man, woman, or child, shall need the rich man's alms. We do not choose, for it is not just, that he should take credit to himself for giving us a shilling when he owes us a pound, ten, a hundred pounds—owes us, in fact, all by which he and his class are richer than us and our class. And we will make him pay his debt."

I do not say that such words are wise. I believe them to be foolish—suicidal. I believe that it is those who patiently wait on the Lord, and not the discontented who fret themselves till they do evil, who will inherit the land, and be refreshed in peace. I believe that all those who take the sword will perish by the sword; that those who appeal to brute force will always find it—just because it is brute force—always strongest on the side of the rich, who can hire it for evil, as for good.

I only say, that so hundreds of thousands think; so they speak, and will speak more and more loudly, as long as the present tone of society endures,—good-natured and well meaning, but luxurious, covetous, ignoble, frivolous, ignorant; believing—all classes alike, not only that money makes the man, but worse far—that money makes the woman also; and all the while half-ashamed of itself, half-distrustful of itself, and trying to buy off man by alms, and God by superstition.

So long as the great mass of the poor of any city know nothing of the great mass of the rich of that city, save as folk who roll past them in their carriages, seemingly easy while they are struggling, seemingly happy while they are wretched, so long will the rich of that city be supposed, however falsely, to be what the French workmen used to call mangeurs d'hommes—exploiteurs d'hommes—to get their wealth by means of the poverty, their comfort by means of the misery of their fellow-men; and so long will they be exposed to that mere envy and hatred which pursues always the more prosperous, till, in some national crisis, when the rich and poor meet together, both parties will be but too apt to behave, through mutual fear and hate, as if not God, but the devil, was the maker of them all.

These words are strong. How can they be too strong, in face of what is now passing in a neighbouring land? Not too strong, either, in view of the actual state of vast masses of the poor in London itself, and indeed of any one of our great cities.

That matter has been reported on, preached on, spoken on, till all other civilized countries reproach Britain with the unique contrast between the exceeding wealth of some classes and the exceeding poverty of others; till we, instead of being startled by the reproach, take the present state of things as a matter of course, a physical necessity, a law of nature and society, that there should be, in the back streets of every great city, hordes of, must I say, savages? neither decently civilized nor decently Christianized, uncertain, most of them, of regular livelihood, and therefore shiftless and reckless, extravagant in prosperity, and in adversity falling at once into want and pauperism. You may ask any clergyman, any minister of religion of any denomination, whether the thing is not so. Or if you want to read the latest news about the degradation of your fellow-subjects, read a little book called "East and West," and judge for yourselves, whether such a population, numbered by hundreds of thousands, are in a state pleasing to God, or safe for those classes of whom they only know that they pay them wages, and that these wages are as small as they can be forced to take. Read that book; and then ask yourselves, is it wonderful that, in one district, before the mission of the society for which I plead was established, the poor used seriously to believe that it was the wish and endeavour of the rich to grind them down, and keep them poor. We, of course, know that the poor folk were mistaken but do we not know, too—some of us—that there are political economists in the world, who, though they would not willingly make the poor poorer than they are, are still of opinion that it is good for the nation, on the whole, that the present state of things should continue; that there should be always a reserve of labour, in plain English, a vast multitude who have not quite work enough to live on, ready to be called on in any emergency of business, and used, to beat down, by their competition, the wages of their fellow-workmen? Is this theory altogether novel and unheard of? Or this theory also, that for this very reason, Emigration, which looks the very simplest remedy for most of this want,—while nine-tenths of the bounteous earth is waiting to be subdued and replenished by the poor wretches who cannot get at it—that Emigration, I say, is an unnecessary movement—that the people are all wanted at home—to be such as the parson and the mission women find them?

And it may be that the poor folk have heard—for a bird of the air may carry the matter in these days of a free press—that some rich folk, at least, hold this opinion, and translate it freely out of the delicate language of political economy, into the more vigorous dialect used in the fever alleys and smallpox courts in which the poor are left to wait for work. But if there be any rich persons in this congregation who hold these peculiar economic doctrines, let me recommend to them, more than to any other persons present, that they would support a society which alleviates the hard pressure of their system; which helps to make it tolerable and prudent by teaching the poor to save; by teaching them, in London alone,—how to save £54,000 in the last eleven years. Let them help this society heartily.

The children of this world are—in their generation—wiser than the children of light. But how long their generation will last, depends mainly (we are told) on how far they make themselves friends out of the mammon of unrighteousness.

But if, again, there be rich people in this congregation, as I trust there are many and many, who start, indignant, at such an imputation, and utterly deny its truth—then,—if it be false, why in the name of God, and of humanity, and of common prudence, why do they not go to these people and tell them so? Why do they not prove that it is not so, by showing a little more human sympathy, not merely for them behind their backs, but sympathy with them face to face? If they wish to know how much can be done by only a little active kindness, they have only to read the pages of that painful, and yet pleasant, book—"East and West,"—which I have just quoted; and to read, also, an appendix to it—a Paper originally read at the Church Congress, Manchester, by the present Lord Chancellor—a document which it would be an impertinence in me to recommend or praise.

Bring yourselves then boldly into contact with these classes, and especially into contact with the women—with the wives and mothers. For it is through the women, through them mainly, if not altogether, that civilization and religion can be introduced among any degraded class. It was so in the Middle Age. The legends which tell us how woman was then the civilizer, the softener, the purifier, the perpetual witness to fierce and coarse men, that there were nobler aims in life than pleasure, and power, and the gratification of revenge; that not self-assertion, but self-sacrifice was the Divine ideal, toward which all must aspire. These old legends are immortal; for they speak of facts and laws which will endure as long as there are women upon earth. Through the woman, the civilizer and the Christianizer must reach the man. Through the wife, he must reach the husband. Through the mother, he must reach the children. I say he must. It is easy to complain that the clergy in every age and country have tried to obtain influence over women. They have been forced to do so, because otherwise they could obtain no influence at all. And if a priesthood should arise hereafter, whose calling was to teach not religion but irreligion, not the good news that there is a good God, and that we can know Him; but the bad news that there is no God, or, if there is, we cannot know Him; then would that priesthood find it necessary to appeal like all other priesthoods, to the women, and to teach them how to teach their children.

But more. It is not religion only which must be taught through the wives and mothers, but sound science also, and sound economy. If you intend (as I trust some here intend) to teach the labouring classes those laws of health and life, on which depend the comfort, the wholesomeness, often the decency and the morality of the poor man's home, then you must teach those laws first to the house-mother, who brings the children into the world, and brings them up, who puts them to bed at night, and prepares their food by day. If you wish to teach habits of thrift, and sound notions of economy to the labouring classes, you must teach them first to the housewife, who has to make the weekly earnings cover, if possible, the week's expenses. If you wish to soften and to purify the man, you must first soften and purify the woman, or at least encourage her not to lose what womanliness she has left, amid sights, and sounds, and habits which tend continually to destroy her womanhood. You must encourage her, I say, to remember always that she is a woman still, and let her teach—as none can teach like her—true manfulness to her husband and her sons.

And how can you best do that? Not by giving her shillings, not by preaching at her, not by scolding her: but by behaving to her as what she is—a woman and a sister—and cheering her heavy heart by simple human kindliness. What she wants amid all her poverty and toil, her child-bearing and child-rearing, what she wants, I say, to keep her brave and strong, is to know by actual sight and speech that she is still not an outcast; not alone; that she is still a member of the human family, that her fellow-woman has not forgotten her; and that, therefore, it may be, He that was born of woman has not forgotten her either. That she has, after all, a God in heaven, who can be touched with the feeling of her infirmities, and can help her and those she loves, to struggle through all their temptations, seeing that He too was tempted in all things like them, yet without sin.

It is only personal intercourse with them—only the meeting of the rich and poor together, in the belief that God is the maker of them all, that will do that. But it will do it.

Only personal intercourse will reconcile these people to their condition, in as far as they ought to be reconciled to it. But personal intercourse will reconcile them to it, as far as it ought, but no further. And I think that the system of personal intercourse attempted by this Society is, on the whole, the best yet devised. It is imperfect, as all attempts to make that straight which is crooked, and to number that which is wanting—to patch, in a word, a radically vicious system of society,—must be imperfect; but it is the best plan which I have yet seen. I find no fault with other plans, God forbid! Wisdom is justified of all her children; and the amount of evil is so great, and (as I believe, so dangerous), that I must bid God-speed to any persons who will do anything, always saving and excepting indiscriminate almsgiving.

But it seems to me that the soothing and civilizing, and in due time Christianising, effect of personal intercourse cannot begin better than through a woman, herself of the working class, who has struggled as these poor souls have struggled, and conquered, more or less, where they are failing. That through her they should be brought in contact with women of the more comfortable and cultivated class, who are their immediate employers, if not their immediate neighbours; and through them, again, brought in contact with women of that class, of whom I shall only say, that if they were not meant for some such noble work as this—and not for mere pleasure and mere display, then for what purpose, in heaven or earth, were they made? and why has Providence taken the trouble (as it were) to elaborate, by long ages of civilization, that most exquisite of all products of nature and of art—A Lady?

Ah! what the ladies of England might do, and that without interfering in the least with their duties as wives and mothers, if they would work together, as a class! If they would work as well and humanly while they are in towns, as most of them do work while they are in the country; as some of them do, to their honour, in the towns already! But how many? what proportion do those who do good bear to those who do nothing? What a small amount of humanizing and civilizing intercourse with some women of the labouring class is there in the case of the wives of rich men who come up to town, merely for the season, and forget that it is their temporary and uncertain stay in London which causes much of the temporary and uncertain employment of the London poor, and their consequent temptation to unthrift and recklessness! How little humanizing and civilizing intercourse with the poor is carried on by the wives of those employers of labour who surely, surely owe something more to their husband's work people, than to be aware (by hearsay) that they are duly paid every Saturday night?

But I shall be told: We need not fear—we can justify ourselves before God and man. I shall be reminded of all that has been done, and done well too, for the poor during the last generation, and bidden not to calumniate my countrymen. True, much has been done; and done well. And true also it is that no effort to make the rich and poor meet together, to bring the different classes of society into contact with each other, but has succeeded—has sown good seed—which I trust may bring forth good fruit in the day when every tree shall be judged by its fruit. The events of 1830, startling and warning, and those of 1848, more pregnant, if possible, with warning than the former, awakened a spirit of humanity in England, which was also a spirit of prudence and of common sense.

But I cannot conceal from myself, or you, that the earnestness which was awakened in those days is dying out in these. The richer classes of every country are tempted from time to time to fits of laziness—fits of frivolity and luxury, surfeits, in which men say, with a shrug and a yawn—"Why be very much in earnest? Why take so much trouble? Somebody must always be rich, why should not I? Somebody must enjoy the money, why should not I? At all events, things will last my time." And that such a surfeit has fallen upon the rich of this land, is a fact; for that this is the tone of to-day, and that the tone increases, none can deny who knows that which calls itself the world, and calls itself so only too truly; the world of which it is written, that all that is in the world—the lust of the flesh, and the lust of the eyes, and the pride of life—is not of the Father, but of the world. And the world passeth away, and the lust thereof. But he who doeth the will of God, he alone abideth for ever.

God grant that we, who have just seen the most cunningly organized and daintily bedizened specimen of a world, which ever flaunted on the earth since men began to build their towers of Babel, collapse and crumble at a single blow, may take God's hint, that the fashion of this world passeth away. Let the idle, the frivolous, the sensual, and those who, like Figaro's Marquis, have earned all earthly happiness by only taking the trouble to be born—let them look back on this last awful Christmas-tide, and hear, speaking in fact unmistakeable, the voice of the Lord. Think ye that they whose blood Pilate mingled with their sacrifices were sinners above all the Galilæans, because they suffered such things? I tell you, "Nay: but except ye repent, ye shall all likewise perish."

There are those who will hear such words with a smile, even with a sneer, and say, Such wholesale judgments of God, even granting that there are such things, are, after all, very rare: it is very seldom that a whole class, a whole system of society, is punished in mass—and why then need we trouble ourselves about so remote a probability?

Then know this—that as surely as God sometimes punishes wholesale, so surely is He always punishing in detail. By that infinite concatenation of moral causes and effects, which makes the whole world one mass of special Providences, every sin of ours will punish itself, and probably punish itself in kind. Are we selfish? We shall call out selfishness in others. Do we neglect our duty? Then others will neglect their duty to us. Do we indulge our passions? Then others, who depend on us, will indulge theirs, to our detriment and misery. Do we squander our money? Then our children and our servants will squander our money for us.

Do we?—but what use to go on reminding men of truths which no one believes, because they are too painful and searching to be believed in comfort? What use to tell men what they never will confess to be true—that by every crime, folly, even neglect of theirs, they drive a thorn into their own flesh, which will trouble them for years to come, it may be to their dying day? And yet so it is.

Though the mills of God grind slowly, yet they grind exceeding small;
Though with patience He stands waiting, with exactness grinds He all.

As those who neglect their fellow-creatures will discover, by the most patent undeniable proofs, in that last great day, when the rich and poor shall meet together, and then, at least, discover that the Lord is the maker of them all.